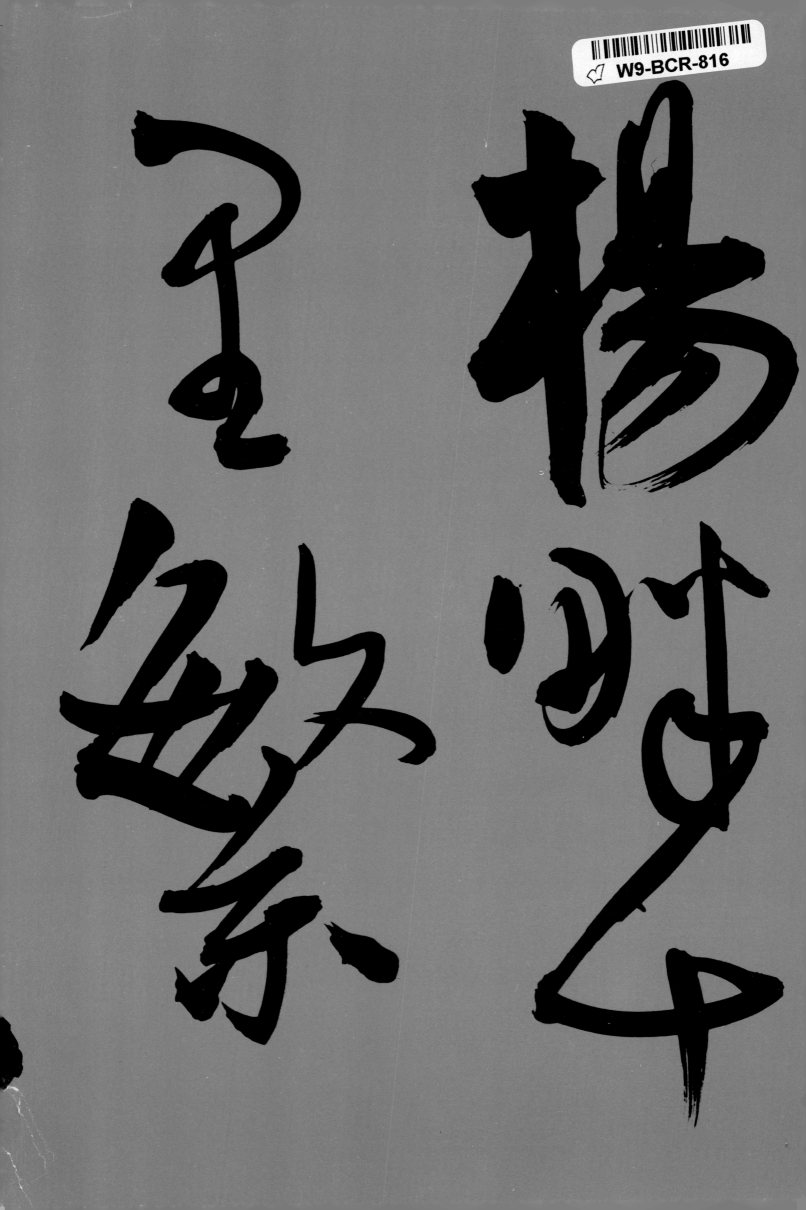

CHINA: A History in Art

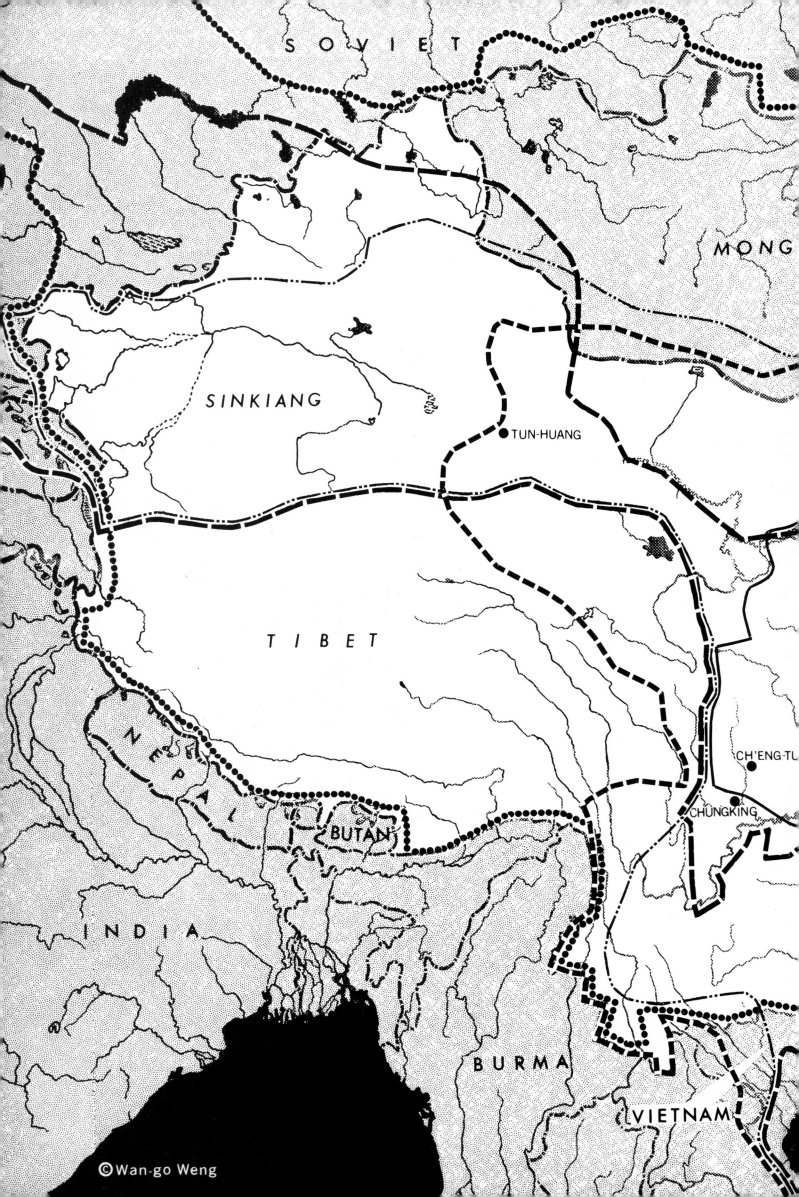

SOVIET

MONG

SINKIANG

TUN-HUANG

TIBET

NEPAL

BUTAN

CH'ENG-TU

CHUNGKING

INDIA

BURMA

VIETNAM

©Wan-go Weng

UNION

MANCHURIA

IA

Great Wall

PEKING

Grand Canal

Yellow River

SIAN
(CH'ANG-AN)

LO-YANG K'AI-FENG

NANKING

SHANGHAI

WUHAN HANGCHOW

Yangtze River

CH'ANG-SHA

KOREA

JAPAN

RYUKYU IS.

TAIPEI

TAIWAN

CANTON

HONG KONG

part of
China
since
Han

A HISTORICAL MAP OF CHINA

☐ Historical capitals

------- *Chou* ___ c. 11th century B.C.

——— *Ch'in* ___ c. 200 B.C.

—·—·— *Han* ___ c. 100 A.D.

——— *T'ang* ___ c. 750 A.D.

– – – *Ming* ___ 1415 A.D.

•••••••• *Ch'ing* ___ 1760 A.D.

China today ___ area in white

0   200   400

miles

CHINA

A HISTORY IN ART

By Bradley Smith and Wan-go Weng / A   *Gemini Smith book published by Harper & Row • New York, Evanston, San Francisco, London*

Consultant CHAOYING FANG
Professor,
Columbia University

FRANK ARUNDEL, *Graphics Director*
The Art Works

FLORENCE KRONFELD,
JUDSON NIVER, *Production Supervisors*

VIRGINIA WENG,
HELEN PAULA SMITH, *Editorial Assistants*

SHARON WELDY,
HUGO WENG,
CAROL GOLDSTEIN, *Researchers*

Typography in San Diego by CENTRAL GRAPHICS

Printed in Japan by TOPPAN

Cover: WAN-GO WENG, *Designer*

Dragon, gilt bronze, T'ang period (618-907); Fogg Art Museum, Cambridge, Mass.

Seal: "Chung-kuo, mei-shu hsü-shih," or "China, history told through art," by Wan-go Weng

Title page   "The Garden for Solitary Enjoyment" (section) by
(pages 4-5)   Ch'iu Ying, 16th century; Wan-go Weng Collection
(Portraying Sung historian-statesman Ssu-ma Kuang in his garden)

Page 1   "Return from Exile" (section) by Li T'ang, 11th-12th century; C. C. Wang Collection
(Duke Wên of Chin returning to power, mid-7th century B.C.)

End pages   Calligraphy by Wang Ch'ung (1494-1533)

Acknowledgments

The authors wish to acknowledge with warm gratitude the guidance and help of friends in the field of Chinese art and history in the preparation of this book. In particular, we are indebted to Professor Chaoying Fang of Columbia University for his detailed reading of the text, many invaluable criticisms and suggestions, as well as his generosity in making available to us the only known contemporary painting of the T'ai-p'ing Rebellion; to Professor Kuang-chih Chang of Yale University, for his reading of the first two chapters, giving us the benefit of his special knowledge of prehistoric China and the Shang and Chou dynasties; to Professor Richard Edwards of the University of Michigan, for his advice on the research related to pictures in the collection of the National Palace Museum in Taipei; to Professor L. Carrington Goodrich of Columbia University, for his kindness in giving us access to research materials and suggestions on certain points of Chinese cultural history, particularly regarding the invention of printing; and to Professor James Cahill of the University of California at Berkeley, for his photographs of the scroll painting "Victory Over Japanese Invaders" in the collection of Mr. Hing-tsang Lee of San Francisco, who graciously consented to their appearance in the book.

We are grateful to all the museums, directors, curators, and museum personnel, private collectors and artists who gave us permission to photograph or reproduce photographs of art objects in their collections. We cannot enumerate here the many instances of kind hospitality, courteous cooperation and special considerations that we encountered in our search for visual material. Names are mentioned in the order of appearance of art objects in the book: Professor Max Lochr, the Fogg Art Museum of Cambridge, Mass; Mr. Per-Olow Leijon, Curator, the Museum of Far Eastern Antiquities, Stockholm; Mr. René-Yvon Lefebvre d'Argencé, Director and Chief Curator of the Avery Brundage Collection, Center of Asian Art and Culture, De Young Memorial Museum, San Francisco; Mr. Henry Trubner, Curator of Asian Art, Seattle Museum; Mr. Thomas Lawton, Assistant Director, Freer Gallery of Art, Washington, D.C.; Mr. Jack V. Sewell, Curator of Oriental Art, the Art Institute of Chicago; Miss Jean K. Schmitt, Assistant Curator, and Miss Marise Johnson, Administrative Assistant, the Far Eastern Department, and Miss Jean Mailey, Associate Curator in Charge of the Textile Study Room, Metropolitan Museum of Art, New York; Mr. Jan Fontein, Curator, Department of Asiatic Art, Museum of Fine Arts, Boston; Mr. and Mrs. Ezekiel Schloss, collectors, New York; Mr. Laurence Sickman, Director, William Rockhill Nelson Gallery of Art and Atkins Museum of Fine Arts, Kansas City, Mo.; Miss Hsio-yen Shih, Curator, Far Eastern Department, Royal Ontario Museum, Toronto; Mr. David Crownover, Executive Secretary, University Museum, Philadelphia; Mr. Chiang Fu-ts'ung, Director and Mr. Wang Chi-wu, Chief, Publications Division, National Palace Museum, Taipei; Mr. Rommel Min Tung, photographer, Taipei; Mr. Roderick Whitfield, Assistant Keeper, Department of Oriental Antiquities, the British Museum, London; Mr. Chi-ch'ien Wang, collector, New York; Mr. John M. Crawford, Jr., collector, New York; Mr. Sherman E. Lee, Director and Mr. Wai-kam Ho, Curator of Chinese Art, Cleveland Museum of Art; Mr. James A. Foster, Director, Mr. Leslie Benji Nerio, Curator, and Mrs. Fritz Hart, the Honolulu Academy of Arts; Mr. K. T. Wu, Head, Chinese and Korean Section, Library of Congress, Washington, D.C.; and Mr. Chen Chi, artist, New York.

Acknowledgment of the assistance we have received from all of the above individuals and institutions does not imply any responsibility for the viewpoints expressed or for any inadequacies in the text. The quotations from Confucius and Lao Tzu in Chapter 2 and Li Ssu in Chapter 3 are as translated in Sources of Chinese Tradition, edited by William Theodore de Bary, and the quotation from Ssu-ma Ch'ien in the same chapter is as translated in Records of the Grand Historian of China by Burton Watson; all other quotations are translated by Wan-go Weng direct from original Chinese texts.

China—A History in Art

Contents

PREFACE

In every country and in every period the artist reveals the life around him. His painting and sculpture become a visual chapter in the history of his civilization. The viewpoint of the artist, influenced by the time in which he lives, may reflect the realities of daily living, the quest for religious meaning, the successes or failures of scientific practices, the affirmation or denial of spiritual values. We can recall past civilizations most clearly through the realism or surrealism or impressionism of their artist-chronicler. Most of the historical art of China falls into the latter sphere. In that now-ancient, now-modern country, the artist has usually addressed himself to visualizing the essential daily living while simultaneously attempting to explore the meaning of life in his creations. In so doing he has illuminated not only passing events in time but also shadings of change in the mores of his contemporaries.

Rather than to realistically portray or "hold as 'twere a mirror up to nature", the Chinese artist often abstracted man and nature into a single form or symbol. He then used symbols as illustration, decoration, and even in communication. It is in this final achievement that the art of China differs from that of other civilizations. With calligraphy, art became a true language. When a Chinese viewed such a symbol he saw not only a pleasing seemingly abstract decoration but within the design a real form (old man, young woman, priest, leaping fish, bird, or flower, and, in the spiritual world, ghosts, dragons, and deities). In many forms abstract and concrete ideas came to be expressed in art.

It is no accident that the Chinese written language was created by artists visualizing their world and communicating its shape and meaning. This is why it is sometimes difficult to discern the line of demarcation between the art of writing and that of painting, for within what appears to be realistic painting there often lies a philosophical concept, and within Chinese calligraphy lie subtle visual experiences. Yet the artists of China did not neglect the representational approach to painting and sculpture. On early vessels of clay and bronze are incised hunting scenes, mountain passes, animals, and insects. In utilitarian vessels an extension of the vision was sought as designers created textures and glazes to satisfy the tactile sense.

In many paintings, ceramics, and sculptured figures, the Chinese artist has graphically realized and reproduced the historical periods in which he lived, but it is necessary for the viewer to look beneath the surface of his art. The reader of this book is therefore asked to search out the nuances in Chinese painting and sculpture to find the key to the country's history. This work is concerned with abstracting the essence of the history of China primarily through its art; to select the visions the artist has used to portray the history of his country. This is not to say that China does not have a great written history. Indeed, because of the calligraphic nature of its written language it has the most definitive and continuous written history of any peoples. No one book could begin to show all the great art of China nor retell but a small fraction of its written history. This work should be viewed and used as a sketchbook of the history of that great Asian civilization.

It is possible to draw a line, sometimes deep and wide, sometimes softly shaded, occasionally almost invisible, through some five thousand years of Chinese history. There is a continuing sequence of visual evidence which, no matter how faintly it be etched in some dynasties, never disappears. We will follow this line from the dimly seen prehistoric ages to the sharp reality of the poised giant standing on the brink of the industrial revolution.

One can follow the art of China in the continuing evolution not only of society but of man himself. In the early stages of cultural evolution much emphasis was put upon the animal nature of man and his gods, but as each changing period overshadowed the last, man soon emerged from his animal-like beginnings to become a socialized, civilized creature. This stage of historical evolution is effectively visualized in the Han period where all the ways of life, of hunters and housewives, of farmers and fishermen, came to life in paintings and sculpture. Humans take on new dimensions, spiritual as well as animal, with the coming of Buddhism. The Chinese is still a farmer, still a fisherman, but he is also a contemplative, studious being relating to the ancestors of his past and projecting his dreams into the future. From the first century onward man became more spiritual, his gods became more human.

In each succeeding generation the Chinese art-historian continuously broadened his scope. Man did not become the conqueror of nature but rather took his rightful place in it. In many Chinese paintings from the tenth to the nineteenth century man seems to have become an insignificant figure against the vastness of his natural surroundings. Yet this is not a distorted view but rather a realistic one. The Chinese began to recognize himself and his place in the scale of his country and the universe. The chronicle of each age, the depiction of poets, heroes, monarchs, and commoners, will be touched on in this visual history. The procession of saints and sinners, human and divine, will appear in these pages. It is hoped that a picture of what China has been will emerge. To create a visual history of a country means to encompass its traditions, its visions, and its reality. As painting moved through one era after another so did the art of writing, which, at times, becomes difficult to separate from painting for in calligraphy there is an evolution of rhythm, analogous to that in music. Words develop meaning by the form in which they are represented. The moving line becomes a picture allowing the viewer to read beyond the form of the letter. This rhythm of line pervades all the visual arts in China. The artist and writer continually attempts to encompass the flow of life in both its real and its imaginary aspects. The choreography and the dance of life itself are deftly and delicately expressed in the ever flowing line of Chinese art and history.

Bradley Smith

Introduction to the History of China

Our word "civilization" goes back to a Latin root having to do with "citizen" and "city." The Chinese counterpart, actually a binom, *wen hua*, literally means "the transforming [i.e., civilizing] influence of writing." In other words, for us the essence of civilization is urbanization; for the Chinese it is the art of writing.

The ramifications of this capsulized distinction have been many and significant. Throughout their literate history, the Chinese have been much more interested in the written than the spoken word. Famous Chinese orators have been rare, famous calligraphers legion. Whereas in India it was the oral recitation of a sacred composition that made it efficacious, in China it was above all its reproduction in written or printed form. Papers bearing writing could not be indiscriminately discarded in the streets of the old China. This was not so much because they polluted the streets as that such an act showed disrespect to the written word. As late as the 1930's it was still possible, in Peking, to see public trash receptacles inscribed with the traditional exhortation: *"Ching hsi tzu chih,"* "Respect and spare written paper."

No doubt this attitude stems from the nature of Chinese writing: a nonalphabetic and basically ideographic script whose thousands of separate symbols or characters each signifies a distinct object or concept and therefore, like the Arabic numerals (1, 2, 3, 4, etc.), are immediately understandable to the eye irrespective of the pronunciations the reader may attach to them. This fact explains why the Chinese script could become the written medium of peoples adjoining the Chinese: not only those, like the Vietnamese, closely related to the Chinese linguistically, but also peoples, like the Koreans and Japanese, whose spoken languages belong to totally different linguistic families.

Because each Chinese ideograph carries from its cultural past its own distinct connotations, the acceptance of Chinese writing by others meant, to a considerable extent, their acceptance of Chinese cultural and moral values as well. Conversely, the Chinese script proved a major barrier to the free *entry* of foreign ideas and values into Chinese culture, because it meant that these values and ideas could reach the Chinese consciousness only through the filter of the ideographs. Resulting frequent failures and distortions of communication were as well known to Buddhist missionaries fifteen hundred years ago as they were to those from the Christian West of the seventeenth century onward.

The prime place of calligraphy among the Chinese arts and its intimate relationship with Chinese painting are both well known. But the significance of their concern with writing has a far wider cultural range. There seems to be a consistent pattern, for example, in the fact that the Chinese were the inventors of paper (first century A.D.), of block printing (ninth century or earlier), and of movable type (eleventh century). Or that, prior to around 1750, they are said to have produced more printed books than the rest of the world put together.

Of particular interest to us here, however, are the social and political consequences. The high prestige of the written language, combined with the tremendous difficulties attached to its mastery, gave to the scholar in China a status unequaled in any other society. During the past two thousand years, speaking very broadly, the Chinese ruling elite consisted neither of nobles, priests, generals, nor industrial or commercial magnates, but rather of scholar-officials. These were men educated from childhood in the Confucian classics who, ideally, became members of officialdom through success in the government's civil service examinations. These examinations, which were written, humanistic in content, and exceedingly rigorous, were conducted periodically throughout the empire at county, provincial, and national levels. In name they were open to all but a very few members of the total male population. In actuality, of course, it was only a tiny fraction of that total who were educationally qualified to take them.

If any single word can describe the imperial state system, it is *bureaucracy*. The government maintained a complex network of official positions which were specialized, ranked according to a fixed scale in the civil service, salaried accordingly, and staffed on the basis of demonstrated intellectual qualifications rather than birth. Career officials moved upward, or sometimes downward, on the bureaucratic ladder according to the merits or demerits regularly entered on their dossiers by their superiors; of course the usual principle of seniority operated as well.

It would be wrong, however, to suppose that these officials were commonly unimaginative, rigid, or lacking in initiative simply because some people today associate these characteristics with the word "bureaucracy." It should be remembered that governmental service was the most highly regarded of all professions for the Chinese educated man and that he came to it trained as a humanist rather than as a technician. As a rule, he had a good appreciation of the accepted literary and artistic accomplishments—notably poetry, calligraphy, and painting— and not infrequently he was a competent practitioner of them. Thousands of Chinese bureaucrats have been passable poets, and most great poets have at some time been bureaucrats.

Like every bureaucracy, that of China generated enormous amounts of paper work, often in multiple copies. These documents, preserved in the official archives, provided much of the raw material that was periodically incorporated into the official or dynastic histories. These histories, normally compiled under imperial auspices from dynasty to dynasty (hence their name), constituted a historical record more continuous, detailed, and precise than those available for any of the other long-lived ancient civilizations.

Although the Chinese bureaucratic system formally began with the creation of the first centralized empire in the third century B.C. (about which more below), tendencies toward bureaucratism may be already detected in the feudal period centuries earlier. If, in fact, the Chinese were not the world's first bureaucrats, they can at least be credited with the creation of governmental forms more complex, more sophisticated, and longer-lived than anywhere else prior to the Industrial Revolution. Indeed, recent research increasingly indicates that certain features hitherto deemed unique in modern bureaucracies were anticipated, and in some cases perhaps even inspired, by Chinese example. There is little doubt that the Chinese form of government has been a major factor in the remarkable continuity of Chinese civilization, both culturally and politically. Another, less formal institution of sterling importance for the lengthy maintenance of Chinese social stability, of course, has been the famed Chinese family system.

We began these pages with the proposition that the Westerner sees civilization as a process of urban development, the Chinese as that of spreading the written word. The role of the city-based bourgeoisie in the rise of modern Western society is known to all. In traditional China, on the contrary, society was strongly rooted in the countryside, cities served often more as administrative than as commercial centers, and the scholar-officials, though necessarily spending much of their lives in an urban environment, usually continued to regard the small rural village of their ancestors as their real "home." Many of them invested their surplus capital in farmland, which they rented to tenant peasants. Perhaps they might retire to their rural communities as landlords or, if continuing an official career, might allow their estate to be managed by a rural branch of the family. Thus our earlier definition of China's dominant elite as consisting of scholars and officials needs to be broadened to include rural landlords as well. Because of the extraordinary cohesiveness and dominance of this interlocking scholar-official-landlord class, Chinese traditional society has sometimes been referred to as Chinese gentry society.

The orthodox ideology of the gentry was Confucianism, but its social and political norms widely permeated all social classes. At the same time, however, the Chinese, perhaps because of their closeness to the soil, were unusually aware of the intimate relationship between man and nature, and the consequent need to harmonize man's movements with the cosmos. Taoism (pronounced "*dow*-ism") was the major philosophy for achieving this goal. Its spirit imbues much of Chinese imaginative literature, especially poetry, and Chinese art, especially painting.

Despite gentry dominance, a great many merchants and entrepreneurs individually succeeded in acquiring great wealth. Never, however, did they achieve sufficient class cohesiveness to seriously challenge the status and values of the dominant elite. On the contrary, in the very course of reaching success, they tended to adopt these values for themselves and thus eventually to convert themselves into members of the elite. Traditionally, Confucianism favored agriculture as the prime basis of national wealth, while showing suspicion toward large-scale private commercial activity. The history of imperial China is filled with examples of the imposition of bureaucratic limitations upon such activity. The resulting contrast with Japan is instructive. Probably it is no accident that modern Japan, with very little bureaucratic tradition, moved successfully from feudalism to massive industrial capitalism, whereas modern China largely jumped the capitalist stage by moving directly from preindustrial agrarian bureaucratism to what might be called socialized bureaucratism. (Of course there is very much more to the present government than this rather forbidding term by itself would suggest.)

How old is Chinese civilization? Roughly, perhaps, the same age as that of India but considerably younger than the major civilizations of the ancient Near East. Neolithic cultures have been uncovered in China, some of them probably going back to the early third millennium B.C., or possibly earlier. They have produced some artifacts of amazing beauty (notably the burial urns of the "painted pottery" culture), but none of the cultures can as yet be identified with any stages of early Chinese history as recorded in later traditional historiography. The earliest confirmation of history by archaeology comes only in the second half of the second millennium B.C., with the discovery of the divination bone inscriptions pertaining to the bronze civilization of the Shang dynasty.

Many major hallmarks of ancient Eurasian civilizations—among them the use of bronze and later iron, the invention of the wheel, the idea of writing, and the cultivation of wheat—all appear many centuries earlier in the ancient Near East than they do in China. This fact has led to a continuing and inconclusive debate between the diffusionists (most of them, unsurprisingly, Westerners), who believe that these techniques and ideas were invented only once in the Near East and then transmitted across the continent to East Asia, and those other scholars (most of them, unsurprisingly, Chinese) who believe in independent invention.

What are the major patterns or movements of Chinese history? Space permits a summary description of only four. By far the most important is the passage from feudalism to empire during the first millennium B.C. During most of this millennium, the then "China" consisted of a coterie of small principalities mostly clustered in the north around the Yellow River valley and westward, plus one or two others in the Yangtze valley farther south. These principalities were ruled by hereditary noble houses. The social and political relationships operating within and between them, as well as with their nominal overlords above, the Chou dynasty kings, were in some ways remarkably similar to those characterizing

feudal Europe during the Middle Ages. Endemic warfare, coupled with other factors, gradually produced increasingly acute social, political, and economic changes. The later centuries of the Chou (fifth to third centuries B.C., appropriately named the Warring States period) were the age of China's greatest intellectual diversity, when many competing schools of thought, including Confucianism and Taoism, arose in response to the needs of the time.

The most important single date in Chinese history before the abolition of the monarchy in 1912 is 221 B.C. In that year the state of Ch'in brought Chinese feudalism to an end by conquering the last opposing principality and creating for the first time a truly universal Chinese empire. (The name "China," from Ch'in, commemorates the Ch'in achievement, but has never been used by the Chinese themselves, who have always termed their land *Chung kuo*, "the Central Country.") This event begins the age of imperial China and with it the bureaucratic state—the roots of which, however, as indicated above, actually go back centuries earlier.

Since the founding of empire, the historical pattern most emphasized by Chinese historians themselves has been that of the dynastic cycle: a sequence of major dynasties, each having a usual duration of somewhat under three hundred years, in the course of which it would come into being, flourish and expand, then decline, and finally disintegrate. Each such cycle would usually be closed by a much briefer period of political disorder and warlordism, out of which, eventually, a new dynasty would arise. Overemphasis on this recurrent pattern has created the traditional belief that nothing much has ever changed in China. That this notion needs correction should, in art at least, be apparent to anyone who turns these pages.

A third pattern has been that of the recurring tension between the agrarian Chinese and the pastoral peoples of the steppes and deserts north and northwest of China proper. The Great Wall was first built under the Ch'in empire as an arbitrary and only partially effective attempt to demarcate the two ways of life. In the long run, neither the Chinese nor the nomads could impose their life patterns on each other, but in the short run (which in China might mean a century or more), China proper repeatedly expanded to embrace greater China during the peaks of major dynasties, but contracted again under "barbarian" pressure during the intervening troughs. Twice in late imperial times, all of China fell under barbarian rule: first under the Mongols (the Yuan dynasty, 1279-1368) and again, more effectively, under the Manchus (the Ch'ing dynasty, 1644-1912).

A fourth and very significant but little understood development is that of the growing urbanization and commercialization of Chinese life beginning during the late T'ang dynasty (ninth century) and perhaps reaching its peak under the Sung (960–1279). During these centuries, commercial and industrial activity, especially in Central and South China, enormously increased. The circulation of metal coins reached a level never equaled before or since, and was supplemented in the eleventh century by extensive issues of the world's first paper currency. A new bourgeois class swelled the population of the great cities, which became major centers of trade as well as administration. The spread of printing brought literacy to a widening sector of the population and fostered the growth of new popular forms of literature. In short, what was to begin in Renaissance Europe several centuries later seemed already to be beginning in China, with all the potential changes this implied. But then something happened or rather failed to happen: the forces that were to lead to capitalism and industrialism in Western Europe failed to achieve ongoing momentum in China. The West was to change into a modern society, China did not. Why this should have been—whether it resulted from the Mongol invasions or the resiliency of the Confucian bureaucratic state or other factors—is one of the major unanswerables in Chinese history.

In the nineteenth century, beginning with the Anglo-Chinese Opium War of 1839–42, the industrializing West came to China in force and irrevocably broke or changed the traditional historical patterns. The monolithic imperial polity disintegrated after more than two thousand years, followed first by Sun Yat-sen's Republic in 1912, and then eventually by the People's Republic of China in 1949. To what extent China today continues to be influenced by more than three thousand years of recorded history is a matter of controversy. At first sight, certainly, the changes seem total. Yet as implied above, when comparing China with Japan, the strength of the past may still be more weighty than appears on the surface. But that is another story.

DERK BODDE
Professor of Chinese, University of Pennsylvania

Introduction to the Art of China

The invisible continuity of the Chinese cultural metamorphosis always seems to me like a giant with his two feet firmly planted in the soil somewhere between Ch'ang-an and Lo-yang in the northern heartland where farther to the east continental Asia meets the Pacific Ocean. Seen from above and judged by the position of his broad shoulders, the giant appears to be facing south-southeast, with his back toward the desert plateau whose western limits border Asia Minor and point to Europe. Rising high over the terrain as he grows, he breathes the pure air from the mountains and streams and absorbs the lives and spirits found there as he moves on. Bypassing culture-pockets imprisoned in deep valleys and regionalized dialects here and there, he changes his accent as he dominates more and more land.

Because of his personified human shape, the giant does not enlarge his form in a radial-symmetrical way; he moves forward and reaches to the left and to the right. The Himalayan Mountains block him from uniting with India, and invaders sneak up to enter him from behind. Nevertheless, his form fills his land to the shimmering waves of the sea. Between the highlands and the water, his two arms reach out to embrace Indochina on his right and Korea on his left. Just beyond his fingertips float the islands of Japan.

If we want to understand the art produced by this culture and to discern the Chinese in his art, we must first learn to become one with this giant, orienting ourselves as he does, and making his right, our right; his left, our left. We must learn to look from the giant's point of view at his physical world. To him, all mankind is but one form of life; and all that is in the universe, his one and only environment. This strikingly modern attitude of the ancient Chinese could not have been the result of ignorance of the existence of other peoples beside his own, since he fought so many of them over the centuries. Still, he holds on to his principles of *ta-t'ung*, "The Grand Union," because of his sheer inability to understand how it could be possible for any human being not to forsake whatever way of life he has been leading and be converted into a Chinese. Indeed, the blood of many a former enemy is now flowing in Chinese veins. Thus, in the mind of the ancient Chinese, the Chinese way *is* the way of man. His art, conceived by man's intelligence, given physical form by man's hands, is also for man. It portrays his image, delineates his aspirations, and is here to complete his total worldly experience. In our mind's eye, this art must be taken down from museum shelves and walls, and out of books, and reassembled in the only permissible way—that in which they were related to the pattern of life at the time of their creation, and ultimately to the position, orientation, and movement of that giant—before any approach to appreciation can be contemplated. A hanging scroll on the wall may very well have been the only survival of a triptych, a fact one should remember to ascertain before rhapsodizing over the dynamic diagonal or the stately vertical quality of the composition. Neolithic painted pottery of the Yang-shao culture is only decorated from the shoulder up, because the vessels were meant to be seen from above surrounding the dead. Roof ornaments glimmering over the treetops beckon the pilgrims to come to the temples. They are not meant to be seen in an exhibition case at eye level.

Even as we relate paintings to walls, sculptures to buildings, or ceramics, lacquers, and jades to furnitures and furnishings, there emerges in our consciousness the necessity of relating all of them to architecture: tombs, houses, palaces, gardens, and temples. This will next bring to our awareness the organization of the cities, and the sensitivity of the Chinese to his terrain, and the art, or should we say "science," of geomancy. As this network of visual forms and visual logic fans wide and far-reaching, we see the Chinese ensconced in it, knowledgeably going about his business: discerning seats of greater or lesser honor around a dining table, or in an assembly hall; ascending or descending the right or the left staircase, walking or scurrying across a courtyard, all according to correct etiquette. It is the self-awareness of the Chinese that has made him aware of his surroundings and caused him to read order into his physical world, which his art illustrates.

The ancient Chinese describes his world with startling lack of ambiguity. A profound statement attempting to define the universe as a time-space continuum is offered under the guise of stark simplicity: Top (heaven), bottom (earth), and the four directions (east, south, west, and north, in that order), plus the past, the present, and the yet to come, constitute *yü-chou*, the Chinese universe. A cosmic diagram is frequently seen in the designs of Han tiles, as well as evident in texts of the earlier Chou period, in which the four borders of this square world are symbolized, or guarded, by four fantastic animals: the Blue Dragon of Spring and the beginning of life for the east, the Red Bird of Summer and the zenith of life for the south, the White Tiger of Autumn and of harvest and death for the west; and most intriguingly, not ending with death, the black *Hsüan-wu*, an intertwined form of a snake and a turtle, two hibernating animals, for winter and preparation for the life of the next beginning. Man, the most fantastic animal of them all, is in the center, facing the Red Bird, fully aware of all the others around him.

Chinese cities, and cities elsewhere built in imitation of the Chinese ones, often adopt the names of these fantastic animals for their gates at these given points, thus making the immediate surroundings of man a miniature cosmic diagram with himself within it. Recent excavations further confirm this manifestation as culturally characteristic: Both the fenestration of the neolithic dwellings and the ramps of the Shang dynasty royal tombs front on the south side. Looking at clusters of these dwellings or tombs from the air, one finds them like iron filings aligned by the invisible force of a magnet. To this Northern Hemisphere culture, the source of this magic power that aligns the architecture is the sun, which traverses the southern sky, going from east to west.

When a visual image is full of symbolism, it is like a written page, transmitting a quantity of information about itself and its maker. These animals of the four directions are here interpreted according to Chou dynasty texts. The meanings of the composite animal motifs found on the ritual bronzes of the Shang and Chou dynasties are less readily deciphered. The ceremonial function of these bronzes, which are made with great skill and dedication, indicates clearly that their role in ancestral worship and in spiritual communication was an important one. The fact that the motifs resemble the ideograms in use at the same time suggests further that these well-written pages of design hold within them messages that will become understandable to us once we learn their visual syntax and grammar. Indeed, the ideograms are frequently found on the ritual bronzes themselves as inscriptions. The nouns that are names of animals and of parts of their bodies are the easiest ones to relate to their counterparts in pictorial design. The composite animal forms thus seem to represent the combined powers of those animals depicted. Since these fantastic forms are not found in nature, they are by their special virtues supernatural, presenting themselves as supernatural beings or, more likely, supernatural powers or forces. It will be naïve to look upon these designs of great imagination, visual strength, and sincerity as simple physical conjunctions of animal parts. As these vessels were used in ceremonies that provided communication between the living and the dead, the motifs and designs found on these food or wine containers, as well as on ceremonial weapons, could not have been for purely decorative purposes as has been suggested. The multiple images seen in the sculptured masses and surface delineations may very well be the medium to tell about the phenomenon or the transformation of life itself; about either its forms or its forces, or both. And the continuity of life involved here is clearly not that of the ox, the deer, the tiger, or the mythical dragon, but that of man himself.

Using the language of symbolism, the ancient Chinese perhaps did not leave us a scientific description of his world and himself. But, then, precisely because it is not expository, the symbols are in themselves complete and absolute, leaving the burden of recognizing and understanding them to the beholder. In this connection, our mute giant offers neither explanation nor apologies, while around him the composite animals of the Shang and early Chou periods yield to the Han dynasty guardian beasts of the four directions and even to common animals, domestic and wild. At this time, plant forms also begin to appear as symbols in art. No longer are human figures hidden beneath the guise of animal features seeking protection from the mythical forces; those made in the late Chou and early Han periods have the look of man just waking up from a superstition-enshrouded past and beginning to inspect his world with open eyes. He has come into his own; his rational ways have compromised the powers of the supernatural. He does not appear to like everything he sees, but he seems man enough to face his unknown future. This is the time of the philosophers and a time of changing psychological outlook. Logical thinking, keen observation, and analytical attitude toward factual information all help to reduce fear of the unknown and dim the luster of the mythical symbols.

Thus, there in East Asia this giant stands like a Chinese counterpart of the Indian *mahapurusha*, the Great Spiritual Man; not holy and eternal, but earthly and earthy. To him and to his world are soon to be introduced the concepts and manifestations of religious India via the vehicle of Buddhism.

The Indian self-image and world-view are so different from those of the Chinese that one wonders how, once they were in confrontation, a compromise could ever have been reached. The Indian cosmic diagram has as its center the concept of god, and its aspiration points heavenward. The universe here is radial-symmetrical and therefore circular or spherical, requiring the central figure to face all directions at the same time. Around this center, the Indians are lifelong pilgrims forever circumambulating it. To install the Buddha, for example, in a space structured according to the Chinese concept would mean the eviction of the Chinese image of man from the center and his reduction to a pilgrim attending an imported higher form of existence. However, no clash occurred; the two cosmic diagrams simply superimposed themselves over one another. As seen in the tympanum of the Ta-yen-t'a, the Buddha is enthroned in a Chinese palace hall. A whole sequence of events takes place here: The domestic house transforms itself into a holy place of worship; the head of the household, or, for that matter, of the nation, becomes the new god-king; the god has come down to earth, bringing with him his heavenly court; and the common people habitually look up and attend to their father-teacher ruler, who is now also a god.

Having absorbed what Indian culture had to offer, the Chinese saw himself still in the center, except that he was not in the center of two worlds: a square one and a circular one superimposed. This visual image worked very well for the benefit of the country. As Buddhism was establishing itself in China, the country was frequently under the patronage of foreign rulers during the tumultuous times following the Han. To both the Chinese and the droves of foreigners who had come to settle in China, this new self-image was miraculously and benevolently catholic, healing, and unifying for a nation invigorated with the massive transfusion of new blood.

The Indian nude figures were not acceptable to the Chinese sensitivity, nor were they comfortable in the colder climate of their new land. The Chinese artists responded positively to this negative challenge, and created some of the world's most imaginative and expressive draperies that reveal the persuasive passions of Buddhism in flowing lines. The development of figure sculpture and painting under Buddhism was a glorious page in the history of Chinese art, in which Chinese artistic conventions were successfully wedded to Indian and Central Asian iconography. The sensitivity to relative positions of objects in a visual composition and the expressive use of lines are but two prominent examples of this achievement.

The problem of religion in art is a good mirror in which to view yet another aspect of the Chinese self-image. I often think that we come to understand the characteristics of a culture not only by what it has created, but also by what it has neglected to create. The Chinese had not formulated an organized church before the challenge of Buddhism. Taoism, while having many commendable features, as a religion is but a weak echo of the overpowering Indian import from which it learned and took much unto itself. Thus, even as Buddhism flourished from the Six Dynasties through the T'ang period, China did not appear to be at a crossroads, about to become a religious nation. Later, in the tenth century, a new visual tradition was developed to satisfy the spiritual need. This "religious" painting of godlike mountains in the vigorous landscape tradition of China has its humble beginnings in the simple backdrops in Buddhist narrative scenes. It is an art very Chinese in origin, enriching the Chinese spiritual experience, and yet, at the same time, independent of any anthropo-morphic god. It added to the rationalized Chinese world a recognition of nature and all its moods and mysteries, but made no attempt to codify these into religious doctrines.

The Chinese world, being record-keeping and history-conscious, does not need Heaven or Hell to keep its citizens fearful and docile. Instead, rewards and punishments are either meted out in this world or entered permanently in the records of history, with a more profound sense of glory or disgrace—of course, all for the living to recognize. This system is also more positive in that it does not end with a Last Judgment, but carries on, with continuing encouragement for action and creativity, all for the purpose of making the world better. So, as the Chinese opens his artistic back door to nature, via landscape paintings and garden design, he learns to provide an arena to express his intellectual energies, which are curious, playful, amoral, not necessarily irrational, but decidedly imaginative.

Here in the realm of the arts, the traditional concern for the welfare of the group yields to the self-expression of the individual. What is official and organizational has no place here; this is the stage for the free and the autobiographical. It is from this point of view that Chinese painting and calligraphy are seen closely related. They are not means to any descriptive end, such as, depicting a flower or a mood. Instead, they serve to make a statement on a flower or a mood, and in this autobiographical act their resultant forms are the end.

In this artistic world the all-important codes of conduct that traditionally safeguard the Chinese social order are temporarily suspended at gatherings of artists and at poetry contests. Rulers of men and their subjects are fellow artists or poets here. In old China, where the realm of activities for women was extremely limited, lady poets and artists enjoyed their status and the mobility it offered.

This concept of the arts as nature-related adds a significant dimension to the Chinese man-centered world and makes it more human. Just as its application tends to minimize the man-made differences among themselves by referring all to nature, the Chinese view of man's universe may indeed one day erase the prejudices among nations, unifying them, by referring all to reason.

NELSON IKON WU

Edward Mallinckrodt Distinguished University Professor of the History of Art and Chinese Culture, Washington University, St. Louis

Legends into History
Prehistory to c.1100 B.C.

Peking Man of about half a million years ago learns to use fire
... Agriculture spreads from the central area in North China to
east coast and west highlands ... Legends of heroes and inventors indicate the early steps toward a unique civilization ...
The emergence of the Shang dynasty with a written language
and unexcelled bronze art objects marks the beginning of Chinese history.

HISTORICAL CHRONOLOGY

*500,000 years ago—Peking Man uses fire and fashions
stone-flake tools.*

*20,000 years ago—in the time span from Middle Glacial to
Late Glacial period (about half a million years) the
Chinese learn to use composite tools, projectile
points and bone implements.*

*10,000 years ago—a slow change from a food-gathering to
a food-producing people through plant cultivation
and animal domestication.*

*6,000–7,000 years ago—Yang-shao culture. Villages divided into
dwelling area, kiln center and cemetery; millet
planted, pigs, dogs and silkworms domesticated;
semisubterranean houses built; painted pottery created.*

*5,000 years ago — Lungshanoid cultures with pottery
made on the wheel; early rice cultivation; stone implements for carpentry and harvesting; divination
and ancestor cult; rise of class society.*

B.C.

*2000 Lung-shan culture in interior and coastal regions;
former believed to be progenitor of Shang dynasty.*

*c.1850–c.1100 Shang dynasty; first record found written on
oracle bones and tortoise shells; a highly organized
society with a ruling class and specialized industries; worship of god and ancestors; building of
walled cities with temples and ceremonial quarters.*

c.1766 King T'ang establishes capital at Po.

c.1400 King P'an-kêng moves capital to An-yang.

c.1100 Fall of Shang.

ART CHRONOLOGY

*12,000 years ago—earliest pottery of coarse paste and dec-
orated with impressions of cord-wrapped sticks and
paddles.*

*6,000–7,000 years ago—Yang-shao culture produces handmade
red pottery with painted designs, often of fertility
symbols; also decorated with cord and mat impressions. Silkworm culture invented.*

*5,000 years ago—Lungshanoid pottery of red, gray and
black indicate the use of wheel; bone, shell and
horn artifacts.*

*4,000 years ago—Coastal Lung-shan pottery are hard,
lustrous and black, usually with ridges and incised
patterns; interior Lung-shan pottery are mainly
gray, made by paddle and anvil technique and decorated with cord and basket markings.*

B.C.

*c.1850–c.1100 Shang period produces writing on bones and
shells; stylized animals and t'ao-t'ieh designs appear on bronzes and pottery; ornaments of clay,
stone, jade, turquoise, bronze and shells; stone
sculpture; sophisticated decorative art; bronze ceremonial vessels; glazed pottery.*

Masklike face found in northwest probably represents a shaman. It is one of earliest intact prehistoric clay human images.

The First Chinese

The origins of the Chinese people date back a million or more years. For in the land known today as China a hardy hominid emerged after the first glacial period. This hominid gave way to Peking Man, who appeared toward the end of the second glacial period, marking the beginning of a significant culture. This ancient ancestor of the Chinese was probably the first man to use fire and cook meat as indicated by bits of charcoal and burned bones found in his caves. He was a hunter of animals, who learned to use traps, snares and throwing spears. He made useful implements of stone flaked from veins of quartz. These crude "stones" were the prototype of the "chopper-chopping" tool complex common to Asiatic cultures.

The long cultural evolution from Peking Man to China's modern man took place in the

A sinuous snake crawls across back of the above head. The snake design led to that of the mythical dragon.

southeast portion of the Asian continent, the land we know as China. It is a country that divides naturally into two major parts: the north dominated by the Yellow River and the south by the Yangtze. In a land of fertile river valleys the Chinese farmer developed and began the Chinese cultural tradition.

18

A human-looking head of same period and origin which has the flat face that is typical of many northerners. Vertical lines on chin may indicate beard. A brush must have been used to paint clay surface.

Belief in an afterlife is shown by food-storage jars provided for the dead. Skeleton's

flexed position is common; others in extended posture exist. Burial patterns in cemeteries hint at early ancestor cult.

21

Skeleton and bold "T" pattern may have imparted magical powers to Yang-shao bowl. Design is precursor of ideographs.

Early Farmers and Potters

The dramatic and critical transformation from nomadic food-gathering tribes to an agricultural food-producing people centered around the confluence of three rivers; the Fên-ho, the Wei-shui, and a major waterway, the broad Yellow River. On these "Central Plains," the heartland of northern China, the Neolithic Revolution took place.

The first staple crop of the new agriculturalists was a cereal grass called millet, which bears nutritious seeds. This they cultivated with primitive hoes and spades. Food was stored in cord-marked pottery. This type of vessel was followed by the earliest well-defined painted pottery called Yang-shao. In the late Neolithic culture, called Lung-shan, wheel-made black pottery characterized the art of the east while gray ware with cord and basket marks typify that of the Central Plains.

Food gathering; hunting with bow and arrow, and spear; fishing with hooks, harpoons and nets continued, but concurrently villages also arose. These first small settlements were divided into three sections: a dwelling area, a kiln center and a cemetery. Later the cemeteries were separated and combined with those of other villages to form a common ancestral ground. Within the villages pigs and dogs were domesticated. Villagers produced fabrics from hemp and later from silk. Farmland surrounded the settlements and cultivators used the slash-and-burn method, shifting the planting site from year to year as they moved to new soil.

Agriculture spread eastward and southward and soon rice, possibly originating in South China, joined millet as a staple crop. Farming and pottery were not the only evidences of an emerging culture. An interest in ideas and abstract thought is seen in the art of divination.

Yang-shao funerary pot with a zigzag design suggests limbs and fingers; top suggests head. Red paint is bloodstream.

Jet black paper-thin pottery, related to Shang period, is typical of the eastern Lung-shan culture.

Simple but graceful and functional Ch'i-chia pottery belongs to advanced farm culture of the northwest.

Legendary Heroes

The ancient Chinese filled their unrecorded yet remembered past with fantastic legends. Even today many Chinese claim to be descendants of the "Red Emperor" (Yen-ti) and the "Yellow Emperor" (Huang-ti), who occupied the Central Plains and the areas to the north and west. After forcing the Red Emperor to flee south, the Yellow Emperor faced another challenger, the horned Ch'ih-yu, the inventor of weapons. In a decisive battle, Ch'ih-yu enveloped his enemy in a dense fog, but a chariot carrying a figure that always pointed south led the Yellow Emperor to safety—forecasting the invention of the compass.

When he finally captured Ch'ih-yu, the Yellow Emperor gained complete dominance over the Yellow River valley. One tradition fixed the first years of his reign at 2698 B.C., on which the old Chinese lunar calendar is based. Important inventions were credited to him: construction of dwellings, tailoring of clothes, silkworm raising and weaving, carriage and boat building, and writing. Fire making and agriculture, however, were attributed to the more ancient sages Sui-jên and Shên-nung.

After many generations, a simple, compassionate legendary leader named Yao ruled with the help of able ministers in charge of law, music, agriculture, labor, education and military affairs. Yao abdicated to Shun, a multi-talented farmer. Shun tamed elephants to work in the fields and inspired potters to improve their craft. He in turn abdicated to Yü, the conqueror of the Great Flood. Yü channeled flood waters into rivers and seas to resettle his people; he defeated the southern Miao tribes, who had troubled the central inhabitants for centuries. At the death of Yü, his son Ch'i seized power to found Hsia, the legendary first dynasty of China.

These myths indicate clearly that in the days of these legendary heroes prehistoric China had learned to domesticate animals, control flood waters, build boats and carriages, and communicate ideas in writing. They also illustrate the concept of transference of power from one ruling dynasty to another.

Stone implements of Yang-shao farmers. Most frequently found are axes and adzes. Ornaments were sometimes of jade.

Earliest sculptures found in China include Neolithic jade "bird," whose form is more abstract than representational.

A powerful sitting bear in marble of the Shang dynasty. Its "cubist" treatment contrasts with the curves of the "bird" above.

Heat-induced cracks on tortoise shells provided clues for omens; the script was often written by brush, then engraved.

The Beginning of Writing

The earliest known Chinese writing appeared on oracle bones and shells which date from the middle of the second millennium B.C., making the Shang dynasty the first verifiable period in Chinese history. Shang priests prepared shoulder blades of animals and tortoise shells by drilling holes through them. Questions were written upon them. When they were heated, the voice of the Supreme God was revealed as the priests interpreted the meaning of the cracks that appeared. They wrote down the answers directly on the bone. Ink and brush were used. Then the question and answer were incised with a sharp instrument, making for a permanent record. This mode of divining the future was consulted in royal courts and common households alike. No important decision could be made without word from the Supreme Power. Farmers asked about propitious times for planting, kings consulted about troop movements; both commoners and royalty had questions about the weather, travel, sacrifice and health.

It is conceivable that writing may even have derived from cracks that resembled actual ob-

Animal bones were also used in divining. Most words have been deciphered and yield descriptions of ancient life-styles.

jects as seen by priests at the dawn of Chinese history. Certainly the priests must have had a hand in shaping China's earliest written language. But inscriptions on oracle bones are not all the evidence we have of the development of early Chinese writing, for inscriptions abound on bronze vessels and pottery, and on stone and jade carvings.

If judged only by the more than a hundred thousand pieces of oracle bones and shells unearthed so far, the Shang script contained some five thousand different characters, basically pictographs representing animals such as horse, ox, sheep and pig; plants such as tree and flower; natural elements such as sun,

moon, water, fire and earth; artificial objects such as house and spear; and human beings. Ideographs were created by combining graphic elements to represent abstract ideas; for example, a hand holding a brush became "to record," a man turning his head away from a food vessel meant he "had finished" (already eaten).

Ancient texts recount that the Shang court archivists used brush and ink to write on bamboo or wooden slips bound into "books." Although these books no longer exist, we know that characters formed vertical columns arranged from right to left. This format has persisted to the present.

This unique wine vessel of the late Shang period has a flattened human face with prominent nose and ears as its cover.

The First Historical Dynasty

With the emergence of the Shang dynasty China's early history becomes a matter of record. For while later annals referring to past eras have been interpreted in various ways, the results of systematic scientific excavations cannot be doubted.

Little is known of the political development of the Shang period but we know that a vigorous people dominated the eastern regions through which the Yellow River flows into the sea. These people grew strong enough to challenge the legendary Hsia dynasty. The deposition of the last monarch of Hsia is attributed to King T'ang of Shang who increasingly extended his influence over North China.

Under Shang rule social classes became more clearly defined: the king and nobility ruled and waged war, craftsmen created artifacts; farm-

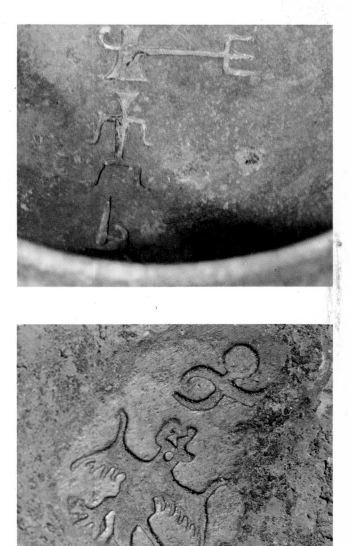

◁ *A Shang bronze ritual vessel with masklike designs is only sixteen inches tall but monumental in concept.*

▷ *Inscription inside Shang bronze represents the insignia of a clan: an ax beheading a standing figure.*

▷ *This clan sign inside another Shang bronze consists of two pictographs: a human figure and a bat.*

Some notable bronze vessels have naturalistic forms. This handsome rhinoceros is a fine example of late Shang sculpture.

ers, laborers and slaves did the work. Much of the slave population was made up of captives taken in frequent raids on neighboring states but luckless individuals and even whole families were sometimes reduced to slave status as punishment. Yet there was some mobility within the social system. We know it was possible for an individual to rise from slavery, for one of King T'ang's two chief ministers was a former slave.

Under the successors of King T'ang the Shang dynasty moved rapidly toward increased centralization of government. Its self-contained settlements were controlled from the capital city. Proliferating agricultural and industrial production extended and increased the distribution of consumer goods. One indication was the importation of cowrie shells which were used for currency.

After ten generations of Shang rule and five changes of the capital site, King P'an-kêng ascended the throne and forced the decaying aristocracy to move to a new seat of government, a city called Yin. This major event occurred in fourteenth century B.C. and gave the Shang period the name of Yin or Yin-Shang, for the same capital served until the end of the dynasty. The buildings were square or oblong and construction was governed by the four cardinal directions and the rule of symmetry. Stone was used for pillar bases and for decorative details. The great variety of the workshops showed a high degree of urbanization and specialization yet the Yin capital is best known for the high quality, originality and beauty of its unexcelled bronze artifacts.

The origins of metallurgy go back to prehistoric China and in traditional texts the originator of bronze casting was the legendary Emperor Yü. Yin craftsmen became masters of the

Pi *disk, probably earliest cosmic symbol, shows heaven as being round; jade is believed to possess protective powers.*

technique of mixing copper and tin to create the desired hardness for such utilitarian objects (of great artistic excellence) as weapons, tools, musical instruments, horse and chariot fittings and vessels. Because alcoholic beverages were popular in the Shang dynasty, drinking and serving vessels were among the most elegant of the bronze objects created. The use of highly polished bones for divination by the priests and for practical (hairpins, etc.) and decorative items for the aristocracy created such a demand that a bone industry resulted. Jade was carved into decorative shapes and used for adornment and ceremonies.

Many of the artistic efforts of the Shang dynasty were motivated by religious fervor based upon a belief in ancestral worship and an afterlife. In rituals for and burial of the nobility no extravagance was too great. In vast tombs the dead were surrounded by useful and ceremo-

nial objects. Birds and animals, real and in effigy, horses and even chariots were interred. Retainers and slaves, sometimes by the hundreds, were beheaded or buried alive to accompany their masters in the next life. Customs such as these reflect the distance between the all-powerful nobility and their defenseless subjects.

With their economic and military power based on slave ownership the later Shang elite placed wealth and pleasure above all other values. Extremes in indulgence were attributed to the last king of Shang who also engaged in large-scale slave raiding against his neighboring states and exacted heavy taxes to build palaces and gardens and to accumulate treasures. Carrying with them ceremonial vessels, a number of high government officials defected to the rising power of the west, the state of Chou, which was to become the succeeding dynasty.

Yüeh *ax blade in bronze at left and* ko *dagger blade in brown jade with bronze handle are both late Shang ritual weapons.*

The Forming of a Civilization c.1100 – 221 B.C.

The Chou dynasty lays the foundation for an agricultural nation ... The royal house reigns over feudal states which finally overshadow the court ... The late period sees the era of the "hundred philosophers" such as Confucius, Mo Ti and Lao Tzu ... The development of iron-working, city building, transportation and irrigation help to shift power and wealth from aristocracy to bureaucrats, warriors, merchants, landowners and intellectual activists ... Finally the state of Ch'in succeeds in crushing other states to unify China.

HISTORICAL CHRONOLOGY

B.C.

c.1100 The last ruler of Shang is overthrown by King Wu of Chou, who begins a dynasty which is to last some eight centuries. Upon Wu's death his brother, the Duke of Chou, assumes the regency. He quells a rebellion in the east, encourages rituals and music, builds the eastern capital at Lo-yang and resettles the Shang people. Within two decades he returns power to King Wu's son.

841 Ministers form a government by council after deposing King Li by popular rebellion (the first exact dating in Chinese history).

771 Invasion of western barbarians, who kill King Yu and sack the capital.

770 Capital moved eastward to Lo-yang, dividing the dynasty into Western and Eastern Chou.

722–481 Spring and Autumn period—Absorption of weak feudal states by strong ones who contend for leadership under the name of Chou.

c.700 Use of iron for farm implements and weapons spreads.

685 Duke Huan of the eastern state Ch'i "nationalizes" the salt and iron industries.

632 Duke Wên of the northwestern state Chin takes over leadership after defeating the southern state Ch'u.

403–221 Warring States period—the seven states fight for supremacy.

361 Shang Yang introduces reforms to strengthen the western state Ch'in. Severe "legalistic" laws are promulgated.

333 Six states form an alliance against Ch'in which lasts for a year.

316 An irrigation project still used in modern times begun by Li Ping and his son.

256 Ch'in removes last king of Chou, ending the dynasty.

246 Ying Chêng, the future emperor, becomes king of Ch'in.

230–222 Ch'in absorbs the states of Han, Chao, Wei, Ch'u and Yen.

221 Ch'in conquers the last opposing state, Ch'i, reuniting China. Ying Chêng takes the title Shih-huang-ti, "First Emperor" of Ch'in (later known to the world as China).

ART CHRONOLOGY

B.C.

c.1100 Official costumes and banners designed; new rituals and music created; colors assume symbolic meanings.

c.1100–770 Western Chou ceremonial vessels continue Shang style but forms become curvilinear with flowing outlines; inscriptions become frequent and lengthy.

c.900 Court historian Shih Chou creates large seal script.

c.900–800 Glass is made.

c.770 Ten "stone drums," engraved with seal script, commemorate a royal hunting expedition in Ch'in.

c.770–200 Lacquer-painted bronze mirrors; woodenware and carvings; bronze coins in shapes of knives and circles with round holes; bronze and marble sculpture in naturalistic and mythological forms; bronze ornaments with gold, silver, jade, glass, mother-of-pearl and turquoise inlay work; bronze vessels with sophisticated designs, geometrical and storytelling decorations; jade carvings; clay and stoneware; paintings in mural form.

c.600 Lao Tzu, supposed author of Tao-tê ching, the poetic and cryptic canon of Taoism.

551–479 Confucius—traditionally acknowledged compiler, editor and commentator of Book of Changes, Book of History, Book of Odes, Book of Rites, Spring and Autumn Annals, etc.; sayings recorded in the Analects.

470–391? Mo Ti, champion of universal love and utilitarianism, critic of Confucius, as recorded in Mo Tzu.

c.500–200 Tso Commentaries—recording events from 722 to 468 B.C.; History of States—covering 990–453 B.C.; History of Warring States—covering 452–216 B.C. Ink-on-silk drawing of lady, phoenix and a dragon-snake (earliest extant painting—from Ch'ang-sha tomb).

372–289? Mencius (Mêng K'o)—philosopher follower of Confucius—sayings recorded in Mencius.

c.369–286 Chuang Chou—author of Chuang Tzu—witty and imaginative essays by himself and disciples.

343–277 Ch'ü Yüan—first "name poet" of China, founder of the Southern School of poetry called Ch'u tz'u, influences lyrical poetry and poetic prose of Han.

c.298–238 Hsün K'uang, author of Hsün Tzu, advances theory that human nature is evil.

280–208 Li Ssu establishes the small-seal script.

Etched shaman figure shows antler headdress. It is representative of China's early southern culture.

The Insiders and Outsiders

In the west the Chou people were the first farmers and the legend of their origin reflects this fact. The "Lord of Agriculture" Ch'i (meaning "The Abandoned") was born after his mother had stepped into a giant footprint. Considering this a bad omen, she left the infant in a narrow lane, but cattle avoided trampling him. Cast on a frozen stream, the birds covered and shielded him. So his mother reclaimed him and he grew up to be an ingenious agriculturist. After many generations, Ch'i's tribe prospered by diligently cultivating the fields and breeding silkworms. One of the poems in the Book of Odes describes how such a ruler treated his peasants. At the beginning of the planting season he brought food to them and after the harvest he offered them feasts.

Pressured by less civilized but more militant neighbors, the Chou tribe decided to move rather than fight. At their new site many other tribes came to join the kind and just leader who was posthumously honored as King T'ai, or the "Great Ancestor." His grandson, King Wên, instituted a benevolent policy: every peasant family was given a piece of land and every eight families cooperated to cultivate a ninth piece for the king. Progressive actions such as this contrasted sharply with the oppressive practices of Shang. In addition, the puritanical King Wên prohibited drinking and hunting for pleasure. King Wên expanded westward by force and southward by cultural absorption. At the time of his death, two-thirds of the civilized world in China was under his influence, and the once "outsider" state of Chou was poised to move into the Central Plains. The penetration succeeded when his son, King Wu, defeated the Shang army and forced the Shang monarch to end his life in self-immolation.

The concept of a "Central Kingdom," or *Chung-kuo*, came into being during early Chou. However, the idea is more cultural than geographical. Inhabitants of the Central Kingdom were the "insider" group who adhered to the cultural pattern and sociopolitical system of the Chou royal house. They called themselves the *Hua* people, because *Hua* represented Chou's color—red. All other people surrounding the Central Kingdom were "outsiders," loosely referred to as "barbarians," since they had not been absorbed into the Chou civilization.

Essentially Chou inherited the Shang culture, but there were important differences: Shang practiced human sacrifice; Chou did not. Shang maintained a system of slavery; Chou did not. Shang believed in divination by oracle bones and shells; Chou consulted the spirits by using the stalks of the milfoil plant. At the time of conquest, Chou was backward economically and culturally, but its more humanistic social and political policies, together with a superior military organization, enabled it to conquer a much larger, more populous and well-entrenched kingdom. The victors faced a problem. Were the conquered to be killed? To be enslaved? Or should they be disturbed as little as possible, simply eliminating the stubborn loyalists and working with the collaborators? The last policy was adopted and the royal heir, Wu-kêng of Shang, was given a fiefdom under the guidance of two Chou princes. The culturally superior Shang aristocrats became, under the new regime, archivists, court scribes, teachers, traders and commanders of their own soldiers, but some were reduced to the status of farmer-laborers, traders and slaves. The former Shang troops did their share in subduing neighboring tribes such as the eastern and southern I (pronounced "yee") barbarians.

At the death of King Wu, his brother, the Duke of Chou, completed the task of unification by crushing the now rebellious Shang prince Wu-kêng and other remnants of Shang power. In the ensuing years of relative internal peace, the Shang and Chou peoples became increasingly integrated and continued to absorb other tribes who worked and lived within the Chou territory. Warfare between the now enlarged circle of "insiders" and the surrounding alien "outsiders" continued, with the Central Kingdom always the coveted prize.

Engravings show hunting and fishing of "outsiders" before they learned farming from the "insiders."

The Son of Heaven and the Lords on Earth

To sanctify the overthrow of the House of Shang, which boasted a royal lineage of godlike ancestors, the Chou conquerors claimed the mandate of Heaven and declared that its blessing was now shifted to the new regime. The throne became the symbol of power of the Son of Heaven, the king, who in turn was all virtuous and deserving to wield absolute political and religious power. To control a far-flung kingdom with limited loyal forces, the dynastic founder King Wu and his immediate successor expanded the feudal system by bestowing land and power on royal princes and kinsmen, Shang princes and other nobles supposedly descended from pre-Shang rulers.

The vision of "Under Heaven All One Family" was realized when Chou instituted *tsung-fa*, a far-reaching concept that merged the political structure with the familial relationship, making all positions in life from king to commoner a matter of birth through the application of the rule of succession. The eldest son became head of family as well as political overlord; other sons were his fiefs and owed him allegiance. Loyalty was the supreme virtue demanded by the king of his dukes, the duke of his ministers and so on down the line to the lowly farmer who toiled in the field to support the entire nation. This system worked well only when the Son of Heaven and all his earthly lords and sublords understood that Heaven's Will embraced the people's welfare. The Duke of Chou did; as regent for young King Ch'êng, he strove for peace and left the peasants alone. It was recorded that he scarcely had time to eat a quiet meal or wash his hair without interruption. But later monarchs, being lesser men, enjoyed their positions without performing the onerous duties of chief of state, religion and family. Power began to fractionalize among the lords. When the western barbarians forced the royal house to move its capital east to Lo-yang in 770 B.C., the Son of Heaven had already become just another lord on earth.

Vessel in elephant form was probably made for Shang king. Shang craftsmen later served Chou rulers.

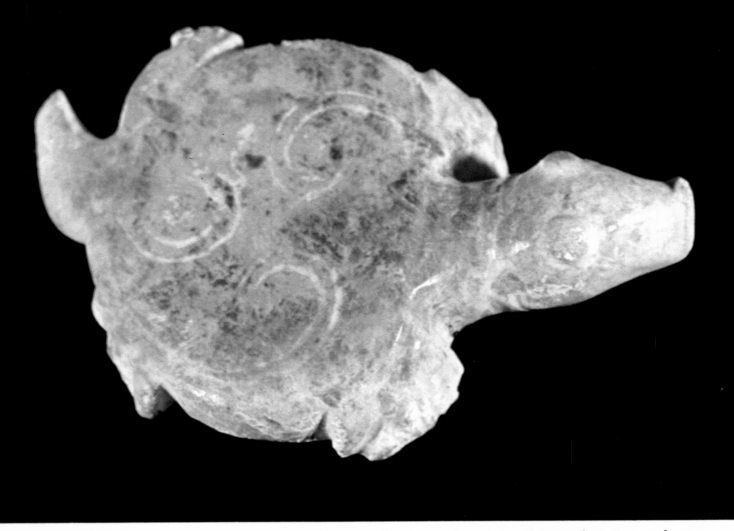

This tortoise has abstract design on carapace; such jade animals were carved for pendants, toys or charms.

Free-sculptured jade salamander was worn as pendant. Visible touch of detail is incisions on tail.

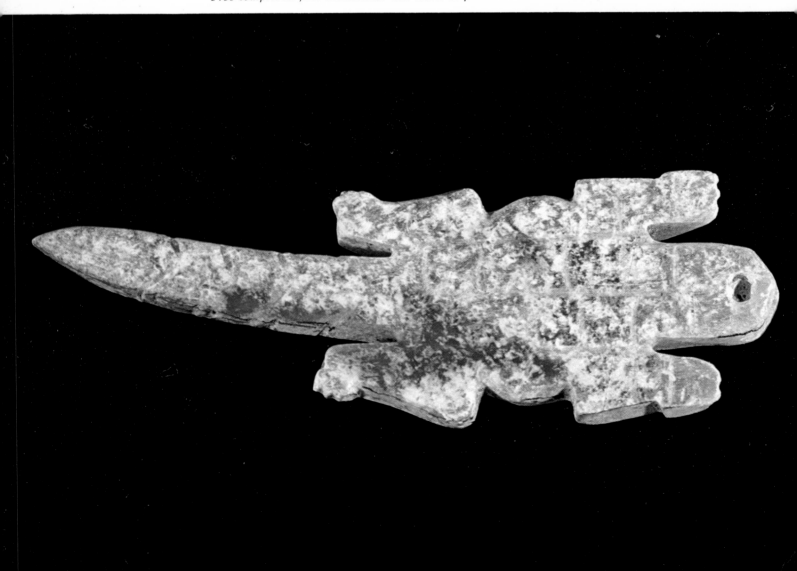

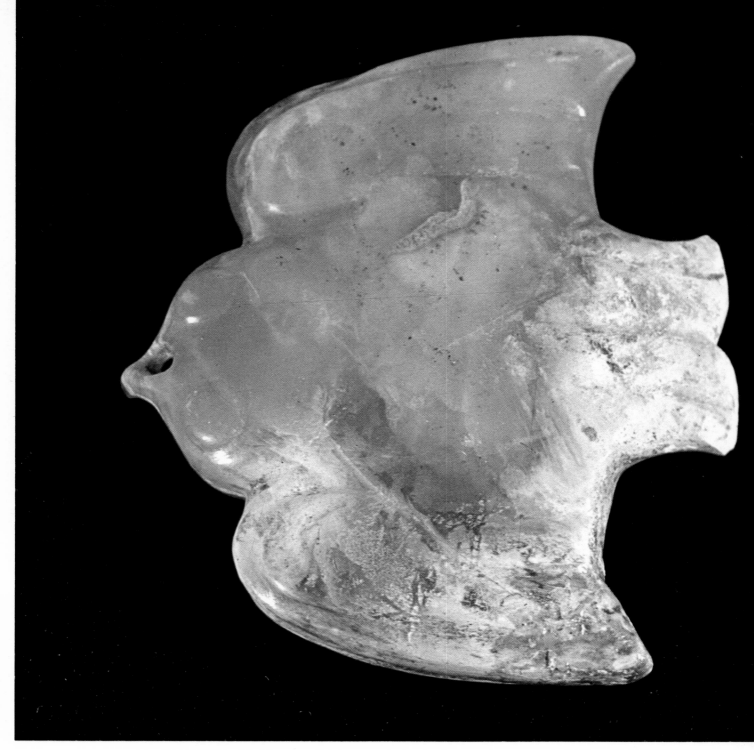

Small jade bird expresses motion; the simple design retains its freshness after three thousand years.

The Perception of Nature

The pre-Shang Chinese are said to have devised a lunar calendar by watching changes in the positions of Ursa Major and the constellations of the northern sky. Shang priests designated the month after the winter solstice as the beginning of the year, somewhat similar to our present solar calendar. The Chou calendar changed the New Year to the time of the winter solstice and by the fourth century B.C. two astronomers compiled the first star catalogue, two centuries ahead of Hipparchus.

Large-scale land reclamation for the increasing farm population necessitated the development of water resources. Following the long tradition of hydraulic engineering from pre-Shang times, a canal was built that connected two rivers north and northwest of the early Chou capital. A talented father (Li Ping) and his son designed an irrigation network for the Ch'êng-tu Plain in the southwest that is still used after twenty-three centuries.

The Bronze Age ended with a technological revolution in the seventh century B.C. when the art of iron-casting spread from the east through China. Iron farm implements allowed deep furrowing and the advent of animal-drawn ploughs (developed in the Near East) in turn increased farm production. A strong economic basis supplied the impetus for the expansion of individual militaristic states. Man's control of nature began to change the nature of man.

Most Chou bronze ritual vessels bear inscriptions; some yield historical information unprocurable elsewhere.

The Rising of the States

When the king of Chou became a figurehead, the stronger dukedoms became sovereign states by absorbing weaker neighbors. In the early seventh century B.C., Duke Huan of the eastern state of Ch'i profited from his minister Kuan Chung's innovations and the monopoly of iron and salt. He conquered more than thirty fiefdoms and repelled invading nomads by rallying other states. His authority, however, was challenged by the southern state of Ch'u. This southern province, by draining vast swamps near lakes in the central Yangtze valley and opening up forests, had grown in power and was expanding northeastward to the Huai River valley. With his allies and a show of strength, Duke Huan intimidated Ch'u, forcing them to pay tribute to the Chou king. He became the first super-lord to preside over other princes in the name of the Son of Heaven.

In mid-seventh century B.C., Duke Wên of the northern state of Chin returned to power after nearly twenty years of exile caused by family intrigue. He pacified border tribes by mutual nonaggression, encouraged farmers by forgiving debts and reducing taxes and sent traders to other states to promote commerce. His decisive victory over Ch'u's army in 632 B.C. made him the super-lord following Duke Huan; his position was sanctified by the king in an elaborate ceremony.

Meanwhile in the west, the land of Chou ancestry was left to the state of Ch'in (not to be confused with Chin) when the royal capital moved east. Living among and fighting with fierce nomadic tribes, its rulers learned to work hard and stay alert. By stimulating farm production and imposing strict discipline, Ch'in rose to become another serious contender for super-lordship. With the intensification of the power struggle, less and less attention was paid to the shadowy authority of Chou.

Stately bronze vessel, with design of twin-bodied dragon, reflects the power and wealth of Chou royalty.

The Land and the Tiller

In early Chou both the land and the subjects living on it were under the complete control of the king. In practice, however, he only administered the land in and around the royal capital and exacted tribute from the dukes. The dukes followed the same procedure with their ministers. The land was actually managed by the ministers and their officials known as *shih*, or hereditary nobles. For example, peasants of a noble household belonged to the "family" for whom they worked and on whom they depended. The ruling class, comprising the king, the dukes, the ministers and *shih*, took everything from the peasants after feeding, lodging and clothing them.

But beginning with the dukedom of Lu in 594 B.C., a twenty per cent tax on produce was initiated to encourage efficiency; the farmers then took care of themselves with after-tax harvests. In effect, they became possessors of the land. Pioneers turned wasteland into new soil that was free from hereditary bondage; brave warriors and other persons of merit were awarded land as a reward for accomplishment. Soon land became real estate to be bought and sold. Then, with the introduction of iron implements, the expansion of industries and trade, and the circulation of money, came the accumulation of capital. The rich began to gather huge land holdings, forcing the poor to become landless tenants. As warfare among states increased, taxes rose to unbearable heights of fifty per cent or more; many tenant farmers, owing more than they could produce, escaped to join indigent, nonproductive and disruptive elements. By late Chou, every rising state was striving to bring the farmer back to the land.

Jade tiger crouching on man recalls a Confucius saying: "Harsh political measures are crueler than tigers."

High-crested bird decorates a ritual wine vessel of bronze. It was hand-crafted in the early Chou period.

Ferocity frozen in bronze. This unique pair of tigers have hollow chamber in center of their bodies.

The Hundred Schools of Thought

An unprecedented explosion of intellectual activity began in the sixth century B.C. It was initiated by those men at the bottom of the ruling class known as the *shih*. Serving as overseers or managers of the peasants who farmed the large estates of the nobles in peacetime, they also led the military in wartime. They were among the best-educated as well as the most industrious class in the Chou dynasty. It was expected that a *shih* would excel in writing, music, archery, chariot driving, arithmetic and "rules of conduct." The continuing expansion of commerce, the technological revolution in metal, the increase in population, all contributed to the rise of the *shih*. It became possible for a member of this class, although not born into nobility, to rise to ministerial status.

A majority of the progressive thinkers came from this class. Most outstanding to emerge was Confucius, who said: "The gentleman makes demands on himself; the inferior man makes demands on others."

After Confucius the most influential philosopher was Lao Tzu, who, with his followers, formed the Taoist group who taught *Tao*, "the way of nature," as a way of life. Lao Tzu said: "*Tao* invariably does nothing [*wu-wei*] and yet there is nothing that is not done."

Still another of the outstanding philosopher-teachers was Mo Ti, who was born shortly after Confucius died. Mo Ti derogated the Confucian inordinate attention to ritual and criticized their fatalism and materialism.

In the succeeding chapters we will examine some of the unique philosophies expounded by these early teachers which included the Logicians, Strategists, Legalists, Militarists and indeed a "hundred schools" of thought which touched upon every phase of the human condition. They formed a base of ideas that permanently influenced the Chinese people.

Tiger on bell top is more naturalistic in feeling than those opposite; it was cast five centuries later.

Like tiger above, this bowl is a product of the Warring States period; it takes the form of a stag.

Two hunters wearing loin cloths use bow and arrow and short sword to corner a wounded stag. This is one of several panels decorating a bronze vase. Other scenes show a snake swallowing

birds, griffinlike monsters and unique supernatural creatures. Other known Warring States art objects have homogeneous designs decorated with geometric borders and reveal similar scenes of men hunting and fighting, and of ancient rituals.

The Teacher of Teachers

The year 551 B.C. marked the birth of China's most honored philosopher. In the state of Lu, an ancient center of traditional learning, a son was born into a poor family which is said to have descended from the royal lineage of the Shang dynasty. The child was named K'ung Ch'iu. Westerners know the name in its Latin-ized form—Confucius. As a young man Confucius tried to find employment in government and for a time held a minor position in the state of Lu. But at heart he was a reformer, not a politician, a dedicated believer in order and virtue for both the rulers and the ruled. Throughout his adulthood he preached that *li*, the rites for functions and rules of conduct, was the binding force and the perfect form for an enduring social order.

Confucius decried use of figurines in burial as too reminiscent of the Shang practice of sacrificing

During much of his lifetime he traveled from state to state trying to obtain a hearing for his beliefs which were based not only upon *li* but upon *jên*, a benevolent humane approach to government. Failing in politics, the philosopher turned to teaching. As an educator, Confucius gained a following. He is said to have had three thousand students, seventy-two of whom became devoted disciples.

In his old age it is believed he edited and interpreted works of history, philosophy and literature, collecting them into six classics that embodied the essence of ancient Chinese culture. Together with his sayings, as recorded by his disciples in the book called Analects, the Confucian works later became a major influence in the Chinese way of life. He died in 479 B.C. before his wisdom was fully recognized by the people who would later revere his memory and adopt his teachings.

human slaves. Yet these were made soon after his death. Excavations of Warring States tombs show vogue of such figurines.

The Art of War and Peace

The intellectual ferment in the third century B.C. was at least partly responsible for the unification of all China. Indeed, there was a great need for thoughtful leadership behind the military effort to unite the seven kingdoms which were in almost continuous conflict as each sought to dominate the country. These warring states varied in size, military and economic strength and especially in leadership.

It was leadership and organization that finally triumphed. The kingdom of Ch'in had a wise and farsighted leader, Duke Hsiao. He employed a resourceful military adventurer, Shang Yang, who in 359 B.C. began to lay the foundations for the first empire of China.

Under Shang Yang and his successors the government pursued a policy of enlisting every available source of manpower. To break up large households that sheltered nonworkers, every male except the first son was required to leave home upon coming of age. Commerce and industry became government monopolies. The population was reorganized into small units of five to ten families, each responsible for policing the others. These small townships were combined into districts that reported directly to the central government. Farmers and weavers whose production was above the average were exempted from labor service. To further increase food production, new land with ownership rights was opened up to homesteaders. Fighting within the country was forbidden but military men in the service of the state were generously rewarded. A most significant reform was the abolition of titles held by royal kinsmen who showed no military merit. The nobility that did not contribute to the welfare of the state were stripped of their privileges. The scholar class was generally distrusted and literary men were barred from the country. Under these stern measures the kingdom of Ch'in became the strongest of the competing states.

When mutual suspicion prevented an effective alliance among the competing states the Ch'in attacked them ruthlessly. In the war for the prize of all China the humane rules of chivalry were forgotten. Surrendering troops were executed, enemy villages were mercilessly destroyed. The destruction was to last for years. But the groundwork for victory and ultimate unification had been laid.

▷ *The tomb of a prince in the kingdom of Kuo. Buried with him were weapons, chariots and his live horses.*

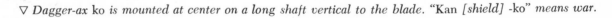

▽ *Dagger-ax* ko *is mounted at center on a long shaft vertical to the blade. "Kan [shield] -ko" means war.*

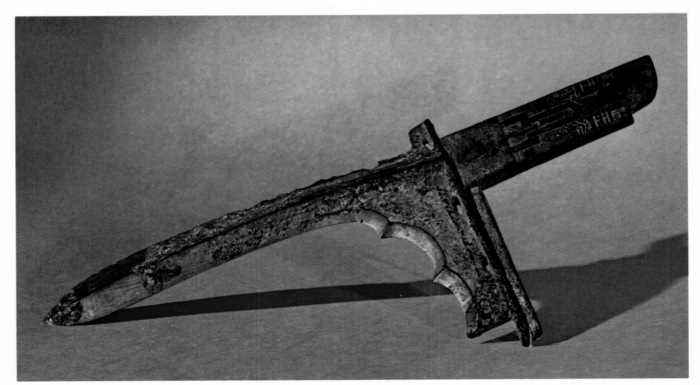

New Wealth and Power

In mid-third century B.C., one of Ch'in's minor princes, I-jên, was held hostage in the kingdom of Chao (all states having claimed the status of kingdoms a century earlier). A merchant-extraordinary named Lü Pu-wei met the young prince and immediately recognized in him a political asset. He asked his rich father: "What is the greatest profit to be earned in farming?" "Ten times," said his father. "In trading pearls and jades?" "A hundred times," answered the old man. "In controlling a future king?" "Incalculable!" was the reply. So Lü Pu-wei began a campaign to repatriate Prince I-jên and to install him as heir to the crown prince of Ch'in. He bribed the envoys and ambassadors to the Ch'in court to praise his puppet.

Knowing that Lady Hua-yang, the favorite mistress of the crown prince, had no heir, Lü bribed Lady Hua-yang's brother to implant the idea of adopting one. As Lü explained, this would return the country to a rightful, yet countryless, prince and give an heir to the barren queen-to-be. Events moved according to his scheme; the mistress became queen and in 250 B.C. I-jên became her heir. In another year he ascended the throne. Lü Pu-wei, the merchant of politics, was now rewarded with the prime ministership and one hundred thousand families as his fiefs. The new prime minister attracted scholars from nearby states and employed them to compile an encyclopedic work touching upon subjects ranging from heaven to earth.

When I-jên died, his son Ying Chêng was enthroned at the age of twelve, and Lü as regent took over control of the powerful kingdom. But Lü lost everything when Ying Chêng came of age and decided to reclaim his kingly powers. The ex-merchant became involved in a palace intrigue which was punishable by death. Lü ended his life with a cup of poison. Yet his meteoric career illustrated the wealth and power of the rising merchant class toward the end of the Chou dynasty.

Carved wood burial figures are typical of the southern state of Ch'u around the third century B.C. These were originally painted in bright colors; now only faint red and black designs remain. The arms are lost.

The Odes and Ch'u Tz'u

The genesis of Chinese literature is *Shih ching,* the Book of Odes, which contains some three hundred verses of which many were set to music. Included are folk songs, ceremonial odes and sacrificial laudations. This work, basic to the understanding of Chinese history, was composed between 1100 and 600 B.C. It represented the poetry of the north—simple, human and sometimes solemn. The memory of every Chinese writer since Confucius has been moved by the sentiments, mild in expression but deep and lasting in feeling. To quote one short love song of a girl:

> Green be your ribbons/deep be my longings
> Even if I do not go/would you not send words?
> Green be your jade/deep be my thoughts
> Even if I do not go/would you not come?
> Back and forth/on the city gate
> Missing you for one day/is like three months!

As Chinese culture penetrated southward, poetry was influenced by the supernatural world of the shamans. An extraordinary scholar, Ch'ü Yüan (343–277 B.C.) nurtured by rich folklore and the religious songs of his native kingdom of Ch'u, almost single-handedly established *Ch'u tz'u* (verse) as the poetry of the south. Ch'ü Yüan was a nobleman with great compassion for the people of his country who, he believed, were being destroyed by a succession of ineffective self-indulgent kings. He foresaw the impending doom of his country but felt powerless to save it. His deep grief and frustration, before turning into desperation and suicide, found sublime expression in his new poetry, which was interwoven with imagery and symbolism. He left very few pieces to posterity, but his major work *Li sao,* or "On Encountering Sorrow," is a magnificent soliloquy. In the periods which followed, Chinese poetry drank deep from these two ever-flowing springs: the odes from the north and *Ch'u tz'u* from the south.

An official-looking figurine, refined in feature, is a made-of-clay attendant found in a Ch'u tomb.

Rare fish-shaped money. Various metal coins gained wide usage by the third century B.C., later were standardized.

The Road to Unity

Toward the end of the Chou dynasty, the last call for benevolent and virtuous rule came from Mêng K'o, or Mencius, the supreme exponent of Confucian precepts. He wrote of the basic goodness of human nature and claimed that the people had the right to revolt when oppressed; but a third influential Confucian thinker refuted him. Hsün Tzu declared that man must be trained to be good; human nature was evil. The idea of molding human nature led Hsün Tzu's two leading pupils to develop the theory of Legalism. The first, Han Fei, rejected individual ethical values in favor of central authority. He soon met death at the hands of the second, Li Ssu, a well-established minister who had similar ideas and wanted no competition at the Ch'in court.

Li Ssu had deserted his native Ch'u as a lowly clerk and gone straight to the center of power to expound his ideas. He instituted the control of human beings to be used as servants of the state and drove them to work and fight with a system of rewards and punishments. Using such dictatorial methods, he helped the Ch'in kingdom establish the first empire in the territory we now know as China. Li Ssu's plans for expansion through warfare were soon realized, for the people were willing to pay any price for the stability of a single empire after centuries of feudal chaos.

Mongolian figure in cast bronze with jade birds comes from vicinity of Lo-yang, the capital of Eastern Chou.

The First Empires
221 B.C.–A.D. 220

Imperial age begins with Ch'in, the unifier, and continues with Han, the expansionist . . . Han's founder rises from ranks of common people . . . Han envoys explore from Japan to Mesopotamia, from Mongolia to India; they establish the Silk Road linking the East and the West . . . Confucianism dominates the ruling ideology; cosmology influences politics . . . Centralization of power degenerates into palace intrigue and abuse, driving peasants into revolt . . . Three kingdoms divide the empire.

HISTORICAL CHRONOLOGY

B.C.

221   *Ying Chêng proclaims himself First Emperor of Ch'in.*

c.220   *Li Ssu standardizes writing style, weights and measures, and chariot-wheel gauge.*

214   *Hsiung-nu (the Huns) defeated. Regional walls joined to form Great Wall.*

213   *Burning of books of history, literature and philosophy unrelated to Ch'in.*

210   *First Emperor dies. Revolts spread.*

206   *Ch'in dynasty ends.*

202   *Lui Pang founds Han dynasty, revives feudalism. Emperor Kao-tsu and next three rulers restore land to farmers and reduce taxes.*

140   *Expansionist rule begun by Emperor Wu.*

138–126   *First mission to the Western Regions by envoy Chang Ch'ien.*

136   *Confucianism becomes official ideology.*

129   *New taxes finance public works and expeditions.*

127–119   *Successful campaigns against the Hsiung-nu (Huns).*

111   *Han armies conquer Vietnam and the Southwest.*

108   *Han colony established in Korea.*

102   *Han forces subjugate Ferghana, take its fine horses.*

36   *Chinese soldiers confront Roman legionnaires in Sogdiana.*

A.D.

8   *Wang Mang founds Hsin dynasty.*

25   *Liu Hsiu begins the Later or Eastern Han period as Emperor Kuang-wu.*

39   *Land registration and census taking.*

57   *Japan pays tribute to the Han court.*

73   *Envoy Pan Ch'ao begins mission in Central Asia and dominates this region until 107.*

166   *Anton of Rome sends envoy to Han court.*

184   *Rise of the Yellow Turban rebels.*

190–208   *Ts'ao Ts'ao consolidates power in the north.*

208   *Liu Pei and Sun Ch'üan defeat Ts'ao Ts'ao at Red Cliff.*

220   *Eldest son of Ts'ao Ts'ao deposes last Han emperor and ends the Han dynasty.*

ART CHRONOLOGY

B.C.

c.220   *Li Ssu unifies writing into small seal style.*

212   *Building activities at height for A-fang palace.*

c.220–120   *Poetic essays in fu style which dominate Han poetry until end of second century A.D. created by Mei Ch'êng and Ssu-ma Hsiang-ju (179–117 B.C.)*

140–87   *Emperor Wu of Han begins Bureau of Music, collects folk songs, commissions music and dance.*

c.150   *Discourses on philosophy and alchemy (Huai-nan Tzu) edited by Prince Liu An (179–122 B.C.).*

117 or later.   *Stone sculpture of horse trampling a barbarian at the tomb of Ho Ch'ü-ping.*

c.120–90   *Ssu-ma Ch'ien (145–90? B.C.) works on Shih chi, the first history with systematic structure.*

c.100   *Jade shroud with golden threads used in burial of Prince Liu Shêng and wife.*

c.50 B.C.–A.D. c.20   *Existing literature classified into six main divisions and 13,269 volumes by 596 authors edited by Liu Hsiang and son Liu Hsin.*

2 B.C.–A.D. 4   *Dated lacquer vessels found in Korea and near Ulan Bator.*

A.D. c.50–90   *History of the Former Han dynasty begun by Pan Piao and written by his son Pan Ku (32–92).*

105   *Paper invented by Ts'ai Lun.*

100–21   *First Chinese lexicography, Shuo-wên, containing 9,353 characters plus 1,163 with double use, is completed by Hsü Shên.*

147–68   *Engraved designs on Wu Family funerary stones.*

175   *Calligraphy in official script by Ts'ai Yung engraved on the stones of Confucian classics.*

196–220   *Eminent poets are Ts'ao Ts'ao, his sons Ts'ao P'ei and Ts'ao Chih together with the Chien-an Seven. Chung Yu creates the regular script.*

Han period develops and exports silk textiles.

The Great Wall was begun twenty-five hundred years ago when feudal states built defense barriers at mountain passes.

The Great Unifier

With the successful reunification of China, Ying Chêng assumed the title *Shih-huang-ti*, the "First Emperor." Following the advice of his minister Li Ssu, he abolished the feudal system and divided the country into thirty-six (later forty) provinces, administered by officials carefully selected. Arms belonging to private citizens and conquered weapons were collected, melted down and cast into twelve gigantic statues which were installed in his palace.

Unification was further achieved by the removal of fortifications between former feudal states, the shifting of thousands of scattered rich and powerful families to the capital, a large-scale transfer of the population to borderlands and the construction of a web of highways. Weights, measurements, currency, axle

They were linked together in the third century. Most of the present Great Wall, above, was rebuilt in the Ming dynasty.

widths and script style were standardized.

To facilitate the conquest of China's extreme south as far as Vietnam, the emperor ordered a canal dug between a north-flowing river and a south-flowing river, making it possible to sail from Central China to Canton.

After General Mêng T'ien defeated the nomadic Hsiung-nu tribe, hundreds of thousands of laborers were conscripted to connect the northern defense walls, built during the past few centuries, into early China's greatest fortification—the Great Wall. The emperor made his presence felt by making five inspection tours to various parts of the empire. On summits of well-known mountains he erected stone steles to commemorate his achievements.

But the Ch'in emperor's most extravagant projects were the building of his palaces and his tomb, which may have employed as many as a million and a half workers at one time. His cavernous crypt was illuminated by ever-burning fish-oil lamps and the entrance is said to have been protected by automatic crossbows.

The Chinese have used cavalry warfare since before 300 B.C. This Han figurine is made of clay and highly stylized.

Following the rigid precepts of the Legalists, Prime Minister Li Ssu induced the emperor to issue the most unpopular edict in Chinese history. He decreed the burning of most of the great books of the past. To quote him:

> Your servant suggests that all books in the imperial archives, save the memoirs of Ch'in, be burned. All persons in the empire, except members of the Academy of Learned Scholars, in possession of the Book of Odes, the Book of History and discourses of the hundred philosophers should take them to the local governors and have them indiscriminately burned. Those who dare talk to each other about the Book of Odes and the Book of History should be executed and their bodies exposed in the market place. Anyone referring to the past to criticize the present should, together with all members of his family, be put to death. . . . Books not to be destroyed will be those on medicine and

pharmacy, divination by the tortoise and milfoil, and agriculture and arboriculture. People wishing to pursue learning should take the officials as their teachers.

Although a most able and energetic organizer the emperor was deeply superstitious. When two trusted magicians escaped after failing to find the elixir of life he had scores of magicians and scholars buried alive. On his fifth journey, in search of a formula for immortality, he died.

Li Ssu, with the powerful court eunuch Chao Kao and the emperor's young second son, quickly organized a plot that resulted in the suicide of the eldest son and rightful heir, and enthroned his younger brother. Reigning as *Êhr-shih-huang-ti*, but controlled by Chao Kao, he was to be the last of the Ch'in emperors.

60

The Peasants Revolt

For the first time in Chinese history, desperate peasants defied their leaders and used their farm implements as weapons. In the first year of the new emperor, a contingent of tenant farmers who had been drafted to guard the borders were caught in a rainstorm as they marched north. Two of the draftees, Ch'ên Shêng and Wu Kuang, calculated that they would never reach the appointed place on time, a crime punishable by death. Calling upon their comrades for help they succeeded in killing their armed escorts. Soon the leaders headed an open rebellion. The government forces quickly quelled this revolt but a second peasant uprising began, this time led by former aristocrats and local peasant leaders. With this rebellion a new leader emerged, the ruthless Hsiang Yü, a grandson of a general who had been among the last defenders of the former kingdom of Ch'u. In 207 B.C., Hsiang Yü had his revenge over the Ch'in for the defeat of his ancestor when he crushed its main force and is said to have massacred more than two hundred thousand war prisoners. The Ch'in dynasty virtually ended when the eunuch Chao Kao murdered the Second Emperor and installed the emperor's nephew as the "king" of Ch'in.

A second rebel leader, Liu Pang, emerged. He was a former minor official and farmer who had been ordered to deliver drafted laborers to the capital. Finding it difficult to prevent their escape, he led them in an uprising against the government. Liu Pang started with less than one hundred men but after three years he entered the capital with a huge well-disciplined

Young girl attendant is a tomb figurine and fine example of Han human form sculpture. Short dress, convenient for work, contrasts with long, flowing garments with train worn by figurines representing ladies.

△Seated laughing statuettes in bronze probably represent the northern "barbarians." Their round faces, high cheek-bones, large eyes and noses are distinctly non-Chinese; triangular caps and bare shoulders are typical of the northern tribes.

Everyday world is well-portrayed by Han tomb pottery which was intended to make the dead feel at home. House with courtyard, wellhead, granary, domestic animals and figures are typical of life as it appeared in first century B.C.

army. The king of Ch'in surrendered. The two rebel leaders confronted one another in Hsien-yang. Hsiang Yü had far superior forces and succeeded in burning the vast palace complex. Liu Pang made a strategic retreat, then came back to engage Hsiang Yü in a series of battles that lasted over four years. The tenacious Liu Pang suffered serious injuries twelve times and lost every battle except the last one. In the end Hsiang Yü lost the support of his people through unnecessary killing and looting. He was only thirty years old when he was surrounded in his final battle. Rather than face capture he killed himself.

Liu Pang, now the victor, became Emperor Kao-tsu of the Han dynasty.

Model of granary in glazed clay shows one man going up ladder with sack while another waits to receive the grain. Two carved animals in front guard building. In prosperous Han around 150 B.C., official granaries were usually overfilled.

Grain mill shows rice husker, left, and winnowing machine with early crank handle, at right; corn grinder is in center.

A Time for Rest

The pattern of empire had been set by the Ch'in dynasty, and now the Han dynasty consolidated and amplified the grand design. Han inherited a ravaged, war-torn but essentially unified country. The short-lived Ch'in dynasty had passed on a fundamentally sound plan of government—and, most important, the concept of a unified China.

The first goal of the Han leaders was to provide a period of peace so that the economy could be repaired. Early Han policies therefore moved toward simplification, restoration and pacification. Ch'in laws were clarified and applied without exceptions. The court staffed a central bureaucracy with able officials from various regions to prevent local discontent.

Veterans were rewarded with land, housing and farming equipment. Merchants who had taken part in war profiteering were prohibited from wearing silk, riding horses and using carriages, or entering officialdom. The government encouraged a return to the farm by reducing land taxes. Heads of families with newborn children were exempted from military service.

The four rulers to follow Liu Pang restored land to the hungry farmers, reduced the military draft and cut taxes. Disfigurement, such as facial tattooing, amputation of feet, hands and toes, and the execution of relatives of criminals, were abolished. The necessity for such reform points up the sadism of previous rulers.

A brief interlude of disunity flared when seven princes rebelled. This abortive attempt to divide the country ended with the killing of their leader and the suicide of the remaining six. By 154 B.C. the Han emperor had established central control over most of the country. China regained its strength. Gradually the scorched earth turned green; the decimated population multiplied and war wounds were healed by a policy of *laissez-faire*.

65

△ *A detail from wilderness scenes on carved lid of a pottery incense burner shows a hunter thrusting his sword into tiger.*

◁ *A Han farmer works a tilt-hammer grain pounder; at right is rotary mill with double hopper; dog and domestic fowls watch.*

▽ *Below, the tiger triumphs over the human. Incense burners, always made with stems and bases, were also cast in metal.*

Minor official and driver in chariot approach gate-tower followed by foot soldier. An official waits to greet them.

The Expansion

The Emperor Wu, an intelligent, active and able leader, led a country that for a time was able to support his ambitions. After sixty years of comparative tranquillity, Han's economic vigor had reached its zenith. But a major obstacle to continuing peace remained. For more than a millennium the nomadic Hsiung-nu in the north had been a scourge to China; they attained unprecedented military strength at the beginning of Han. The domain of these fierce tribesmen extended from Manchuria to Lake Balkhash, with their southern border abutting on Han's northern provinces. Every year, in two provinces alone, thousands of inhabitants were killed or captured. Emperor Wu fought back. His grand strategy was to sever the enemy's liaison with their eastern and western vassals, and finally to confront them with superior manpower.

As part of this plan, the Han envoy Chang Ch'ien ventured westward to contact the Hsiung-nu's former adversary, the Yüeh-chih, but he was captured by the enemy. After ten years he escaped and reached the Yüeh-chih. Although he failed to persuade its ruler to join the fight, Chang Ch'ien returned with a wealth of information about the Western Regions, as Chinese Turkestan and the lands beyond were called at that time.

In 127 B.C., Han's first victory against the Hsiung-nu reclaimed the fertile Ordos region on the Yellow River, into which the emperor promptly moved one hundred thousand families as settlers. Six years later, a second campaign resulted in a complete victory after which a Hsiung-nu chieftain surrendered with thousands of his troops. Two years later the Mongols' main force was crushed in a costly battle.

Again, colonization followed conquest as seven hundred thousand people were moved to

This is typical design on stones, bricks and tiles in Han dynasty tombs. Rank of deceased is reflected in type of carriage.

the northwest, converting more grazing lands into farms. Meanwhile the Great Wall was extended westward to protect the corridor that linked China with Central Asia.

In 115 B.C., Emperor Wu sent Chang Ch'ien on his second western expedition with selected soldiers, six hundred horses, herds of cattle and large quantities of gold, silks and other goods. Chang established his base at Wu-sun, a country just east of Lake Balkhash. From there his emissaries reached many countries of the West, including Bactria, Parthia and India. Chang returned and died not long after, but he had opened the overland route later known as the Silk Road, which became the main artery of material and cultural exchange between the East and the West, from the Han capital Ch'ang-an to the Mediterranean shore.

Over the new route and from conquests in the northwest, China imported horses, alfalfa, furs, grapes and walnuts, as well as Central Asian music and musical instruments; silk and other textiles were exported. From the Han people the outside world learned how to build underground irrigation channels and of new metallurgical formulas. What began as a strategy to defeat Hsiung-nu now assumed far greater significance in world history.

Between 112 and 110 B.C., Han armies conquered China's extreme southern provinces and Vietnam. The colonization of Korea came after a military campaign by land and sea. Through this outpost, and over the Korean straits of the Sea of Japan, Chinese culture slowly began to infiltrate Japan.

But was this expansion worth the price in lives lost in war and in the resulting agricultural crisis? During the fifty-four years of Emperor Wu's reign his military expeditions drained the national economy and reputedly killed half the population. But the emperor did achieve a China growing rapidly in territory. In his last years, realizing that the nation was near exhaustion, he concentrated on bringing

Bronze mirrors originated around 500 B.C. and gained wide usage. They were often exported to Western Regions and Japan.

about an agricultural revolution by using newly developed farm implements and techniques. Seed spreaders and tandem ploughs drawn by two oxen increased productivity, while the new method of rotating planting every three rows maintained the earth's fertility.

The two succeeding emperors continued his efforts and gradually replenished the national strength. However, from the middle of the first century B.C. onward, corruption spread through the court and the bureaucracy. This intensified the polarization of the rich and the poor and provided an opportunity for Wang Mang, a royal kinsman, to usurp the throne. His short-lived Hsin dynasty adopted economic measures which enabled dishonest officials to exploit the peasants who, following the previous pattern, were driven to rebellion. In the wake of these revolts, China experienced another traumatic upheaval as warfare broke out among contenders for the throne. When stability returned under Liu Hsiu, a member of the royal house who proclaimed himself emperor, the capital was moved eastward to Lo-yang, and the next two centuries became known as Eastern or Later Han, as distinguished from the first period Western or Former Han.

This kneeling pottery warrior once held his shield in one hand and his sword, or a lance, in the other.

Guardians holding halberds and swords stand guard over the deceased. These "printings on clay" were stamped on tiles.

A New Wind

By A.D. 2 the population had climbed to some sixty million. But the concentration of land ownership among the rich and noble had forced many peasants back into the slavery that had been abolished by previous rulers. In the current struggle to revive the Han fortunes Liu Hsiu, now known as Emperor Kuang-wu, issued seven edicts within twelve years releasing slaves. To prevent peasants from being sold, he supplied aid to the desperately poor. Relief measures, together with strict punishments for corrupt officials, reasonable taxation, and infrequent military campaigns brought the country to a precarious stability. But once again the traditional enemy, Hsiung-nu, arose.

In A.D. 73 General Pan Ch'ao led thirty-six men on a mission to reopen negotiations with the Western Regions in order to undermine the enemy's alliances. Not far from his starting point he detected the presence of an enemy camp. His surprise attack in the night wiped out one hundred and thirty Hsiung-nu. His continuing campaigns eventually won for Han the allegiance of fifty-five small countries north and south of the Tarim Basin. Later, as governor-general of Central Asia, Pan Ch'ao dispatched his envoy Kan Ying to Roman Syria, but after passing through Parthia and reaching

Splendid funerary clay house has paintings on exterior walls. Post and beam construction is clue to wooden architecture of Han, none of which has survived. Multistoried structures were apparently common.

Mesopotamia, the emissary, facing a vast sea (probably the Persian Gulf), is said to have been discouraged by reports of dangers ahead. This journey to Mesopotamia marked the westernmost point of Han's explorations.

A pattern of palace intrigues developed beginning in A.D. 88 and lasted until the end of the Han dynasty. A legitimate child-emperor was placed on the throne under the influence of female relatives and palace eunuchs. Because of his complete seclusion only the women and eunuchs came in intimate contact with him. The royal wives and concubines and their relatives were no match in palace intrigue for the eunuchs who soon rose to ministerial status. The scholar class, many of whom were ministers, resented the eunuchs' influence and opposed them. Ceaseless conflicts among these three power groups: royal relatives, scholar-officials and eunuchs, gradually weakened the government and caused its collapse.

The first blow came when Emperor Huan branded more than two hundred scholars who protested the dominance of the eunuchs. Two years later, just after twelve-year-old Emperor Ling was installed, the powerful eunuch clique wiped out the empress dowager's family and killed more than one hundred of the scholar class. Six hundred more were imprisoned and a thousand Imperial Academy student protestors were arrested. But in A.D. 189 a general from a scholar family disposed of the eunuch problem by massacring two thousand of them. The last child Han emperor was enthroned soon after and survived only until A.D. 220, a puppet of the militarists.

73

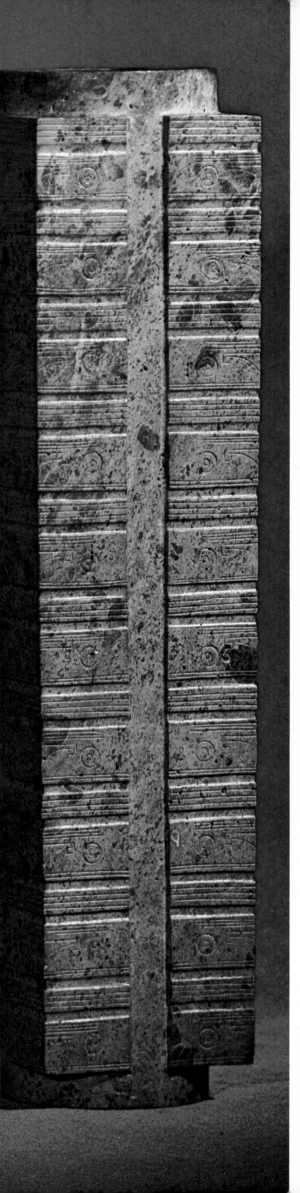

Men of Science

In the second century B.C., naturalists completed the book *Huai-nan tzu*, which contains much early Chinese scientific thought. Among later thinkers, two stand out. Wang Chung's (A.D. 27–c.96) method was based upon the examination of actual objects and events. He believed Heaven and Earth to be natural objects devoid of will, that the human body ended with death without leaving any spirit and that hallucinations were caused by sickness.

Chang Hêng (A.D. 78–139) also studied natural phenomena, and denied that they were caused by Heaven's anger. He designed a weather vane and a jar-shaped seismograph with eight dragon heads, capable of expelling a ball in the direction of an earth tremor. Chang theorized that Heaven was like an egg with the earth its yolk. He found the positions of the equator, the ecliptic, and the polar star, and he wrote an explanation of why days were long in summer and short in winter. He discovered that the moon received light from the sun and rotated around the earth, that the changing positions of the sun, moon and earth caused it to wax and wane, and that the shadow of the earth was the reason for the eclipse. Improving on early models, he developed the first armillary sphere with horizon and meridian rings and later succeeded in making it rotate by water pressure. He checked its indications against actual observations of celestial phenomena.

During the Han dynasty calendars that predicted eclipses were devised, and a south-pointing spoon (simulating the shape of the Big Dipper) was made from magnetite—forerunner of the magnetic needle compass. The foundation of systematic botany was laid through medicine, since doctors relied on plants and herbs for pharmaceuticals. Acupuncture, which probably had been discovered earlier, gained widespread usage.

The invention of paper was credited to Ts'ai Lun in A.D. 105. His method found its way to Europe via Samarkand some six hundred years later.

Jade pi *disk, the symbol of Heaven, and* tsung *column, symbol of Earth, are traceable to the Neolithic and Shang periods respectively. Heaven is round, the Earth is square. The disk also represents the sun.*

Symbols of the Universe

Nature and human events were viewed through a strange mixture of mysticism and rationality in the Han dynasty. The belief already existing by late Chou that the universe was made of five elements—water, fire, wood, metal and soil—and the concept of *yin* (negative) and *yang* (positive) forces, were combined into a formula for interpreting and predicting the

Mating of tortoise and snake, both yin *animals, probably symbolizes birth of spring from winter,which they represent.*

Gilt bronze toilet box painted with clouds and symbolic bird (phoenix) inside lid. Bird is symbol of yang *and summer.*

past and future. Each direction acquired a color, element, animal, season and position in the *yin-yang* cycle. For example: east—blue, wood, dragon, spring and minor *yang*; south—red, fire, phoenix, summer and major *yang*; west—white, metal, tiger, autumn and minor *yin*; north—black, water, tortoise, winter and major *yin*; center—yellow, earth, and man, the super animal for all seasons, capable of harmonizing with both *yin* and *yang*.

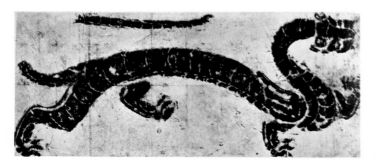

A Han tile rubbing is divided into two scenes: the upper panel shows men shooting birds in flight with bow and arrow; the lower one shows men harvesting and threshing. Except for the oversized fish in lotus pond, the drawing is naturalistic.

A Han nobleman and lady sit on mat to watch a juggler and a sword dancer. Below, a girl with streamer performs to the music of flutes played by sitting musicians. The conductor is waving drumstick. Both tiles show free-flowing art form.

The Confucian Legacy

Confucianism gained eminence during the Han period because of the meeting of minds of a monarch in search of a clear mandate from Heaven and a scholar with an ambition to dominate the current ideologies, which included earlier Legalist, Taoist and Confucian theories. Their formula was simple—they interpreted the past to suit the present. The scholar Tung Chung-shu, hand-picked in an examination by Emperor Wu soon after his ascension to the throne, claimed authority from the Confucian ideal of a perfect social order and from the cosmological theory of the Book of Changes and the Yin-yang Five Elements School to support his own concept of the "Oneness of Heaven and Man."

From the earlier Confucian doctrine he took the view that stability in society depends on three major human relationships: ruler and subject, father and son, and husband and wife; that the morality of the individual depends on five constant virtues: humanity, righteousness, propriety, wisdom and good faith.

From the Book of Changes and the Yin-yang School he adopted the concept that the universe comprises Heaven, Earth and Man—the basic trilogy. These are made up of five elements: wood, fire, soil, metal and water. They are controlled by two primal forces: *yin*, the negative, and *yang*, the positive. *Yin* and *yang* complement each other; therefore, when there is high, there must be low; left, right; front, back; outside, inside; good, bad; cheer, anger; cold, warm; and day, night. *Yang* may be equal in quantity to *yin*, but never in quality, because *yang* is inherently nobler than *yin*. In human relationship, the ruler, the father and the

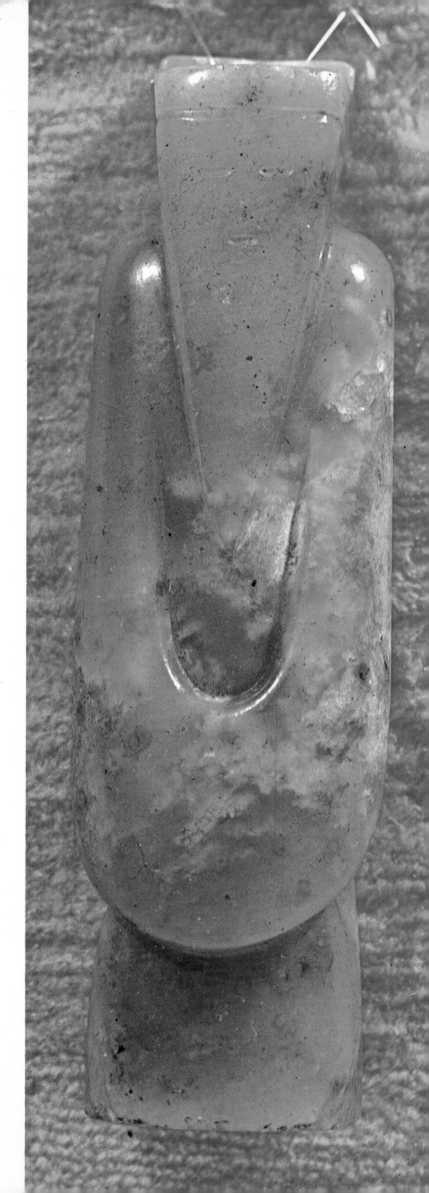

A dignified elder was stylized to complete simplicity, as the sculptor brought out the beauty of the green jade in this pendant. This abstract charm, for the dead or the living, probably symbolizes longevity.

Before paper was invented books were made
by stringing together writings on bamboo or wooden slips.

Bronze seal of a Han general and its impression
in red; Chinese seals have same authority as signatures.

husband are *yang*, while the subject, the son and the wife are *yin*. *Yang* is the substance and always leads, but *yin* is the shadow and always follows. *Yang* and *yin* wax and wane alternately. The essence of Heaven and Earth, when combined, is oneness; when separated, becomes two, *yin* and *yang*. These in turn are divided into four seasons which harmonize with the five directional elements; namely, wood/east, fire/south, soil/center, metal/west, and water/north. In a forward order, each element produces the one following; for example, wood produces fire, and fire produces soil. In reverse order, each element overcomes the next; for example, water overcomes fire, and fire overcomes metal. Man is born with the nature of Heaven; therefore, he also inherits the qualities of *yin*, *yang* and the five elements and is responsive to Heaven. When human events are in harmony with Heaven, great peace prevails; when they are contrary to Heaven, great upheavals occur. Heaven produces the ruler for the people, but not the people for the ruler. At the same time, Heaven favors *yang* and shuns *yin*; therefore, favors benevolence and shuns punishments. Thus Heaven always supports the benevolent ruler and removes the tyrant.

Tung Chung-shu put his theories into practice when he acted as judge in two hundred and thirty-two controversial cases. His decisions put emphasis on magnanimity and avoidance of the death penalty. He recommended limitation of land ownership in order to curb the oppression of the poor by the rich and powerful. By injecting political significance into natural disasters, such as earthquakes and floods, Tung Chung-shu was able to derive constructive results from his emperor's belief in cosmology. Citing political philosophy, implied by Confucius in the "Spring and Autumn Annals," he pointed out that unity was the universal virtue and Confucianism the only way to unified authority. Yet many of his philosophical ideas had no relationship to earlier Confucianism. He reinterpreted history and arranged the past dynasties as Three Reigns and Five Sovereigns (to match the three relationships and five virtues) to prove that Han was now the dynasty favored by Heaven. Hearing Tung's arguments and those of his scholar-disciples, Emperor Wu established Confucianism as the official government doctrine.

The Grand Historians

The first complete history of China and foreign peoples known to the Chinese was written by Ssu-ma Ch'ien in the first century B.C. From his distinguished father Ssu-ma T'an young Ch'ien learned of astronomy, Taoism, Confucianism and the Book of Changes. He later inherited his father's position of imperial historian. It is written that before the age of ten, Ssu-ma Ch'ien learned farming and animal husbandry; before twenty he studied ancient classics; as an adult he traveled throughout China to interview people on past events and to acquaint himself with historical settings. After taking over his father's office, he read voraciously in the palace libraries but remained independent of the prevailing Confucian ideology and the Yin-yang Five Elements School of thought.

A great tragedy befell him as a result of his honesty and loyalty. He voiced sympathy for General Li Ling after the general had surrendered to Hsiung-nu. Emperor Wu condemned his historian to the punishment of castration. Yet he continued to write fearlessly for posterity and wrote in a letter to a friend, "If it

Rubbing shows Confucius and disciple paying respects to Lao Tzu (left). The meeting was a Taoist invention, but the story gained such acceptance that even Confucianists repeated it to prove their founder's receptiveness to noble teachings.

Acrobats, animals and birds are painted on a granary jar that has three feet in the form of bears.

[my work] may be handed down to men who will appreciate it and it penetrates to the villages and great cities, then though I should suffer a thousand mutilations, what regret would I have?"

He channeled his passion for truth, his scope of knowledge and his balance of judgment into a monumental work called *Shih chi* or "Records of the Historian." In more than twenty years he wrote one hundred and thirty chapters, synthesizing all available materials into one coherent history, from the legendary "Yellow Emperor" to his own monarch.

He recorded past and present knowledge by writing chapters on astronomy, the calendar, religious affairs, ritual and music, and economics. His biographies of medical men, merchants, assassins, roving knights and diviners broadened the field of history which had been

hitherto largely the record of kings, princes, generals, ministers, and scholars. His concept of cyclical growth and decay in human affairs was not new, but his vivid narrative breathed life into complex events and resulted in both history and literature.

By the end of the first century B.C., another father-and-son team accomplished the gargantuan task of reviewing existing written works collected by imperial librarians and covered the entire range of Chinese learning. Liu Hsiang headed a team of specialists who analyzed various versions of each selected work in order to make a final version, which he reviewed and summarized. After his death, his son Liu Hsin carried on. By careful screening, checking and digesting, a definitive analytical bibliography was compiled. It consisted of six major divisions: (1) Confucian classics and studies of the written language; (2) schools of philosophy and agricultural arts; (3) poetry; (4) military affairs; (5) astronomy, mathematics and calendrical science; and (6) medicine, alchemy and ways of achieving immortality. With another division comprising the introduction and a table of contents, this grand summation of the cultural heritage was called *Ch'i lüeh* or the "Seven Summaries."

A third father-and-son team, Pan Piao and Pan Ku, continued the tradition of Ssu-ma Ch'ien by writing the "History of the Former Han Dynasty," which originated the dynastic divisions of Chinese history followed by all later historians. Pan Ku was the older brother of Pan Ch'ao, an intrepid explorer of Central Asia. When Pan Ku was imprisoned on false charges of having privately revised national history, Pan Ch'ao hastened to request an audience with the emperor, who then appointed Pan Ku to carry out the project under the imperial aegis. Using his father's unfinished work as a base, Pan Ku added material from a broad spectrum of sources. He enlarged Ssu-ma Ch'ien's coverage on social, scientific, and artistic events by adding chapters on the penal code, portents, geography and literature. He died just short of completing this opus, but his sister Pan Chao, who was also a poet and essayist, carried the work to its conclusion. With the achievements of this remarkable family and their predecessors, Chinese history as a science and as an art came into being.

The Revival of Taoism

Early peasant revolts had their origins in the usual droughts, floods and ineffectual rulers. In the Later Han period a new element was added. The philosophy of Taoism which had deeply influenced earlier China was revived as a new, vigorous religion.

Three major factors led to the development of new Taoism and to its influence on the decline of the late Han period. First the position of the emperor had been weakened by his dependency on the court eunuchs and their disaffection for the scholarly Confucian bureaucracy. Neither of these groups had provided a viable economy. This gave the Taoist leaders an opportunity to declare that the mandate of Heaven had been taken away from the Han emperor and passed to them. Second, the peasants desperately needed a religion that offered some rewards. This popular Taoism did. It offered a doctrine of healing for the body and immortality for the soul. In a strife-torn age it promised a way to peace. The final factor was the emergence of an extraordinary leadership. In eastern China three Chang brothers who were descendants of highly revered earlier Taoists gathered hundreds of thousands of followers under the banner of *T'ai-p'ing tao*—"the way of peace."

In the west, the leader was Chang Ling, a prophet, practitioner of magic, and a faith healer. Sickness was believed by the religious Taoists to be an indication of evil within. Chang Ling cured by isolating the sufferer. Then he offered prayers and asked that the supplicant write his sins on slips of paper which were offered to Heaven, Earth, and Water. Grateful families paid the priest's fees in rice, and the movement became known as *Wu-tou-mi tao*, the "Way of Five Pecks of Rice." After the death of Chang Ling, leadership of the western Taoists passed to his son and grandson.

But the first Taoist rebellion began in the east. Because yellow was believed to be the color of the future dynasty, the religious peasant soldiers wore yellow turbans for identification. Unfortunately, their initial plan of attack was discovered and more than a thousand

Pavilion offers grand view from top; its towering structure foretells the building of pagodas.

A stone slab in high relief shows tumblers with horses at top, musicians and dancer, and two horsemen.

sympathizers were executed. This did not deter the Chang brothers and their adherents. For a time the rebels beat back the government troops, but as individual war lords were given an opportunity to carve out their own domains, the Chang brothers were defeated. Although Chang Chüeh, leader and oldest of the Taoist brothers, had died of illness, his coffin was violated and he was decapitated. His two brothers were captured and suffered the same fate.

The most colorful of the victorious war lords to emerge in the east was Ts'ao Ts'ao, a talented poet and ruthless general, who had been reared by a palace eunuch. After the defeat of the eastern Taoists a new rebellion arose in the southwest. This uprising was led by Chang Lu, called "Lord of the Teachers" *(Shih-chün)*. He founded and stabilized a Taoist state within the Chinese state for some thirty years.

After defeating one of the Taoist armies in the southwest led by Chang Lu's younger brother Chang Wei, Ts'ao Ts'ao moved against Chang Lu but he refused to do battle. The Taoist leader and the war lord made peace and Ts'ao Ts'ao supported Lu's claim to his small fiefdom. He also diplomatically arranged a marriage between one of his sons and Chang Lu's daughter.

As the Taoist revolts subsided, China, because of the rise of the war lords and the division caused by revolution, was split into three spheres of influence. Ts'ao Ts'ao, ever hopeful of more victories, turned to the rich lower Yangtze River valley, which was prospering under the rule of Sun Chüan. There he was defeated by a coalition of Sun Chüan and Liu Pei at the crucial battle of Red Cliff. This engagement decided the division of China at the end of the Han dynasty. The Wu kingdom in the southeast was ruled by Sun Chüan; the Shu in the southwest by Liu Pei; and the Wei kingdom in the north by Ts'ao Ts'ao.

The last Han emperor had been kept captive by Ts'ao Ts'ao. A year after Ts'ao Ts'ao's death his son Ts'ao P'ei arranged the abdication of the puppet emperor and ascended the throne as Emperor Wên. The Han dynasty, one of the greatest in all Chinese history, was over.

Watchdog in glazed pottery is so expressive one can almost hear its bark. Clay animals unearthed from Han dynasty tombs also include pigs, cocks and hens, drakes and sheep, but dogs are the most realistic.

Stone chimeras that guard royal tombs originated in Mesopotamia, but the style of this statue is thoroughly Chinese.

Darkness and Light
A.D. 220–581

As Chinese political structure and social order collapses, nomad hordes overrun North China, stimulating the spread of Indian Buddhism, challenging Confucian orthodoxy and Taoist popularity ... Absorption of "barbarians" invigorates the declining Central Kingdom ... Chinese development of the Yangtze valley enlarges the cultural and economic base for a reunited empire at the end of the sixth century.

HISTORICAL CHRONOLOGY

A.D.

220   Ts'ao P'ei proclaims himself emperor of Wei.

221   Liu Pei continues the House of Han by becoming emperor in Shu.

229   Sun Chüan declares himself emperor of Wu, formally dividing China with Wei and Shu into the Three Kingdoms.

263   Wei annexes Shu.

265   Ssu-ma Yen usurps the throne of Wei, establishes Chin dynasty (historically known as Western Chin).

280   By conquering Wu, Chin reunites China.

301–06   Eight Chin kings fight each other, enlisting aid of Hsiung-nu and other nomadic peoples.

304   A Hsiung-nu general rebels against Chin. His kingdom and fifteen others are formed by five major "barbarian" groups.

316   Hsiung-nu forces end of Chin rule.

317   A member of the Chin royal clan rallies Chinese support in the south. Next year he founds the Eastern Chin dynasty.

354–69   General Huan Wên of Eastern Chin leads three northern expeditions without success.

383   A northern Tibetan power encounters defeat in invasion of the Chinese south.

386   T'o-pa people found Northern Wei dynasty, which unites North China in 439.

420   A usurping general ends Eastern Chin. Sung and the following Ch'i, Liang and Ch'ên constitute the southern dynasties, as against the partially non-Chinese northern dynasties.

534   Northern Wei splits into Eastern and Western Wei.

550   Eastern Wei usurped becomes Northern Ch'i.

557   Western Wei usurped becomes Northern Chou.

577   Northern Chou conquers Northern Ch'i.

581   Northern Chou general, Yang Chien, father of the empress, founds Sui dynasty.

ART CHRONOLOGY

c.250   Juan Chi (210–63) writes eighty-two poems on inner thoughts. He and six others of the "Seven Sages of the Bamboo Grove" engage in Neo-Taoist dialogue.

276   Wu stele calligraphy attributed to Huang Hsiang.

280–90   T'ai-k'ang Era poets excel in five-word poetry and parallel prose; they include Lu Chi (261–303) whose Wên fu is the first essay on theory of literature.

281   Discovery of bamboo-slip books on history in third century B.C. tomb.

c.300   Kuo Hsiang (d.312) develops Neo-Taoist philosophy in "Commentary on the Chuang Tzu." Ko Hung (253–c.333) writes Pao-p'u Tzu, principles of popular Taoism.

348   Indian orchestra of twelve musicians comes to Northwest China.

353   Wang Hsi-chih (321–379), regarded as greatest calligrapher, composes and writes "Orchid Pavilion Preface."

366   Cave temples started at Tun-huang.

c.375   Ku K'ai-chih (c.345–c.406), the first great Chinese painter and theorist.

405–27   T'ao Ch'ien (365–427), greatest hermit poet.

c.410   Hsieh Ling-yün (385–433) creates landscape poetry.

460   Colossal Buddhas in Yün-kang cave temples begun.

c.500   Hsieh Ho, portrait painter, writes "Classification of Painters," stating his famous "Six Principles." Chung Hung writes "Classification of Poets," the first systematic evaluation of poetry.

c.525   Hsiao T'ung (501–31) compiles "The Anthology of Literature."

c.550   Hsü Ling (507–83) compiles Yü-t'ai hsin-yung, an anthology of love poetry; he also writes poems in the often erotic "Palace Style."

c.570   Yü Hsin (513–81) writes "Lament for the South," outstanding and moving example of fu style poetic prose, which has become fully developed during this period.

Foreign warriors on armored horses, foot soldiers with mixed facial characteristics, and Chinese-looking civil

The Great Decline

The Three Kingdoms were born in the midst of continuing civil strife and in the wake of widespread hunger and epidemics. Out of the chaos four folk heroes, gallant, audacious and brave, arose. All were of the kingdom of Shu Han in the west. Three of them, like the three musketeers of Alexander Dumas, were close friends bound together by an oath of loyalty. They were Liu Pei, a Han prince who became emperor of Shu Han, and his loyal companions Chang Fei and Kuan Yü. The fourth hero was Chu-ko Liang, premier of Shu Han, an inventor of devices for warfare and a master strategist. The chivalrous adventures of these folk heroes supplied the material for innumerable popular tales and plays as well as a historically based novel, the *San-kuo-chih yen-i*, which has been translated as the *Romance of*

the Three Kingdoms. But even with the daring and resourcefulness of these folk heroes, Shu Han was the first to be defeated and absorbed by the kingdom of Wei.

This manifestation of faith in courage and chivalry is understandable when viewed against the continuing civil strife, widespread famine and epidemics, and the burning and looting of the capitals. It is pertinent to note that, after his death, one of the folk heroes, Kuan Yü, became transformed into Kuan Ti, a god of war whose ultimate goal was peace.

The Three Kingdoms were a brief but bloody interlude. Within sixty years both Shu Han and Wu had been conquered by the Wei. Ssŭ-ma Yen, its *de facto* ruler, forced the last of Ts'ao's line to abdicate. He founded the Chin dynasty and China was reunited.

In a desperate attempt to ensure the survival of his newborn empire, the ruler used drastic measures. To secure the royal house, he reverted

officials are pottery figurines from different tombs. They are representative of the northern power structure in sixth century.

to the Chou feudal system. Each small kingdom selected its ministers and controlled its army. Realizing the dangers inherent in such a system, he tried to balance their power through an alliance with the scholar-officials.

These scholar-officials had gained status and power as a result of the "Nine Grades" system which had been established some forty years earlier. Under this method, candidates for government positions were chosen by a Greater Selection Officer in each province and a Lesser Selection Officer in each prefecture. Since these key officials all came from high ranking scholar families, they naturally awarded the upper-grade positions to the most prominent families. To balance the power of his newly formed empire, the emperor chose his queen from this influential class.

Another difficult problem faced the emperor. The loss of manpower, through incessant warfare, famines and pestilence, had greatly re-

duced the population of the newly united country. It was decreed that daughters of commoners marry at seventeen or submit to the state's choice of husbands. To rebuild the population of the decimated north, immigrants from the conquered states of Wu and Shu were exempted from labor and military draft for twenty years. In a further attempt to reverse the acute population decline, the emperor made his greatest error. He opened the borders to the barbarians from beyond the Great Wall. Six entries in the history of the Chin Dynasty record the immigration of 265,000 men and women from non-Chinese tribes.

The result was a calamity. The feudal princes fought among themselves and even enlisted aid from the barbarians. The total chaos that ensued gave the barbarians their opportunity. The capitals of Lo-yang and Ch'ang-an were conquered and the Chin dynasty, later known as Western Chin, was ended.

Conquests were made by armies but the governments were run by bureaucrats like these from a sixth-century tomb.

A Time of Division

The rise of the border barbarians was slow but inevitable. The Chinese formed close alliances with first one northern tribe then another. Through these alliances the northern tribes gained strength as Chinese energies were drained by continuing internecine warfare. The northern states were ripe for conquest. The conquerors swept across the almost undefended states like wildfire.

A descendant of the leader of the conquering Hsiung-nu tribe claimed descent from the house of Han and founded a dynasty sometimes called the Pei, or Northern, Han. Liu Yüan took the title of emperor, thereby establishing the first non-Chinese dynasty. Upon his death his son Liu Ts'ung extended his domain by crushing the state of Western Chin.

For the next two and a half centuries non-Chinese controlled the north. Chinese historians refer to them as the "Five Barbarians": Hsiung-nu, long in contact with Chinese; the Chieh, a less civilized band; the Hsien-pei of

the Northeast; and two Tibetan groups, the Ti and the Ch'iang. Of these the Tibetan state known as the Early Ch'in succeeded in dominating most of North China after absorbing and utilizing Chinese men and skills in warfare and agriculture. For a time an excellent cavalry and well-trained Chinese infantry made them invincible. At the peak of Tibetan dominance its leader Fu Chien attempted an invasion across the Yangtze to South China. But the south had grown too strong.

When the Hsiung-nu invaders ended the Chin dynasty by the capture and destruction of the capitals at Lo-yang and Ch'ang-an, the royal family, officials, scholars and millions of commoners fled south across the Yangtze River to Chien-k'ang, now modern Nanking. There they continued the Chin dynasty, later known as Eastern Chin. The south had a more solid base of traditions and skills. Great families native to the south joined with them. The new southern dynasty of Eastern Chin ultimately was replaced by a series of short-lived dynasties.

Gilt bronze seated Buddha, inscribed A.D. 338, is the earliest known dated Chinese Buddhist sculpture.

Foreigners and the Foreign Religion

With the "barbarian" invasion came a system of thought more dangerous to the Confucians than physical conquest. The threat was Buddhism. As early as the first century A.D., this Indian religion had filtered in via the Silk Road and the sea route in the south. The first historical mention of a Chinese Buddhist community was recorded in A.D. 65. One hundred years later Buddha was being worshipped along with Taoist deities. But the ideological fortress of Confucianism, armed with an ethical system governing man's social relations, was not easily penetrated. Not until the collapse of both the social order and the political system with the subsequent invasion of foreign forces did Buddhism gain momentum.

Three extraordinary personages laid the foundation. The first was Fo-t'u-têng, a monk from Central Asia whose magic power in rainmaking and prophecy won the confidence of Shih Lo, a Chieh ruler. His nephew and successor, Shih Hu, listened to Fo-t'u-têng's preaching of compassion and love and the Buddha's doctrine against killing. He was sufficiently influenced to decree that any Chinese could enter the Buddhist monkhood. Many peasants, preferring to be serfs in temples rather than slaves of officials, did so. The second notable Buddhist monk, Tao-an, who concentrated on teaching Buddhist philosophy, gained hundreds of adherents and penetrated the intellectual community north and south of the Yangtze. The third was Kumarajiva, an Indian who was brought to Ch'ang-an under the patronage of an enlightened Tibetan ruler. He led a translation project which rendered into Chinese some of the most important scriptures.

In 399 the Chinese monk Fa-hsien traveled to India. This was the beginning of the Chinese quest to find Buddha's truth at the source. After fifteen years Fa-hsien returned and settled in Nanking, where he translated the sutras.

Rising to a height of some forty-five feet this colossal but benign Buddha is one of five carved in memory of northern Wei rulers. This cave temple at Yünkang is Indian in concept but Central Asian in execution.

Altar piece in gilt bronze dated 538 shows Buddha of the Future framed in a superbly realized nimbus. His right hand is raised signifying protection and his left hand is extended to indicate charity.

Buddha's Teachings

About the same time that Confucius in North China was teaching his doctrines of orderliness, an Indian prince named Siddhartha Gautama, in a tiny kingdom at the southern foot of the Himalayas, was seeking an understanding of the inevitable cycle of human existence—birth, age, illness and death. He left the pleasures of his royal home and family to go into the wilderness to live as an ascetic. After years of meditation he attained enlightenment at the age of thirty-four when he emerged to preach his philosophy until his death at eighty. He became known as *Sakyamuni,* or "the Buddha, the Enlightened One."

Buddha accepted the Indian religious concepts of *karma* or "deeds and acts," and reincarnation. He saw life as a stream of countless individuals going through endless rebirth, with every life the result of a former life and every fate the effect of former good or evil deeds. He taught that *karma* included not only deeds and their results, but also intentions behind the deeds. Within the cycle of rebirth, misery and suffering are inevitable, and to liberate oneself, one must enter into a state of absolute transcendence called *nirvana.* Toward this goal, Buddha formulated a doctrine of four noble truths: all of life is suffering; suffering is caused by desire; suffering can be ended because the cause is known; and suppression of desire can be accomplished by following the eight-part path of right views, intentions, speech, actions, livelihood, effort, mindfulness and concentration. Moral conduct, deep contemplation and intuitive wisdom can then lead to nirvana.

Before the death of Buddha, and for many years afterward, there was only one Buddhist doctrine. It was called *Theravada,* "The Teachings of the Elders," but at some point in the first or second century a schism occurred and the new doctrine of *Mahāyānā* arose. In China the Mahayana School gained acceptance.

Buddha's birth is etched on a stele dated 546. Center, he is born from his mother's armpit. Below, lotus blossoms spring up as he takes steps on the eightfold path. On left he is bathed under dragon tree.

An arhat, or "perfect being," is shown in center in monk's robe. On each side are Bodhisattvas. Note the delicacy and softness the artist has given these figures. These sixth-century fragments come from a cave temple at T'ien-lung Shan.

From Speculation to Faith

As Buddhism moved slowly into China, the intellectual movement of neo-Taoists, the Hsüan School, was threatening the position of official Confucianism. Studying the works of Lao Tzu and Chuang Tzu and the Book of Changes, these scholars searched for deeply hidden and mysterious truths as they reinterpreted traditional Taoism.

The neo-Taoist sages did not withdraw from life but did insist upon living it on their own terms. This sometimes led to what their Confucian critics called hedonistic escapism, lack of moral responsibility and "emptiness." But the daily lives and the philosophy of these free thinkers were anything but empty. True, they indulged in long, and to the realists, seemingly pointless dialogues. But their dialogues were a protest against society's insistence upon formalism, ritualism and conformism. They indulged themselves in the art of "pure conversation," seeking and occasionally finding new answers to ancient questions.

The most celebrated of the Hsüan assemblage were known as the "Seven Sages of the Bamboo Grove." These nonconformists sought enlightenment in study, enjoyment of the arts and in the forgetfulness of wine. Their impact on the literature, music and the visual arts was impressive and permanent.

But this new approach to Taoism did not offer a desperately needed religion for the masses. This requisite was met by the foreign religion, Buddhism, which infiltrated through the south. Buddhist monks such as Chih-tun and Hui-yüan became conversant with neo-Taoism and soon a rapport existed between the radical literati and the proponents of the new faith.

By no means all of the neo-Taoists agreed with the disciples of the Indian religion but a noteworthy incident occurred in 402 when the priest Hui-yüan assembled one hundred twenty-three followers, including many neo-Taoists, before a statue of Amitābha, a *Mahāyāna* Buddhist deity who offered a Heaven for his followers. There they made a collective vow to seek rebirth in his "Pure Land."

Apsarases are the flying spirits of the Buddhist world. They are usually shown playing musical instruments but this one offers an alms bowl. Intricately carved wind-blown draperies and the placement of the figure create an airborne effect.

The Greatest Calligrapher

Chinese written characters are highly systematized and abstract versions of pictographs and ideographs that lend themselves to an infinite variety of expression through the simple medium of brush and ink. To many Chinese calligraphy is more exalted than painting.

Wang Tao, the head of a great northern family, emigrated to the south and there became the chief architect of the Eastern Chin dynasty,

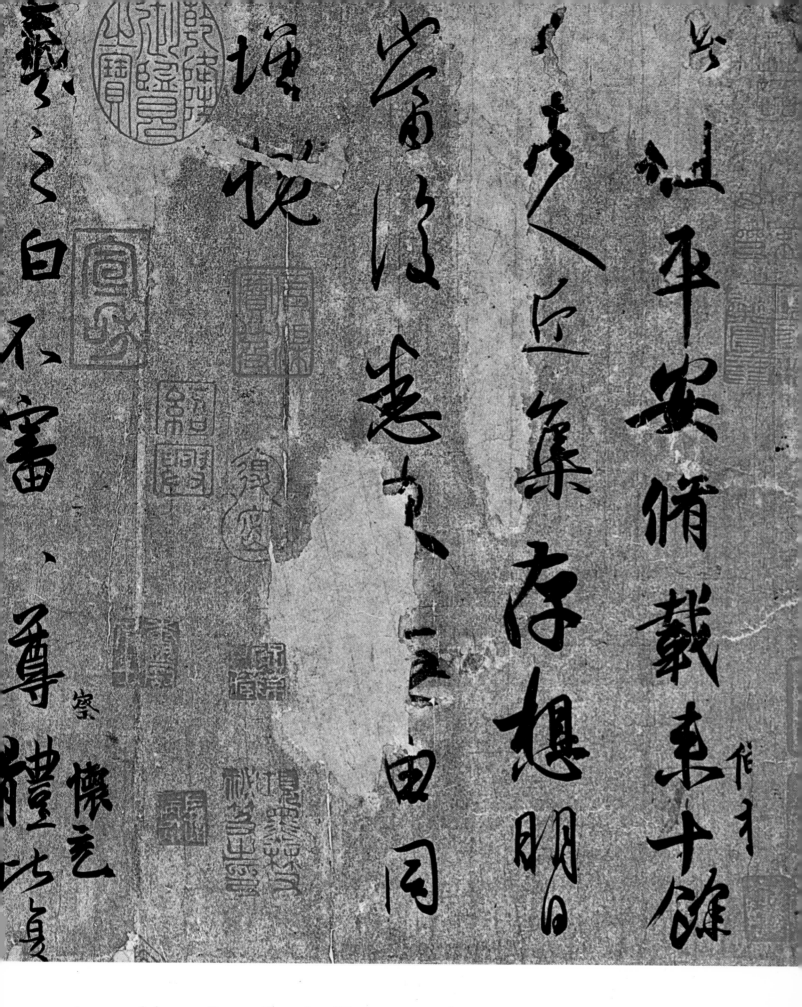

a regime noted for excellent calligraphy. His son, Wang Hsi-chih (303–79), reached a position in calligraphy comparable to that of Confucius in philosophy. All that remains of his original work are a few traced copies, such as the one above, much damaged but greatly treasured and laden with seals of collectors. A later emperor was moved to compare Wang Hsi-chih's work to a "dragon leaping over the Heavenly Gate" and a "tiger crouching in the Phoenix Pavilion." His brush imparted life, tension and movement to the script.

The Supreme Painter

Ku K'ai-chih (c.345–c.406) was the first Chinese artist to combine a talent for poetry, calligraphy and painting into creative forms which transcended technical excellence. He was also noted for his critical judgment, which established a tradition in Chinese aesthetics.

To judge by the writings of his contemporary critics, he excelled in painting on all subjects: figures, landscapes, animals, flowers, religious

portraits and supernatural creatures. Regrettably, only two early copies of his works remain today. One is the "Admonitions of the Instructress to the Court Ladies," one panel of which (below) shows the courageous Lady Fêng shielding the emperor from an escaping bear (a legend of c.48–33 B.C.). From this example we can discern his style and technique. Fine lines as free as floating silk threads but as strong as metal wires delineate the scene. In Ku K'ai-chih's own words, painting is "spirit in the heart, and hands that satisfy the eyes" and "great thoughts, deftly captured." This was his legacy to all Chinese painters of the future.

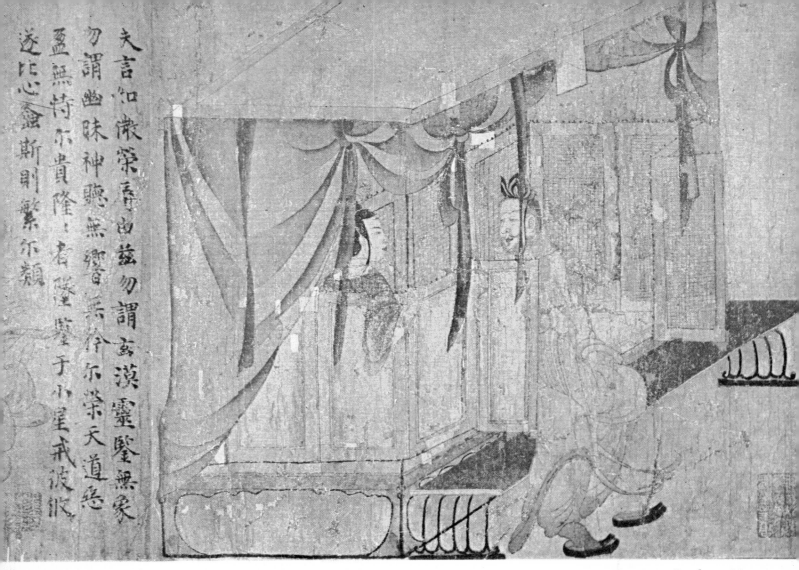

夫言如微榮弄由茲勿謂玄漠靈鑒無象
勿謂幽昧神聽無響無矜尔榮天道惡盈
無恃尔貴隆竝君隆鑒于小星武彼徒歟
逐比心盈斯則繁尔類

Ku K'ai-chih's scroll shows man and wife in canopied bed; text reads: intimacy without faith cannot dispel suspicion.

The Hermit Poets

During the period of darkness the negativism expressed by the literati was a method of escaping the tyrant's sword. Such escape from the official world was, in fact, an affirmation of life. Rather than becoming vulnerable by criticism of the venality around them, the best of the Wei and Chin poets turned their thoughts inward to commune with themselves and sought wisdom by looking backward to the ancients. Physically they escaped by fleeing to the shelter of mountains, riversides and farms.

One of the Seven Sages of the Bamboo Grove was Juan Chi, whose collection of eighty-two poems on his inner thoughts spoke for many sensitive souls. He indulged in drinking to avoid dwelling on the sorrows of his official duties. Often he would impulsively drive aimlessly in his carriage to a dead end in the road; there he would stop to relieve his anguish with tears. Kuo P'u matched him in depth of feeling with fourteen poignant poems devoted to the Taoist roving immortals.

But it was T'ao Ch'ien who transformed unrelenting pessimism into peace of mind and a love for simple, natural and commonplace things. He achieved greatness as a hermit poet. His youthful ambition had been to play a role in the regaining of North China, but after years of frustrating service as a minor official, he retired. On his humble farm and garden he devoted the last twenty-two years of his life to tilling the land, writing and drinking. His widely quoted "Fifth Poem on Drinking" reveals his treasured private world:

A hut built among people's habitat.
Yet noiseless of horse or coach.
How can this be?
An aloof mind keeps the place remote.
Picking chrysanthemums under the eastern
    hedge,
The southern hills in leisure come to view.
The mountain air is fine in setting sun,
When flying birds return together.
In this there is a truth;
Trying to say it, I have forgotten the words.

Ladies dressing hair and applying cosmetics learn another lesson: character building is more important than appearance.

The Severe Critics

In art and literature, the Chinese south in the fourth to the sixth centuries established a cultural cleavage between the old (Chou, Ch'in and Han) and the new ways of the Sui and T'ang which would follow. This area of intellectual ferment produced titans such as Wang Hsi-chih in calligraphy, Ku K'ai-chih in painting, and T'ao Ch'ien in poetry, and exceptional men of letters with knowledge and taste who evaluated the achievements of the past and set goals for the future.

Hsieh Ho, critic and artist, formulated six ways for excellence in painting: first, liveliness in breath and rhythm; second, technique in structure and brushwork; third, definition of forms according to objects; fourth, use of colors that follow nature; fifth, planning in com-position; and sixth, transmission of tradition through copying. His grading of twenty-seven famous painters may not be definitive, but his clear statements of critical standards have exerted a paramount influence.

In the field of poetry Chung Hung was equally notable. He judged one hundred and twenty poets by their inner strength and outer style; he considered direct feeling and rhythmic flow as virtues, but literary allusions and tonal regulations as burdens. For a thoroughly developed canon of literary criticism and theory, none surpassed Liu Hsieh (sixth century) in his "The Literary Mind and Its Carving of Dragons." This sweeping and penetrating review of Chinese letters covering fifteen hundred years expresses the belief that observation, feeling, analysis and distillation of essence, not mere flashes of genius, lead to supreme achievement. From the writings of these critics, the Chinese learned standards of excellence that stressed spirit and ideas over virtuosity and decorativeness.

105

Reason and Invention

Progress in science and technology was not interrupted during this politically and socially complex period. The engineer Ma Chün designed an efficient silk loom. He also improved the water-pumping machinery essential for rice-growing so that it could even be operated by small boys. His rotary ballista, a military weapon, was capable of hurling large stones continuously. Ma Chün's most intriguing invention was the legendary south-pointing carriage in which a replica of a human figure was mounted on top of a vertical shaft; one arm pointed to the south no matter how the carriage was turned. This device used gears and had nothing to do with the magnetic compass.

In the Eastern and Western worlds, mathematicians had been struggling for centuries to find an accurate ratio between the diameter and circumference of the circle. A rough but unsatisfactory approximation of three had been known. Around 250 B.C., Archimedes was the first to arrive at an accuracy to the second decimal point (3.1428) by using a 96-sided polygon for his calculations; but no evidence exists that this idea was ever transmitted eastward. Five hundred years later Liu Hui achieved an accuracy to the fifth decimal place (3.14159), but the greatest advance was made by the versatile Tsu Ch'ung-chih, mathematician, astronomer and engineer. He found that the value lay between 3.1415926 and 3.1415927. It was a thousand years before the West equaled his accuracy. In 463, Tsu devised a new calendar giving the number of days in a solar year as 365.2428148, only some fifty seconds from our present-day figure. History records that Tsu also invented a ship with hidden paddles, but details are unknown, and that he reconstructed the then obsolete south-pointing carriage. A son, Tsu Kêng-chih, distinguished himself by calculating the volume of the sphere through the use of solid geometry and by building a calibrated bronze instrument to measure the sun's shadow; he also built a water clock that indicated time with great accuracy.

The abacus was probably a Chinese invention which benefited scientists and mathematicians and influenced the daily life of all Eastern peoples. The earliest mention of "ball arithmetic" appeared in a book attributed to the second century that may have actually been written by the commentator Chên Luan around 570. It contained a clear description of a proto-abacus, not too different from the modern calculator.

In geography achievements were remarkable. P'ei Hsiu was known as the father of Chinese scientific cartography. His eighteen sheets of maps were the result of research based on his six principles, two dealing with the scale and the rectangular grid, four others dealing with actual measurements of distances, elevations, slopes and curves. Li Tao-yüan wrote the all-encompassing "Commentary on the Waterways Classic," a description of China's waterways and environs, based upon firsthand studies. He was the first Chinese to undertake extensive travels solely for the purpose of geographical research.

A woman attends the fire beneath the stove; another cooks, surrounded by pots. This same type of stove is still in use.

Figures from funerary jar have masklike faces, may be dancing and singing. One seems to be running with bag of grain.

The "Barbarian" North and the Chinese South

During the years of destruction and fragmentation of North and South China a vigorous process of regeneration was at work. In the northern regions cultural assimilation of the invaders began to make the distinction between "barbarians" and Chinese meaningless. Intermarriage was common as the divergent cultures intermingled. The Chinese language was slowly adopted by the outsiders. In the fifth century, a non-Chinese emperor in the north decreed that the use of the Tartar language be prohibited in favor of the Chinese.

Inspired by the spread of Buddhism advances of great significance were made in the field of art. Cave temples with colossal images, five to ten times life size, were carved out of living rock. The earliest of these tremendous monuments extant is in the present province of Shansi on the side of Yün-kang Ridge. Here thousands of artisans worked for decades to create towering Buddhas and Bodhisattvas (disciples of the master who had earned *nirvana* but delayed their entrance to assist the earthbound sufferers).

The Chinese language was deeply influenced by Buddhism as previously unknown concepts such as *lai-shêng* ("next life"), *yin-kuo* ("cause-effect"), and other words for new ideas were added. A new awareness of tonality was learned during the recitation and translation of the *sutras*, the Buddhist canons. The tradition of Buddhist storytelling and singing led to the adoption of new forms of popular drama and literature.

In the south the influx of Chinese refugees into the Yangtze River valley caused a shift in the center of Chinese civilization. The former economic pattern resisted change; great wealth

A northern warrior and a horse heavily burdened with a grain sack are reflections of actual types of the sixth century.

109

A lady donor arrives at a Buddhist shrine with her impressive retinue and her canopied ox cart. Such scenes engraved on steles or sarcophagi may have been copied from lost early scrolls or paintings. The date of this relief work is A.D. 525.

On another side of above stele base a male donor arrives with offering. Retinue includes attendants with canopy and fan. Lotus blossoms, signifying purity of the spirit, decorate the scene. On right is his splendidly caparisoned horse.

continued to be concentrated in the privileged families who shielded their slaves, servants, and tenant farmers from the government's forced labor and military draft. A new wealth-power bloc was the Buddhist Church patronized by the imperial houses and rich landowners. Even though power, privilege and wealth were abused, these groups stimulated production of goods for consumption and trade. Great strides were made in the technologies of iron, paper and ceramics. Trade with Indochina, Ceylon and India prospered. Important cultural contact was made with Japan. Shipbuilding increased so much that a storm in the fifth century is said to have damaged thousands of ships in Nanking harbor.

Even more than the north, the south had grown enormously economically and in population. When a general of the reconstructed north amalgamated both the north and the south to create the next empire a united China was to enjoy a cultural and economic base far greater than that of the Han dynasty.

Holding a skull, this fierce-looking ascetic is a statuette of gilt bronze. An object was once held in the right hand.

The Golden Age
A.D. 581–907

A reunited China under ambitious and enlightened emperors . . . extends its influence from Japan to Caspian Sea, from Mongolia to Annam . . . absorbs foreign cultures and spreads its own . . . creates great poetry and art, and invents wood-block printing and true porcelain . . . promotes Buddhism to its historical height and becomes the "Light of the East" for two and a half centuries, a period constituting perhaps the most brilliant era in early Chinese history.

HISTORICAL CHRONOLOGY

A.D. 581 *Yang Chien, known as Emperor Wên founds Sui dynasty.*

589 *He reunifies China after three centuries of chaos.*

604 *His son, Emperor Yang begins a tyrannical but constructive rule.*

605-610 *Emperor Yang mobilizes millions of workers to construct the Grand Canal linking North and South; also builds a river capital Chiang-tu.*

612-614 *He wages costly and unsuccessful campaigns against Koguryo (Korea).*

618 *Emperor Yang assassinated in the new river capital; in the north, Li Yüan declares himself first emperor of T'ang.*

621 *The civil service system is re-established, emphasizing literary examinations.*

626 *T'ai-tsung (reign 627-649) son of Li Yüan, seizes power and becomes one of the most enlightened rulers in Chinese history.*

657 *T'ang armies defeat the Western Turks, leading to other conquests in the west, culminating in a victory over Turfan in 692.*

668 *The fall of Pyong-yang signifies T'ang's victory over Korea.*

690 *Empress Wu usurps the throne. The commoners gain power.*

713 *Hsüan-tsung begins his reign, which prospers in initial period but slowly deteriorates.*

751 *Moslem forces rout T'ang armies at the Talas River, ending China's influence in Central Asia.*

755 *Powerful northeast governor An Lu-shan rebels against the Royal House, forcing Emperor Hsüan-tsung to flee to Szechwan.*

756 *The new emperor Su-tsung asks Arab help to subdue An Lu-shan.*

880 *Huang Ch'ao, leader of rebellious peasants, sacks Lo-yang and Ch'ang-an, the eastern and western capitals.*

907 *Rebel Chu Ch'üan-chung removes the last T'ang emperor.*

ART CHRONOLOGY

A.D. 581 *Restoration and construction begun on Great Wall and Buddhist temples. Cave temples at Tun-huang, Lung-mên and Mai-chi Shan created.*

583 *New design and construction of capital Ch'ang-an. Its plan later adapted by Japan in building Nara (710) and Kyoto (794). Construction of eastern capital Lo-yang in 604.*

c. 590 *Creative calligraphers Yü Shih-nan, Ou-yang Hsün and Ch'u Sui-liang excel.*

c. 600 *Invention of wood-block printing. Refined white stoneware appears. Painted and lead-glazed earthenware and feldspathic stoneware leading to the invention of porcelain by 9th century.*

c 650 *Yen Li-pên designs the bas-relief stone panels called Six Horses at Emperor T'ai-tsung's tomb.*

c. 680 *Blue-green landscapes created by General Li Ssu-hsün and son Li Chao-tao, the father considered the founder of the Northern School of painting.*

706 *Wall paintings and terracotta figurines in tomb of Princess Yung-t'ai. Throughout T'ang period, voluminous creation of glazed and unglazed mortuary figures.*

c. 720 *Wu Tao-tzu paints Buddhist and Taoist temple walls. Wang Wei, poet-painter famous for snow landscapes, known as the founder of the Southern School. Li Po and Tu Fu rank highest in poetry.*

758 *Protest over Seating, essay written by Yen Chên-ch'ing. He exerts vast influence in calligraphy.*

819 *Memorial on the Bone of Buddha composed by Han Yü, outstanding essayist.*

868 The Diamond Sutra Scroll, *finest among the oldest extant printed works, produced.*

Sui-T'ang period also produces intricately designed and exquisitely executed bronze mirrors, gold and silver jewelry and utensils. Designs show influences of India, Persia, Mesopotamia, Byzantium and Hellenistic Orient.

Emperor Wên, the founder of the Sui dynasty, is portrayed by Yen Li-pên in his "Portraits of the Emperors." Behind him is his son and successor Emperor Yang. The less important figures are smaller in scale.

The Tyrannical and Benevolent Rulers

Three exceptional leaders emerged during the first seventy years of the Sui and T'ang periods. The Emperor Wên, founder of the Sui dynasty, began as a reform-minded ruler, but became a despot; his son, Emperor Yang, was an ambitious and cruel tyrant; the third, Emperor T'ai-tsung of T'ang, was a brilliant and benevolent ruler.

Forging a powerful union after centuries of chaos, Emperor Wên, who ruled for twenty-four years, began the Sui dynasty most promisingly. To the common people he distributed land and direct relief. He reduced taxation and shortened military service. He promoted industry and trade by standardizing currency,

weights and measures. He minimized injustice by simplifying and humanizing criminal laws. He improved the quality of the bureaucracy by instituting a civil service selection system. He centralized governmental power in the capital.

Setting a personal example of frugality, he imposed thrifty habits throughout the nation: silk disappeared from the gentleman's wardrobe; and gold and jade ceased to be used for adornments. Within a quarter century, the government filled its storehouses with enough grain and cloth to offset fifty years of harvest failures.

But during the twilight of his rule, Emperor Wên became irrational toward subordinates and resorted to excessive punishments. Disregarding his earlier legal reforms, he sometimes executed the entire families of those he suspected. Few of the top aides who helped him gain imperial power survived his fury. Finally when the Emperor fell ill in 604, the crown prince reportedly hastened the natural process by having his father strangled.

Emperor Wu, left, was the forceful leader of the Northern Chou dynasty who suppressed Buddhism. Facing him is the Emperor of Ch'ên captured by Sui. The artist allowed the Ch'ên leader one attendant.

The second Sui ruler, Emperor Yang, was cunning and ruthless yet constructive. During his youth he used kindness, diligence, obedience and austerity to build for himself an impeccable reputation and win his father's approval as successor. After his seizure of power, he inaugurated a series of grandiose plans; the building of a new capital at Lo-yang, a more central location for controlling the nation's wealth; the construction of the Grand Canal to link the north and the south for commerce as well as his pleasure trips; the strengthening of the Great Wall's frontier fortifications; the building of thousands of boats for imperial travel and military expeditions; the opening of international marketplaces with silk-decorated trees and free restaurants to impress visitors and merchants.

The enormous financial, natural and human resources nurtured and accumulated by his father hardly sufficed his extravagance and licentiousness. It was recorded that in 607 more than a million men were conscripted to labor on the Great Wall and five or six out of every ten died. He raised huge armies for territorial expansion, but his victories against Khitan in the north and T'u-yü-huen in the west could not balance three disastrous campaigns against Koguryo in Korea. In these gigantic expeditions he used such oppressive means that the strong among the conscripts escaped to become thieves and the weak sold themselves into slavery.

An unusually energetic and strong-willed man, Emperor Yang took no advice he did not want to hear and showed no mercy for aristocrats or commoners. Uprisings among his generals and impoverished farmers finally blocked his return to the capital. In 618 his life was taken by an aide in his palace on the Grand Canal.

The founder of the succeeding T'ang dynasty was Li Yüan. With a well-established power base in the northwest, he swiftly quelled the local rebels and remnants of loyal Sui forces and regained unification of the country in 624. His brief but constructive reign was, however, overshadowed by that of his son, Emperor T'ai-tsung, a monarch as close to perfection as China ever produced. This young ruler likened himself to a ship and the people to the waters that support it or let it sink. The power of a happy and peaceful population is to be treasured, he taught, while the wrath of angry and desperate mobs is to be dreaded. Surrounding himself with honest, courageous and able officials, his willingness to accept fair criticism, even when harsh, became legendary. At the death of his most severe critic Wei Chêng he lamented: "With bronze as a mirror one can correct his improper appearance; with history as a mirror one can understand the rise and fall of a nation; with good men as a mirror one can distinguish right from wrong. I lost one mirror with the passing of Wei Chêng."

With a rare genius for military strategy T'ai-tsung was primarily responsible for quickly unifying his own realm and subsequently pacifying neighboring kingdoms in the north and the west. As a patron of the arts, he established an academy of literature to attract the best scholars and writers, and he promoted calligraphy by becoming a collector and calligrapher himself. He forbade extravagance in imperial living and sent home three thousand court ladies to be married to commoners. He allowed prisoners to visit their homes for the New Year holidays. Such thoughtful and benevolent acts won the loyalty and admiration of his subjects.

Early T'ang political and economical measures largely improved upon those of the previous dynasty. A projection of the bureaucratic organization achieved central control and a combination of land distribution through which soldiers were converted into farmers during

When an arrow struck the mount of the emperor, a general quickly exchanged horses with him. This relief in stone showing the general removing the arrow from the wounded horse was in the tomb of T'ai-tsung.

peace time and farmers into soldiers during war time was instituted. The useful civil service examination system was completed. One salient feature was the addition of poetry to examinations which in no small measure contributed to the flowering of that branch of literature.

T'ai-tsung especially appreciated the importance of appointing good local officials who would concern themselves directly with the welfare of the common people. He worried over the selection of governors and magistrates and once confessed to his aides, "Sometimes I remain sleepless until the middle of the night, considering the capabilities of various officials. I list their names on the screen and review them, marking good deeds under the doers. Being isolated in the palace, my contacts do not extend far; thus the prosperity or degeneration of the empire depends upon them."

Two arrows penetrate the flanks of Emperor T'ai-tsung's battle charger in another of six panels on his tomb.

A portrait of the emperor shown with female attendants (above) is also by Yen Li-pên.

Three men wait respectfully as T'ai-tsung's entourage approaches. The one in the center is the Tibetan envoy.

A lion carved from white marble is a rare work sculptured in the cultural peak of the T'ang period.

The Heavenly Khan

In 630 Emperor T'ai-tsung crushed the nomadic eastern Turks who had been pressing southward from their base in Mongolia. This momentous event heightened China's prestige in Central Asia. Many northwestern tribes sent envoys to seek T'ang protection and presented the emperor with the title of Heavenly Khan, or the Khan of Khans, thus marking the beginning of a remarkable political-military alliance under China as the leader-arbiter and made up of kingdoms in East, Central and South Asia including at various times India and Persia.

In Japan it was Chinese cultural influence rather than military might that prevailed. Beginning in 600 Japan sent envoys to China to

T'ai-tsung granted the wish of the Tibetan King to marry a Chinese princess, assuring his allegiance.

study Buddhism, art and architecture, language and literature, as well as administration and law. After repulsing a Tibetan invasion, T'ai-tsung pacified his foe by marrying a kinswoman, Princess Wên-ch'êng, to the first king of Tibet in 641, thus spreading Buddhism and Chinese culture to the roof of the world. T'ai-tsung suffered defeat in 645 in northern Korea but in 648, when a T'ang envoy encountered rebellion in Assam, he was able to command troops from Tibet and Nepal to capture the usurper and restore friendly rule.

The death of T'ai-tsung did not diminish Chinese pressure against the western Turks, whose influence extended from Chinese Turkestan to the Caspian. In 657 the Turks were defeated and scattered in all directions, fleeing as far as Hungary. In the eight years between 660 and 668 T'ai-tsung's successor brought Manchuria and most of Korea under the T'ang military governorship. All the countries in the Western Region were now under the protection of the Heavenly Khan. His satellites comprised nine kingdoms situated in and around Samarkand, Tashkent, and Merv and sixteen others in Kashmir, Afghanistan and Iran. The T'ang court sent military governors as far west as Teheran. The common aim was to prevent a Turkish reconquest or the emergence of any other power such as the Tibetans or the Arabs who for a time acknowledged T'ang suzerainty and paid tribute to the capital of the government at Ch'ang-an. Important garrison posts included one in Kucha and another at Tokmak, both near Lake Issyk-kul in present-day Russia. These guarded East-West trade routes and facilitated the flow of goods and people, religion and culture. Despite minor setbacks, T'ang power dominated the Asian heartland until 751 when the battle of Talas signaled the beginning of its end. In that battle the Islamic Arabs decisively routed the Chinese. With the death of the great general, Kuo Tzu-i, feared and respected by foreign troops, the 150 year old alliance under T'ang domination collapsed. It had been the largest empire on earth in the 7th-8th century.

The Transformation of Buddhism

A thousand years after the historical Buddha attained enlightenment in India his teaching began to undergo extensive enrichment in 6th century China. For the next three hundred years while Buddhism sank deeper into mysticism in the land of its origin, in China it exploded into ten major disciplines influencing all East Asia. During the long incubation period of the Six Dynasties its roots spread far and deep from the royal court to the villages. A short and violent repression of Buddhism in 574 ended with the founding of the new Sui dynasty. Emperor Wên revived the propagation of this popular faith by permitting his subjects to enter monkhood at will. During his 24-year reign one and a half million statues were restored and more than 100,000 new ones created; nearly 4,000 temples were constructed. In his empire the number of copies of Buddhist sutras (canonical writings) exceeded Confucian classics by a hundredfold. When Wên-ti died, his son Emperor Yang assembled monk-scholars to edit Buddhist scriptures in the Chinese language's eleven encyclopedic divisions. The dynastic change in 618 did not dampen the momentum for growth. Imperial patronage, although shared by Taoism and Confucianism, was continued by the house of T'ang, further encouraging the development of Buddhism.

The path of Buddhism as it moved through Chinese Turkestan is recorded by these fragments: a bejeweled head of a bodhisattva, an image of a buddha in contemplation and a monk holding a lotus blossom.

The Buddha Amitabha (opposite page) in Western Paradise captured the imagination of the public in the Sui dynasty as shown by this exquisite bronze shrine of the period honoring him.

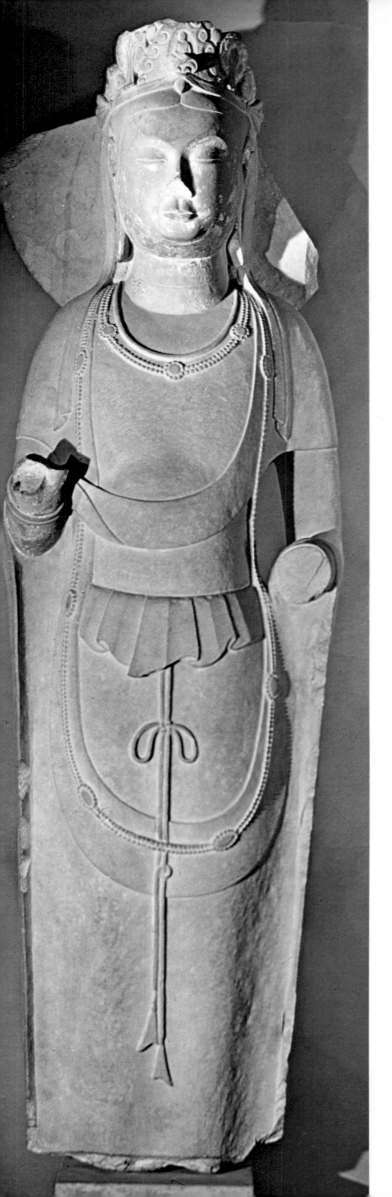

Buddhism in the T'ang Dynasty

Of the many Buddhist schools that flowered in the T'ang dynasty four are pre-eminent. First, the T'ien-t'ai School representing the Chinese attempt to synthesize all Buddhist teaching into a final and rounded doctrine which would be intellectually all-encompassing and spiritually comforting in its belief in universal salvation through the presence of Buddha-nature in all beings. Second, the Hua-yen School, which tries to explain the nature of things by pointing out the inseparability of phenomena and principle: all phenomena are identified with each other and are representations of the same supreme mind of the Blessed One; thus the One contains many and the many are One. Third, the Pure Land School with its appeal to the multitude by the promise of the Western Paradise of Ami-

A reputation for rescuing believers from fire, bandits and other perils made Kuan-yin a popular deity.

Two gilt bronze buddhas show the assimilation of Buddhism. The contemplative one with wing-tipped flames is in the older Indian style. It contrasts with the preaching buddha of naturalistic Chinese design.

tabha, attainable simply through the repeated invocation of the holy name: *namo* (revere)*Amitabha!* Pure Land also boasts the most popular bodhisattva in East Asia: Avalokitesvara, or Kuan-yin, a male deity who changed sex and evolved into the goddess of mercy. He or she is everywhere, delivering people from suffering, granting children to the childless and saving the faithful from peril. Kuan-yin, who is capable of assuming any form or shape, is often depicted as having several heads, or with a thousand eyes and hands, the better to help mankind.

But if Pure Land comes close to superstition, the fourth and perhaps most important school, called Ch'an (or Zen, in Japan) is extreme in sophistication. It has its origin in *dhyana,* the religious discipline that aims at tranquilizing the mind in order to look inward at one's consciousness. Thus, all the paraphernalia of images, rituals and scriptures are superfluous and detract from the true teaching of Buddha. Ch'an preaches instead concentrated meditation, such as the nine-year wall-gazing practiced by its founder Bodhidharma. In 734, however, a southern monk named Shên-hui, claiming authority

from the monk Hui-nêng, known as the founder of the Southern School, championed the concept that wisdom is indivisible and therefore attainable only suddenly and totally or not at all. Ch'an Buddhism split in two—the south believing in the flash of revelation and the north adhering to the principle of gradual enlightenment. The free and unstructured doctrine of Ch'an mocked the pomp and pageantry of all other established schools and exerted a profound influence over Chinese philosophy and art for more than a thousand years. Its nonverbal, non-analytical approach to the ultimate reality that unites all differences, called the "mind" or "Buddha-nature," which is supposed to exist in all beings without discrimination, constitutes a challenge to the notion of objective existence. Ch'an Buddhism may have impeded the development of the scientific spirit in China, but it has also contributed to the uniqueness of the Chinese culture. It has remained an anti-intellectual movement of the intellectuals for its exercises in intuition are incomprehensible to the masses, who decidedly prefer the easier way to salvation offered by Amitabha and Kuan-yin.

The 10,000 Mile Quest for Truth

The most famous human in Chinese Buddhism is the monk Hsüan-tsang (c. 596-664) who began a secret journey to India in 629 without official sanction. His mission was to seek answers at the source for unresolved doubts he found while studying Buddhist texts. After evading frontier guards, escaping an attempted murder by his first guide and successfully crossing the trackless desert, he was detained by an admiring Turfan monarch. His sincerity won his release and the king's assistance for the remainder of his journey across Central Asia. Hsüan-tsang descended from the Iranian plateau into the Indus valley, sailed down the Ganges and saw the bodhi tree under which, it is said, the Buddha attained enlightenment. Later he went to the famous Nalanda Temple to perfect his knowledge of Buddhist philosophy.

His fame soon spread throughout India. When he presented himself to the Emperor Harsha, the ruler bowed to the ground to kiss his feet. At Harsha's behest a grand assembly was convened which debated for eighteen days with Hsüan-tsang emerging triumphant over all disputants. With escorts provided by the Emperor, he returned home through Central Asia arriving in April of 645.

His return to the Chinese capital was tumultuously greeted by high officials and common people alike and a few days later he was welcomed by the Emperor T'ai-tsung who offered support for his translation project. At his death Hsüan-tsang and his disciples had completed 73 out of 657 sutras brought back from his 16-year pilgrimage. His book "Records of the Western Regions" gave the T'ang court a first-hand knowledge of that great frontier. His travels became the subject for a legendary novel cherished by the children of China.

125

Vairocana Buddha, the Brilliant One, is attended by huge bodhisattvas and guardians at Lung-mên in the valley of the Yellow River. In this form of Chinese Buddhism (Hua-yen)

he represents the universal principle underlying all phenomena. This belief formed the base for totalitarian rule with the emperor as the secular counterpart of the all powerful spiritual buddha. Imperial patronage is evident in this work. 127

Buddhist piety is shown by this polychrome bodhisattva from one of hundreds of cave temples in Tun-huang.

The Union of Three Teachings

The door was open to foreign ideas and trade during the first two hundred years of T'ang rule. As early as 635 Emperor T'ai-tsung received a Nestorian monk and allowed this type of Christianity to be freely preached throughout the empire. In the latter half of the 7th century Persian refugees escaping the onslaught of Arabs established Zoroastrian temples and formed congregations in Ch'ang-an, the capital. Another Persian faith, fire-worshipping Manichaeism, was embraced by the Uighurs of Turkic stock, whose military assistance in quelling a serious rebellion in 756 led to the introduction of this exo-

Taoism taught immortality or a higher form after death. Its doctrine was both mystical and realistic. Confucius, shown as a wise sage, was not concerned with afterlife but with the responsibilities of the present . . .

tic cult. The Arab mercenaries who joined the same campaign doubtless helped to found the minority Mohammedan community in China.

But none of these religions compared in followers with Buddhism. When a native resistance to Buddhism arose, led by Taoists and Confucianists, the enlightened T'ang court initiated a series of open forums at which all the spiritual leaders presented their arguments. The dynastic founder who convened the forum in 624 set the tone with the statement: "Though the three teachings are different, their benefits are the same." The first round of debate in which the most respected scholars and priests participated resulted in a clear-cut victory for the Confucianists. In the 638 forum, under the auspices of the second emperor, a margin of advantage appeared to be held by the Taoists, who exploited the fact that their founder bore the same surname as the royal house. The third emperor

continued the dialogue.

It was the succeeding Empress Wu who elevated Buddhism over Confucianism and Taoism. Her attitude induced the Taoists to take a more conciliatory position and the concept of one philosophy with diverse rituals gained acceptance by all, especially the Confucianists, who had found nourishment in both Taoism and Buddhism. For the forum in 735 the liberal minister Chang Chiu-ling adopted the theme of harmonizing the three ways to reach the same goal. By now the struggle for supremacy had been resolved in typical Chinese fashion—synthesis rather than exclusiveness; compatibility rather than conflict. From 624 to 870 this institution of open discussions continued through nine emperors, establishing the foundation for Neo-Confucianism in the Sung dynasty and the tradition for eclectic thinking among the masses.

Court ladies painted on the wall of the tomb of Princess Yung-t'ai indicate a belief in a royal afterlife. The tomb is dated 706. On an adjacent wall of the royal tomb chamber grooms and guards are depicted.

Luxurious Living and Extravagant Dying

Peace and prosperity prevailed for nearly 140 years after the founding of the T'ang dynasty. Farmers increased production with technical innovations: plows designed for both shallow and deep furrowing, wheels rimmed with bamboo buckets to move water from low to high grounds and water mills for grinding grains.

Population tripled from the 630's to 755, the year when nearly 9 million families and 53 million people were recorded, not counting many who eluded the census. Meanwhile officials, noblemen, merchants and Buddhist temples multiplied their land-holding either legally or otherwise, turning the rich into super-rich. Some even surpassed the royalty in wealth.

A great merchant once offered to Emperor Kao-tsung (reign 650-683) one bolt of silk for each tree on Mountain Chung-nan, boasting that after paying for all the trees he would still have silk left. A similar boast was made by Wang Yüan-pao, about whom Emperor Hsüan-tsung (reign 712-755) remarked: "I am the noblest under Heaven, but Wang is the richest." Another tycoon owned villas from city wall to city wall. Wealth bred idleness. Day-long parties were common in the great halls and elaborate gardens. In the pleasure quarters of the capital, after examinations were successfully passed, candidates celebrated their bright future with beautiful and witty courtesans. Celebrations extended beyond death. Funeral processions bore burial vessels and figures created to dazzle the public. Roadside tents, complete with variety shows, entertained the "mourners." Such excesses finally prompted the imperial edict in 714 limiting the size and number of mortuary objects and forbidding luxurious houses and gardens for burial grounds.

Music and sports were part of both life and

death in this affluent society. In the Sui and T'ang dynasties they were enriched by importations. Musicians from Kucha in Central Asia probably exerted the most influence. To this day Chinese names for many instruments betray their foreign origin.

Polo came to China in the early 7th century. Its demand for superb horsemanship made it a natural game for military men. The playground must be large, level and smooth; sticks must be fashioned by expert craftsmen. Only the rich could afford this fancy Persian sport. The imperial court adopted polo during Emperor T'ai-tsung's reign but not until the 8th century did the sons of Heaven become star players themselves. The multi-talented Emperor Hsüan-tsung, when he was a prince, together with three other royal relatives, beat the best Tibetan players. Another emperor, shocked by a fallen team mate, died of a stroke. His 18 year old heir continued to indulge in this game right after the father's death, and soon the new emperor was

Female musicians, above, from Chinese Turkestan played
for the court and for merchant princes. This high life of the T'ang dynasty is recorded in a variety of precious ceramics

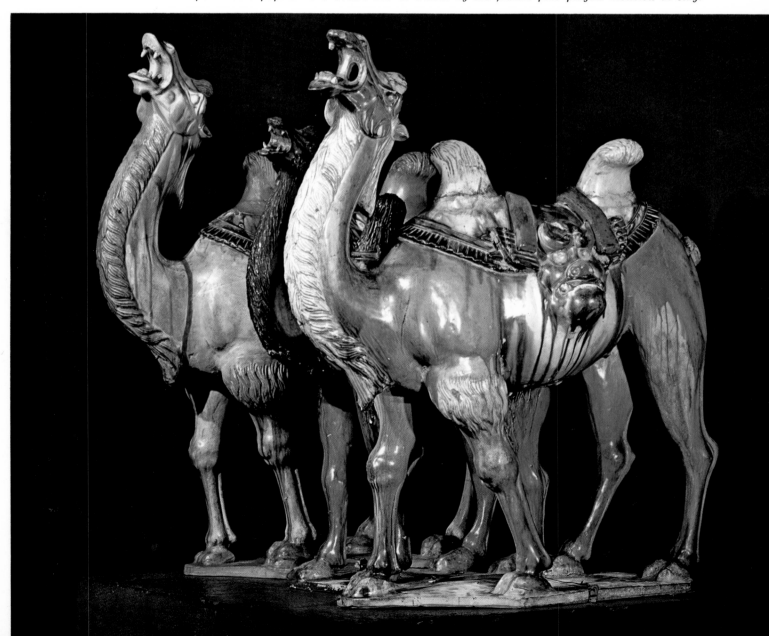

murdered by his polo-playing generals during a drinking bout.

Toward the end of T'ang, clever eunuchs used music, women, hunting and polo-playing as means to corrupt the monarch and usurp power. The fashion spread far and wide. Court ladies, dashing youths and even some of the scholar elite played well, and polo grounds became available all over the countryside. Some games lasted into the night, with large candles costing tens of thousands of coins lighting up the park.

The same grounds were also used for another popular game, the tug-of-war. Ministers, generals and noblemen joined in this rough sport to amuse the emperor and empress. On one occasion seven thousand soldiers exhibited their strength and vigor to impress foreign dignitaries. The origin of the game of two teams pulling in opposite directions on a rope was Indian. In ancient times it had been used as part of the religious ritual to bring about a good harvest. But by late T'ang this meaning was lost.

which were created to be buried with the rich and powerful. Horses and camels, many with handsome trappings, filled the stables and the roads. Sports were popular and democratic as shown by the female polo players modeled in clay.

Gold and silver often decorated intricately designed mirrors which incorporated both foreign and domestic motifs. The one shown has lions and grapes traced to Persian origins. In Chou Fang's painting (right) a servant holds the mirror for a lady arranging her hair.

A royal lady rests while a servant cools her with a decorated fan. Phoenix were popular as decorations on fans, textiles, jewelry and household utensils.

A high degree of artistry is shown in this wine cup and saucer. It is gold plated with turtle, fish and shell-fish designs. Such creativity abounded in T'ang dynasty.

Beauty for Utility

The T'ang government promoted industry by setting up special bureaus which employed thousands of highly skilled craftsmen whose children, once enlisted in the trade, were not allowed to change their occupation. However, the expansion of trade and rise of cities stimulated private enterprises even more. One manufacturer in the industrial center Ting-chou owned five hundred silk-weaving devices. The textile business became specialized with subdivisions in weaving, braiding, spinning and dyeing. Silk and cotton cloths were graded according to quality. Various localities across the nation excelled in different products. Fabrics with wood-block printed patterns, though started in secrecy for exclusive customers, spread widely to brighten the wardrobes of even the lowliest subjects. Exotic materials using golden threads and bird feathers adorned only the rich. One quality of light gauze, its process closely guarded by two families, gave the effect of smoke and fog.

In the 8th century, the fashionable circles loved foreign clothing. The aristocratic ladies often dressed like men. Metalwork of bronze, gold and silver flourished. At Yang-chou, the river capital, a shop once cast a ten-foot square mirror decorated with a bronze tree of gold flowers and silver leaves so that the emperor could see himself riding by on his charger.

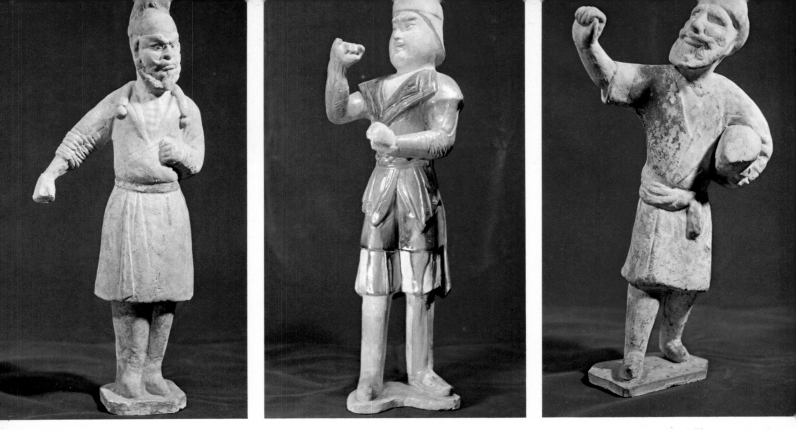

Tomb figurines captured the exciting cosmopolitan life of their times: left to right, an Iranian groom, a Western Turkish groom, and a Semitic merchant with trade goods.

A Cosmopolitan Culture

The great Emperor T'ai-tsung, in a moment of self-admiration, attributed his success in pacifying border kingdoms to his equal treatment of foreigners, a practice contrary to the Chinese tradition of discrimination against "barbarians." This enlightened policy was derived partly from his family's intermarriage with an eastern Mongolian tribe of Turkic stock.

After the military conquests of T'ang, large foreign communities formed within China, among which were a settlement of more than 100,000 Turks in the northwest and another of over 30,000 Koreans in the plains north of the Yangtze River.

Talented aliens attained fame and fortune: the Yü-ch'ih father and son artists from Khotan, the lute player Ts'ao Pao from Kebud. From Bokhara came the brothers An Hsing-kuei who became famous generals and upon whose descendants was even bestowed the royal surname of Li.

Thriving commerce attracted merchants from everywhere. They came by caravans from Persia and the Central Asian kingdoms through the well-established silk routes, by ships from Korea and Japan through the eastern ports and from India, Indo-China and Indonesia through the southern sea routes. The capital Ch'ang-an was also a commercial metropolis where hundreds of shops lined the streets in two markets east and west of the city.

Horses were imported from Karashar and Kucha, glass goblets from Byzantium, jade from Khotan, medicine from Kashmir and India, crystals and agate from Samarkand and cotton from Turfan. In exchange, silk textiles, tea, paper, ceramics and above all, ideas and technology moved into these regions.

To the great learning center called the National Academy, students came from Koguryo, Paekche, Silla, Japan, Turfan and Tibet to study Confucianism, Buddhism, literature, art and architecture. Some competed with the Chinese in civil service examinations and one Japanese envoy-student loved the Central Kingdom so much that he adopted a Chinese name and served the T'ang court, staying in China for fifty years. Even more profound was the influence exerted by students who returned to their own countries. The Japanese borrowed Chinese writing characters and adapted them into phonetic scripts, thus giving that island nation its written language.

Opposite, a foreign trader with a huge wineskin.

136

Poetry, Calligraphy and Painting

The civil service examination system, instituted in Sui, but fully developed in T'ang, included a category called *chin-shih* for the testing of scholars. The tests attracted the most talented men in the country. This literary tradition traces its roots to the southern dynasties when the ability to versify was an absolute requirement for entering high society. Poetry became more than an art form, loved not only for its intrinsic enchantment but also as a road to fortune. In T'ang, the "regulated" five- or seven-word poems, which demanded tonal euphony and parallel construction of imagery and allusions, were perfected.

Among thousands of poets writing during this time, five were most influential. The earliest were Wang Wei and Li Po, both born

Han Huang (723-89) excelled in painting humans, animals and farm life. He undoubtedly portrayed some of his close

about 701. Wang not only pioneered to combine poetry with painting, but also excelled in calligraphy. The tranquillity of his lyric poems reveals a deep devotion to Ch'an (Zen) Buddhism. He is considered to be the founder of the Literati, or Southern School of painting. Li was a Taoist poet known for his gusto and imagination. His gift for extemporaneous composition won temporary favor with the emperor, but his unconventional life-style and temperament could only be tolerated by loyal friends. Among them was the Confucian Tu

Fu, generally considered China's greatest poet. His work reflects a compassion for humanity, diligent scholarship, and a highly developed technique. Tu Fu was the first poet to depict social conditions and may be considered the originator of the realistic school.

Po Chü-i learned well from Tu Fu and gained such popularity that hand-copied and possibly printed editions of his work were sold and exchanged for tea and wine in markets as far away as Japan. His plaintive narrative verse, such as "Everlasting Remorse" and "The

friends in this scene of a literary gathering; one is reflecting on the composition of a poem, a common social activity.

Han Kan (c. 750) painted these two valuable blooded horses from Ferghana and Khotan perhaps for his emperor.

Lute Song," became household literature, and later, drama. The fifth of these famous poets was Han Yü, a leader of anti-Buddhism who rebelled against restrictions and decorative trifles in both poetry and prose. In poetry, he championed "hard style" as an antidote to the facile and sweet writing of his time. In prose, he ignored the prevailing "parallel prose" of four- and six-word sentences and revived ancient free style prose.

Calligraphy was also a category in the examinations and a ladder to success. Emperor T'ai-tsung honored Wang Hsi-chih (see Chapter 4) as perfection. All the leading calligraphers of his time belonged to the Wang School, characterized by elegance and leanness of style. A new departure was created by Yen Chên-ch'ing (709–83) whose strong and full strokes combined power with grace. Chang Hsü and Monk Huai-su brought a new sense of freedom to cursive script. Both also indulged in excessive drinking, which may have contributed to their wild style. Chang found inspiration in the rhythmic movements of the sword dance, recognizing a kinship between the two arts as an expression of inner vitality. This same principle was applied to paintings by one of Chang's students, Wu Tao-tzu, who was known as the "Sage of Painting." His works are now lost, but from early copies and ink rubbings, one can see that his brushwork, characterized by wind-blown streamers draped over his figures, flowed with spirit and force. Undulating lines of varying thickness modeled and shaped the forms. His landscapes, swiftly and succinctly executed, contrast with the meticulous and elaborate compositions of General Li Ssu-hsün (651–716), founder of the older Northern School of painting. General Li and his son Li Chao-tao catered to the taste of kings by using blue, green and gold colors to enrich the magnificent settings of palaces among mountains and rivers.

Thus the expansive and powerful age of T'ang found expression in virtually every field of art, but in poetry, calligraphy and painting it produced even more than its share of innovators and masters.

Five characters from Huai-su's "Autobiographical Essay" dated 777. Free cursive style at its best.

China, China

True porcelain appeared in late T'ang, but its development was a gradual process. The final result—an invention which made the word "china" a common noun in every modern Western nation—was achieved through a series of improvements and refinements that took centuries. The clays became more and more purified; kiln temperature was raised steadily until about 1,300 degrees centigrade was reached; and finally, body and glaze were fused completely to form a glossy, translucent ware that produced a clear ring when struck. With this final refinement, the Chinese potter had realized his dream of creating a substance resembling jade.

In T'ang, one of the criteria for judging ceramics was the compatibility of their colors with tea. An eighth-century authority on tea, Lu Yü, prized celadon Yüeh ware over white Hsing ware, for this reason, among others. The former complements the greenness of tea while the latter shows up its undesirable reddishness. Another standard of his had more universal applications; he preferred the translucency of Yüeh ware to the opaqueness of Hsing ware, comparing Yüeh to jade and ice and Hsing to silver and snow. Modern aesthetics value not only color, form, texture, design and decoration, but intangibles such as the potter's feelings. As a result, many types of ceramics, from earthenware to porcelain, are treasured today.

Judging by the thousands of shards deposited near Cairo, Egypt, and Samarra, Iraq, as well as in Southeast Asia and India, T'ang's thriving maritime commerce must have dealt extensively in ceramics. We learn from an Arabian record that only T'ang ships were large enough to negotiate the rough waters of the Persian Gulf; even Arabs depended on Chinese ships for transporting their exports to the Far East. Chinese porcelain trade continued to prosper down to our century.

The lady, a tomb figurine, is holding a vase similar to the contemporary real one on the opposite page.

A phoenix-headed ewer suggests the influence in design of Persian (Sasanian) bronze and silver vessels.

Marbled jar and dish were made by intermingling clays of two colors, then covering them with lead glaze.

The amphora with dragon side handles and cup-shaped mouth inspired by West is a favorite T'ang type.

The "pilgrim bottle" with relief decoration has Hellenistic elements: dancing figures, grapes and lions.

143

Elaborate illustrations such as this for hand-copied sutras gradually gave way to printed versions.

A detail of the above shows the earthly ruler kneeling on rug in prayer before the Sakyamuni Buddha.

Thousands of hand-copied sutras were preserved in cave temples. This scroll is probably eighth century.

To Spread the Word

The earliest form of Chinese printing, if printing is defined as multicopy reproduction, was seal impressions made before 1000 B.C. By late Han (A.D. 200) stamped designs were used extensively on tomb tiles and rubbings were made from stone-engraved texts to meet the growing demand for official versions of Confucian classics. But popular demand for Taoist

This 868 Diamond Sutra, of which only the illustration and a few lines are shown here, is the oldest printed book known that is authentically dated. Note similarity in design with painting at left and the already advanced printing technique.

and Buddhist charms gave the greatest impetus to the invention of wood-block printing. The perfection of an indelible ink, unaffected by water when properly applied, was credited to Wei Tan (d. 251), whose success was attributable to the use of lamp black as the key ingredient, although some form of black pigment had existed even in the decorations of Neolithic pottery.

Taoist priests made impressions from large wooden seals around A.D. 600 and a few years later the monk Hsüan-tsang distributed printed images of a Bodhisattva to his followers. The oldest existing true block printings in the world are various Buddhist sutras written in Chinese: a scroll hidden in a 751 stone stupa in Korea; scrolls printed by order of the Empress Shōtoku of Japan about 770; and the illustrated Diamond Sutra of Tun-huang, dated 868, which is much more fully developed than the two earlier ones. The fact that the earlier Chinese printed sutras were found abroad rather than in China is understandable considering that the greatest persecution of Buddhism took place in 845–46 when 4,600 temples were destroyed and 260,500 monks and nuns defrocked.

Nation Shattered

As T'ang reached its apogee in power and glory during Hsüan-tsung's early years, a sense of complacency pervaded the entire empire. The emperor occupied his time with music and dancing, ignoring court intrigue and leaving border regions to the control of powerful governors. The dream ended in 755, when Governor An Lu-shan suddenly led his army toward the capital. The emperor fled to Szechwan, and the resulting civil war devastated the country. In 757 the poet Tu Fu wrote:

> Nation shattered, mountains and rivers stay;
> The city is in spring, deep in trees and weeds.
> Lamenting the times, flowers shed tears;
> Regretting the parting, birds cry in bleak heart.
> Three months long warning-fires burn on towers;
> A letter from home is worth ten thousand gold.
> The white hair thins from fingering;
> There's hardly enough to hold a hairpin.

Tu Fu also saw the cruelty of conscription:

> By evening I lodged at Shih-hao Village;
> An officer came to take men at night.
> My old host fled over the wall;
> His old wife went to answer the door.
> Why so angrily shouted the officer?
> Why so bitterly cried the old woman?
> I listened to her words:
> "My three sons went to guard the city Yeh;
> One wrote me a letter, just arrived;
> The other two died newly in battle.
> The living live on stolen time;
> The dead are gone forever.
> There's no man left in this house,
> Save a suckling grandchild.
> Having a child, the mother has not left;
> She comes and goes without a whole skirt.
> Though old woman here has little strength,
> I beg to go with you tonight,
> To answer the urgent call at Ho-yang.
> I can still prepare morning meals."
> Night deepened as voices trailed;
> I seemed to hear subdued sobbing.
> As I began my way at dawn,
> Alone to the old man I bid farewell.

The "Thatched Lodge" attributed to Lu Hung may be similar to one built by Tu Fu in Szechwan in 760.

In the midst of mysterious mountains it is related that Emperor Hsüan-tsung was forced to see his beloved Lady Yang

148

青綠湖山迥
嶇嶇道路長
人多結束行
字白周詳錄
向名和利那
勞勞興忙年
小失姓氏北宗
此乃唐
甲午新秋
御題

strangled before his rebellious troops would retreat to Szechwan. This painting of the retreat shows emperor in red at right.

The Twilight

The breakdown of the T'ang empire in mid-eighth century reflected both the basic weakness of imperial rule, dependent upon the ability and character of a single person, and the underlying strength of Chinese civilization: the sense of unity engendered by cultural traditions and long-standing institutions. The second half of the dynasty, from the recovery of Ch'ang-an in 757 by Hsüan-tsung's son Su-tsung to its end in 907, saw a series of capricious emperors who nearly cut the dynasty short many times and outstanding generals who averted disaster an equal number of times. The period also demonstrated the durability of the people as reflected in the poetry of Tu Fu.

Emperor Su-tsung was exceedingly suspicious of capable men, fearing they would take away what they gained for him. At the same time, he was susceptible to flattery, making him easy prey for schemers such as eunuchs and their allies. His other weakness was reliance upon foreign militarists, under the mistaken notion that they cared only for treasures and women, not territory. In one case, he invited the Uighurs into China to fight the forces of An Lu-shan with cavalry, resulting in ever-increasing intervention by border tribes.

Two of T'ang's saviors during this time were the Taoist Li Pi and General Kuo Tzu-i. Li Pi advised Su-tsung, but wisely declined the position of chief minister; General Kuo, equally loyal, was also careful to avoid too much glory. The emperor following Su-tsung was no better. Whenever rebel leaders were eliminated, he allowed their subordinates to retain power and territory simply by agreeing to surrender, while at the same time he relieved his own loyal men of their armies. When Tibetans

Far outnumbered by invading Uighurs and Tibetans, General Kuo Tzu-i, who enjoyed tremendous respect from

looted and burned Ch'ang-an in 763, General Kuo was recalled from retirement. Although he was given only a few troops, his reputation frightened the Tibetans into withdrawing without a fight. In the next few years, he also succeeded in pacifying the Uighurs and defeating the Tibetans, but the emperor minimized these victories by crediting them to the blessing of Buddha. The court depended on the loyalty of regional governors and continuous uprisings threatened its very existence. Li Pi, one of the skillful scholar-officials who sustained the vitality of the central administration, effected an alliance with Uighurs in the north and the Nan-chao kingdom in the south to counteract the Tibetan threat.

Echoing the final days of Han, the last eighty-seven years of T'ang saw intensified struggles between eunuchs and court officials. Socially disdained, the eunuchs sought allies among rich merchants who bribed their way into official positions previously earned by scholars in examinations. This in-fighting destroyed the effectiveness of the central government, which became a mere collection agency for the emperor's luxurious living and incessant expeditions against insubordinate generals. The burden placed upon the peasantry was totally disregarded until farmers in the Shantung peninsula finally revolted. They joined Huang Ch'ao, a frustrated scholar, whose followers ravaged the Yangtze valley and Fukien and sacked Canton in 879. According to one Arab report, he killed nearly all the inhabitants, including 120,000 Mohammedans, Jews, Christians and Mazdeans. Though Huang Ch'ao, too, was subdued, his subordinate Chu Ch'üan-chung eventually slaughtered the eunuchs and court officials that surrounded the last emperor. He set up a boy monarch, but displaced this pitiful puppet in 907 and established the dynasty known as Later Liang.

foreign armies, visited the Uighurs unarmed. The Uighur leaders, having served under him, immediately paid their respects.

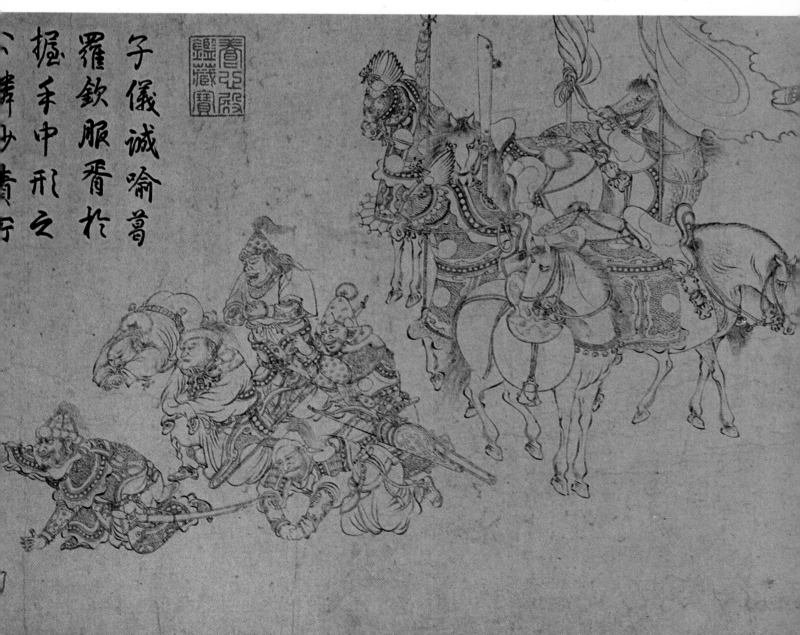

This event of 765 was painted by Li Kung-lin in the eleventh century. It symbolizes the ideal Chinese victory: virtue over force, culture over the uncivilized. At this meeting General Kuo persuaded the Uighurs to join in attacking the Tibetans.

Division and Maturity A.D. 907–1279

China turns from military to cultural and commercial growth . . . Sung court buys peace from powerful nomadic neighbors, builds centrally controlled bureaucracy and army . . . Develops urban centers . . . Its cultural accomplishments lead the world . . . Loss of northern heartland in 1127 stimulates the south, resulting in economic prosperity, thriving oceanic trade . . . Rise of Neo-Confucianism, spread of education . . . Deficit-ridden government falls prey to conquering Mongols.

HISTORICAL CHRONOLOGY

A.D.

907–60 Period of disunion: Five Dynasties and Ten Kingdoms.

960 Chao K'uang-yin usurps last of Five Dynasties and becomes founding emperor of the Sung dynasty; known later as T'ai-tsu.

979 Emperor T'ai-tsung, brother of the founder, reunites China by conquering last of the Ten Kingdoms but suffers defeat from Liao, the Khitan empire in the far north.

1005 Sung becomes subject state of Liao.

1043 Hsi Hsia, a Tibetan state in the west, exacts annual payment from Sung.

1069 Sweeping reforms in finance and defense.

1085 Ssu-ma Kuang, now prime minister, terminates all reform measures.

1114 The Jurchen from Manchuria defeat Liao armies, marking shift of power in the north.

1125 Liao dynasty (the Khitan) is conquered by Chin (the Jurchen people).

1127 Sung ex-emperor, emperor and royal family members removed to the north. End of Northern Sung. The throne in Nanking is ascended by Emperor Kao-tsung of the Southern Sung.

1138 Kao-tsung establishes Hangchow as capital and appoints Ch'in Kuei prime minister. Sung court begs peace from the Jurchen.

1140 Yüeh Fei and other Sung generals score big victories against the Jurchen but are stopped by order of Ch'in Kuei.

1142 Yüeh Fei is executed as part of peace price; Sung court persecutes antiappeasement officials.

1227 Jenghis Khan conquers Hsi Hsia. He dies same year.

1231 The Sinicized Khitan scholar Yeh-lü Ch'u-ts'ai (1189–1243) becomes prime minister of the Mongols.

1234 Mongols end the Jurchen's Chin dynasty and shift their military pressure to Sung.

1260 Kubilai Khan becomes ruler of the Mongols.

1271 Kubilai Khan names his empire Yüan.

1276 Sung emperor surrenders.

1279 Yüan armies chase the last nominal ruler of Sung to suicide in the sea.

ART CHRONOLOGY

A.D.

Early tenth century Monumental landscapes by Ching Hao and Kuan T'ung.

932–53 Revision and printing of texts and commentaries of Confucian classics directed by Fêng Tao.

c.950–80 Basic style of Southern School created by landscapist Tung Yüan and pupil Monk Chü-jan.

972–83 The library of Buddhist canon, the Chinese Tripitaka, printed by imperial order.

c.975 A deposed ruler, Li Yü (937–78) writes tz'u poems of deep pathos.

c.1000–1127 Period of classical renaissance: art, philosophy and literature flourish. Important figures are:

Liu Yung (c.990–1050), lyric poet.

Ou-yang Hsiu (1007–72), poet and essayist.

Chou Tun-i (1012–73) together with brothers Ch'êng Hao (1031–85) and Ch'êng I (1033–1107) found Neo-Confucianism, emphasizing universal principle.

Ssu-ma Kuang (1019–86), historian and statesman, completes The Comprehensive Mirror for Aid in Government in 1084.

Su Shih (1037–1101), poet, essayist, painter, calligrapher and statesman.

Huang T'ing-chien (1045–1105), calligrapher.

Li Kung-lin (1049–1106), leading figure painter.

Li T'ang (1049–1130), leading landscape painter.

The three most influential calligraphers of Sung are Mi Fei, Su and Huang. The former is also a painter, connoisseur-collector.

Li Ch'ing-chao (1081–1140), poetess, the foremost literary woman in Chinese history.

1101–26 Painting Academy organized by Emperor Hui-tsung, calligrapher, painter and collector.

c.1150 Greatest Neo-Confucian philosopher, Chu Hsi (1130–1200) writes and teaches. Major patriotic poets are Lu Yu (1125–1210) and Hsin Ch'i-chi (1140–1207).

c.1190 Leading Southern Sung landscapists are Ma Yüan and Hsia Kuei.

From twelfth century on, playwriting for popular theater flourishes both in Peking (Chin) and Hangchow (Southern Sung). Art of architecture, silk textiles and ceramics reach new heights.

153

The artistic tradition of the T'ang period was continued by the Khitan, a Mongolian people. Above, a Khitan nobleman balances an arrow; a decorated quiver hangs at his side. His sturdy Mongolian pony is efficiently bridled and saddled.

A herald gallops ahead of a richly dressed, well mounted nobleman, probably a prince of Khitan. His em-

"*Hunters with Falcons*" *was attributed to the Khitan artist Hu Huai (c. 930), famous for painting his countrymen's nomadic life. His style is completely Chinese, indicating the degree of Sinicization of Liao people in their higher culture.*

broidered robe is made of Chinese silk. In the Five Dynasties leaders such as this one controlled most of North China.

An excellent view of the architectural style and the amenities of the living quarters of the Chinese nobility is afforded by this tenth-century painting. The detail shows court ladies preparing a feast, perhaps for the emperor.

The Turning Point

The fifty-three years between the end of T'ang and the beginning of Sung was a new turning point in Chinese history. The outward looking empires of Han and T'ang began to turn inward as China suffered foreign encroachment and domination. The influence of the peoples below the Yangtze accelerated, transforming the country into a southern-based culture. Great families became less dominant as the development of commercialism lessened the significance of land as a foundation of wealth and a new scholar "gentry" class rose to prominence, allowing entry for the poor.

A series of power struggles during this period produced Five Dynasties in rapid succession in the northern region. A fierce contest over control of North China between Li K'o-

yung, a governor of Turkish origin, and Chu Ch'üan-chung, a surrendered rebel general, ended with Chu's founding Later Liang, the first of the Five Dynasties. Governor Li's son won the next encounter and founded the second dynasty but Li's son-in-law, Shih Ching-t'ang, also of Turkish origin, usurped the throne with the help of the Liao River valley Mongols known as Khitan. Shih's Later Chin dynasty became a vassal state of the Khitan, to whom he offered tribute and sixteen northern border prefectures inside the Great Wall, signaling the beginning of Chinese military weakness for the next four and a half centuries. In 946 the Khitan, now calling their nation Liao, succeeded in crushing Later Chin completely; they looted the capital before being forced back to the north. The fourth dynasty lasted only four years before being succeeded by the last of the Five Dynasties, Later Chou, whose rulers began the task of reunifying China once again.

Stylized portrait of Emperor T'ai-tsu, founder of the Sung dynasty. He reunited China by his generosity to both friends and enemies. To keep his country united, he paid high tribute to the invaders for border peace.

Troubled Borders and Stable Center

Shih-tsung, the second emperor of Later Chou, combined unusual military and administrative talents. He continued the trend toward personal control that rulers of former dynasties, who rose from local governorships, had started. This meant strengthening three elements of his court: the bureaucrats, who contributed continuity to the government by serving in more than one regime; palace officials, who took over functions performed during T'ang by eunuchs; and the emperor's army, which counterbalanced the forces of local governors. The emperor's bravery and planning ability enabled his army to expand southward to the Yangtze and press northward toward Liao's southern capital in Peking. During the latter campaign, however, he died and General Chao K'uang-yin seized power from the child heir. The year was 960, the beginning of the Sung dynasty.

Rising as he did, the former general was preoccupied with strengthening his central control. One evening, during a drinking party, he remarked to his generals, "Being a governor is better than being an emperor." Asked why, he replied, "That is plain. All governors desire the throne. Even if you don't, one day your subordinates might force you to take over, and you will not be able to refuse." The generals understood his meaning and turned over their forces to T'ai-tsu, who organized them into a national army under his direct command. He consistently pursued this policy of transferring the best troops to his personal command, but minimized resistance by being generous with former rivals and meritorious military officers. Before his death in 976, he had subjugated six of the eight remaining peripheral kingdoms. His brother and successor, Emperor T'ai-tsung, completed the task in 979. Flush with victory, Sung forces rushed toward Liao to recover the sixteen Chinese prefectures inside the Great Wall, but they suffered overwhelming losses under the arrows of the enemy's cavalry near Peking. After years of indecisive warfare, the Sung met another catastrophic defeat in 986. Its weakness was apparent. Liao marauders were able to capture cattle and inhabitants from border areas at will. A few years later the emperor agreed to appease Liao with annual tribute of large quantities of silver and silk.

Thirty years of peace followed. Then trouble developed in the northwest. The leader of the Tibetan Tangut state declared himself emperor of Hsia dynasty (known in Chinese history as Hsi Hsia) and decided to expand into China. Hsi Hsia territory extended from the Ordos to the Kansu corridor, and from this base their cavalry raided Sung's northwestern frontier. The Hsi Hsia forces were stopped but the strain on Sung's economy was considerable. The emperor's army more than doubled and food became available only from the agriculturally rich southeast. The supply line was long and arduous. So another peace treaty came into being. As a result Hsi Hsia acknowledged its subject status, after extracting heavy gifts of silver, silk and tea from Sung.

Early Sung rulers were noted for being humane and fair in the dispatch of justice. The first emperor, T'ai-tsu, administered the capital penalty himself to curb the abuses which existed in the Five Dynasties. The second emperor limited the time for trying cases to forty days for the most serious and three for the least and worried constantly about wrongly punishing the innocent. The third emperor, hearing that starving people in a drought-stricken locality had raided the granaries, instructed his officials not to punish them, since they robbed only to keep alive.

The civil service developed to a high point following three methods instituted in former periods; examinations, recommendations through high officials and special interviews. The examination system was by far the most effective in identifying and attracting talent from all sources. Its emphasis shifted between belles-lettres and analytical reasoning, depending on the preferences of rulers and ministers; many high officials achieved distinction in art, literature and philosophy. To assure a constant supply of educated men, the founder of Sung set up an Imperial Academy and, in the eleventh century, the fourth emperor established the T'ai-hsüeh, a university for the sons of officials to which common people's children were also admitted. This institution gradually assumed great importance, especially when the emperor suspended the examination system at the beginning of the twelfth century.

Reform and Reaction

Peace in China proper resulted in spectacular population growth, which by the early eleventh century had already made up for all the losses caused by the chaos and warfare that marked the time between An Lu-shan's revolt in 755 and the end of the Five Dynasties in 960. Wealth generated by a large, stable population, together with improvements in farm techniques, repair and building of irrigation systems, expansion of acreage and more intense cultivation, made early Sung more prosperous than any previous dynasty. In addition, government monopolies of the salt, tea and wine industries, and commercial taxes derived from the thriving domestic and foreign trade, provided the imperial treasury with an even larger revenue than did the land tax. But government income, which reached a high point in 1021, started to slide downward. The large landowners and merchant princes had numerous ways to escape their share of the tax burden, while taxes levied on peasants eventually reached the point of diminishing returns. Government expenditures, on the other hand, kept rising. When this trend continued there could be only one result. The central administration faced serious deficits. The military budget and administrative costs were the two major expenditures. The number of soldiers had increased from 378,000 in 976 to 1,259,000 by 1041. These men, who had little interest or skill in military matters, added much to the taxpayer's burden. As to administrative cost, every examination yielded five hundred to one thou-

◁ *The ruggedness and towering majesty of the northern landscape near Ch'ang-an is revealed by the Taoist painter Fan K'uan.*

Detail shows two men driving donkeys. Roofs of a temple or a palace rise above the densely wooded hill at top right.

An important scroll, "The Ching-ming Festival on the River," by Chang Tsê-tuan, shows daily life in and near Sung capital.

sand successful candidates to swell the ranks of a civil bureaucracy so massive that one emperor removed nearly two hundred thousand from the rolls in a single sweeping move. But since the influx of new officials continued unabated, even dramatic cutbacks could not stem the tide.

The sixth emperor, Shên-tsung, recognized that he faced a number of problems in addition to the bureaucracy and decided to take strong action to meet them. In 1069 he appointed scholar-statesman Wang An-shih as prime minister, and directed him to make sweeping reforms to bolster finances, eliminate inequities in taxation and strengthen the national defense. Among Wang's measures were low-cost credit for farmers, irrigation projects, a graduated land tax, exemption from labor draft, price regulation, neighborhood self-policing, a militia system, delegation of horse-raising to the militia

and reorganization of army units.

Formidable and determined opposition immediately challenged him: representatives of the large landowners, big merchants and money lenders, who stood to lose financially; conservatives who saw the drastic changes as an opening for opportunists; and political enemies who resented the dictatorial power he assumed. Some of the most respected elder statesmen of the day attacked Wang ruthlessly, resorting to assassination of his character, which proved to be honest and selfless. Unable to overcome bureaucratic resistance, Wang resigned after seven years in office and his adversaries regained their power after Emperor Shên-tsung's death in 1085.

Preparing for festival, man in center raises pennants. Ships carried grain from south to K'ai-fêng.

The "Rainbow Bridge" appears as the scroll is unrolled. A boat lowers its mast, attracting crowds who shout

The Flowering
of an Urban Culture

With one exception, the second dynasty, all the rulers in the Five Dynasties chose K'ai-fêng as their capital, a move further eastward from the ancient eastern capital of Lo-yang. Emperor Shih-tsung of Later Chou took the first steps in building this secondary city into a great metropolis. He ordered all burial grounds moved more than two miles away from the outer walls, laid down a city plan, enlarged the main streets and left home construction to the wishes of the people, provided their plans fit into the overall scheme. Equally important were his systematic efforts to improve and expand waterways that radiated from K'ai-fêng to the centers of agricultural production and commerce in the Yangtze delta, the Shantung peninsula, the inland prefectures directly to the south, and the seaports of Chekiang. With Central Asia in hostile hands, China was forced to turn east for trade with the outside world via the open sea. With the north and northwest

advice from above. Chang Tsê-tuan was noted for his lively architectural drawings and developed a high degree of realism.

constantly threatened by invaders, China relied more and more on the stable, prosperous southeast for its economic base. The shifting of her political center was therefore of much more than transitory significance; from Sung onward, the cities Ch'ang-an and Lo-yang represented the glories of the distant past and never again resumed their place as the seat of power.

The flowering of K'ai-fêng marked the rise of a new urban culture in China. The number of districts with more than 100,000 households increased from thirteen in the middle of the eighth century to forty-six in the late eleventh century. K'ai-fêng was recorded as having 260,000 households in 1105. With urbanization came sophistication, diversity, specialization, commercialization and a view of life that was decidedly luxury-loving and antimilitary. The new gentry class, which rose through education and competitive examination to achieve social prestige and political status, set high standards in taste and pleasures, adding luster as well as ease to metropolitan living.

A writer named Mêng Yüan-lao completed in 1147 a "Remembrance of the Eastern Capital," which describes life in K'ai-fêng:

A train of camels passes through the city gate as Chang's scroll continues. An ornate gate tower guards the entrance.

The Imperial Avenue, more than two hundred steps wide, was lined with black lacquer rib-like barricades on both sides; two rows of red lacquer barricades further to the center defined the emperor's road, forbidden to the people and horses. Between the black and red barricades were imperial ditches paved with brick, stone and tile and planted with lotus, and along these ditches were flowering trees. The total effect in late spring and early summer was one of brilliant embroidery.... Ordinary traffic was not permitted through the Gate of Southern Breeze, since it directly faced the Imperial Palace; but the farmers' pigs must pass here in order to supply the city. From morning to evening, each herd of thousands, driven by a dozen or so herders, would enter in procession without any disorder.... In the southeast of the city was a street named Pan Pavilion; on the south side there was a Hawk Hostel only for sellers of falcons and hawks. Other stores on the street sold pearls, silk, incense, spices, herbs and mats. Further south, the street was connected to a lane of gold, silver and fancy textile shops in magnificent buildings with wide imposing frontage. Inside these shops transactions took place involving thousands in cash, astonishing to ordinary ears. Eastward, there was a Pan Pavilion Restaurant below which a market would open at dawn to trade in clothing, painting and calligraphy, rare works of art, rhino horns, and jade articles.... Nearby was an amusement center with some fifty song and dance houses;

Willows planted along the river bank to hold the earth are beginning to turn green as the spring-festival time approaches.

some of the theatres could seat several thousand. . . . There were also shops for medicine, second-hand clothing, fortune-telling, food and drinks, barbers, art materials and song books. One could loaf around the whole day without noticing the approach of evening. . . . The Jên Restaurant had a long corridor beyond its entrance, lined with upper-floor partitions on either side. In the evening, lamps and candles shone brilliantly on upper and lower floors; brightly dressed and painted girls gathered at the rail near the eaves, waiting to be chosen by customers. From a distance, they looked like fairies. . . . The restaurants line the streets with decorated towers that faced each other, embroidered banners waving and shielding the pedestrians from the sky and sun. . . . Regard-

less of rain or wind, warmth or cold, day or night, the restaurants and amusement centers were always crowded and filled.

One particularly illuminating entry reported:

The sentiment generally cherished was friendship. If an out-of-towner was mistreated by a city resident, an indignant crowd would come to help. . . . If a stranger or new family moved into the city, the neighbors would lend things and render service, bring gifts of soup and tea, and offer advice about shopping. . . . Every day, neighbors called on each other to have tea and talk about what was going on. For special events of happiness or bereavement, houses would be filled with well-wishers or comforters. [Abbreviated and free translation.]

Within the city gate is a two-storied restaurant. The street floor is a maze of small shops. People on the

Detail below shows archery shop. A customer tries out a bow. Note height of bow in background.

With the development of cities came growth in use of currency. The annual production of copper coins increased from 880,000 strings in the late tenth century to 1,830,000 in the eleventh century; yet the demand always outstripped the supply. Thus gold and silver came to be used for larger transactions and the "flying cash," or money-draft system, initiated in the early ninth century, became popular with merchants as a supplement to cash. The next natural step was the development of paper money, which began as certificates of deposits issued by private banks. In 1024 the government took over this function and created the

busy street represent all classes; rich men in sedan chairs, laborers with wheelbarrows, monks, entertainers and merchants.

world's first national banknotes. Unfortunately, confidence in this money gradually dwindled as government receipts fell off (see last section). Officials even tried adding a perfumed mixture of silk and paper to give the money wider appeal, but it didn't help. Runaway inflation and depreciation followed.

Despite these problems, which have plagued governments inside and outside of China ever since, the significant fact is that nearly one thousand years ago China had an advanced money economy which remained viable in all essential features until the nineteenth century.

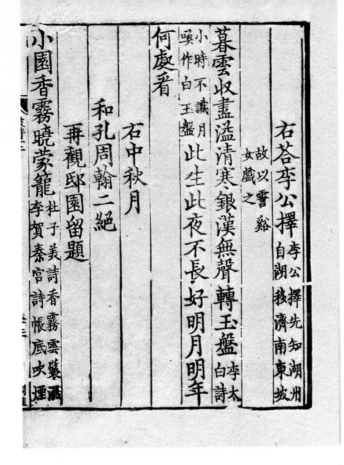

The Era of Civilized Men

The rising importance of education created a great demand for printed matter, and the printing industry had made rapid progress by the middle of the tenth century. In a southwest kingdom of Szechwan, a high official who had been unable to afford books before he attained success, ordered the printing from wood blocks of an "Anthology of Literature" for the benefit of impecunious scholars. On seeing these printed books being sold in Szechwan and the Yangtze delta, Fêng Tao, a durable prime minister who had served four of the Five Dynasties

A page of "Su Shih's Poems," woodblock print of 1213.

Su Shih leaves his home to join his friends revisiting the Red Cliff. He carries a fish and a bottle of wine, gifts

under ten emperors, decided that it would be an excellent service to scholarship to revise the Confucian classics, have them cut in wood, and published. Notwithstanding political and military upheavals during the twenty-one years it took for research, writing and printing, this monumental project of "Nine Classics and Their Commentaries" was completed in 953. After the founding of Sung in 960, a variety of Confucian texts were printed, but the landmark effort was the Chinese Tripitaka, the library of Buddhist canon. Ordered by the new emperor in 972, it required eleven years and 130,000 wood blocks to produce the 5,048 volumes. Some forty years later, the Taoist canon was also prepared and its 466 cases containing 4,565 rolls were presented to the emperor. Ac-

tual printing, however, was delayed and not completed until nearly one hundred years later, in 1117.

Private printing, though less spectacular, was more indicative of the general level of learning. The industry spread throughout the empire, with hereditary houses flourishing for centuries; one family continued publishing for over four hundred years, well into the Ming dynasty. In quality of calligraphy, cutting, pressing and paper, Sung woodblock books have never been surpassed; editions of classics, commentaries, histories, collected works of essayists, poets and philosophers, and even an illustrated description of crop plants, have survived to this day to become treasured collector's items.

A section of the first "Red Cliff Ode" copied by Su Shih himself: "Looking from the changing aspect of things, the universe cannot hold for a wink; from the unchanging aspect, all things are immortal."

from his wife. This is a section of a scroll by Ch'iao Chung-ch'ang illustrating poet Su Shih's second "Red Cliff Ode."

如彼而卒莫消長也蓋將

自其變者而觀之則天地

曾不能以一瞬自其不變

者而觀之則物与我皆無

盡也而又何羨乎且夫天地

One of the widest published literary figures in his own time as well as during later periods was Su Shih, known also as Su Tung-p'o. Unmatched in versatility in a remarkable age of brilliant men, he was at once a poet, essayist, calligrapher, painter and statesman, and achieved greatness in all of these categories. His famous prose-poems on the Red Cliff contrast the insignificance of man with the infinity of the universe, but also emphasize man's eternal oneness with nature. This blending of philosophy and poetry distinguishes Sung verse from that of T'ang, which is more purely lyrical or narrative. In addition to his skill in poetic prose, Su Shih was equally at home in the traditional five- and seven-word poems and the relatively new *tz'u* form, consisting of long and short lines. *Tz'u* originated from lyrics written to music for courtesans and adapted by some major poets of the eighth century, but did not reach full development until the late T'ang and Five Dynasties. Early works tended to be sentimental songs of love and sorrow. In the hands of Su Shih, *tz'u* became freed from music and matured in depth and scope. One illustration is this poem on his longing for his brother when exhilarated by wine during the moon festival:

> How often does the bright moon come?
> With wine, I ask of the blue sky.
> In the heavenly palaces,
> What year is it tonight?
> I wish to return there, riding the wind,
> But fear that in the high places of jade halls and eaves,
> I cannot fend off the cold.
> Rising to dance with my clear shadow,
> Scarcely possible that I am among men.
> Turn around the red lacquered pavilions,
> Dip below the silken-curtained windows,
> Shine on the sleepless.
> There ought not be regrets,
> But why so often full at times of parting?
> Men have sorrow and joy, farewell and union,
> The moon has clouds and clear skies, waxing and waning.
> Perfection is rare since days of old,
> So wish only that the years be long,
> To share beauty even across a thousand miles.

Though he was a daring ground-breaker in art, Su Shih was conservative in political views and allied himself with the respected arch-conservative Ssu-ma Kuang in opposing liberal reforms. Ssu-ma Kuang followed the tradition of the Grand Historian of Han, whose family name he shared, by collaborating with three other scholars in compiling and writing a chronological history of China from 403 B.C. to A.D. 959 entitled *Tzu-chih t'ung-chien,* or "The Comprehensive Mirror for Aid in Government." By pointing out the successes and failures of former dynasties, he hoped that the work would become a reference for men in power. He wrote in a simple and lucid style whose beauty greatly enhanced the content. His history set a high standard in accuracy and comprehensiveness. This passion for accuracy is illustrated by the fact that thirty of the book's 354 chapters are devoted to an appendix listing and commenting on conflicts in facts Ssu-ma discovered in the 322 books used as source material.

Ssu-ma Kuang, Su Shih and Wang An-shih, though differing in political views, all represented the best of the Chinese civilization of their time; they embodied the ideal of integrity, loyalty and talent. An anecdote concerning Wang An-shih, the great reformer, and Su Shih, conservative poet-painter-scholar, illustrates their high-mindedness: After he retired from the government, Wang An-shih lived in Nanking. One day in the tenth year of his retirement and after a serious illness, his old opponent Su Shih passed through and decided to visit him. Wang met his guest by the only mode of locomotion he could afford, on the back of a donkey; and Su rushed off the boat to greet him without even taking the time to put on his hat. Laughing at themselves, the two erstwhile high officials remarked: "Official ceremony is certainly not designed for us!" They immediately went to a small wine shop to drink and chat. During the next few days, they roamed about the mountains, resting in temples and carrying on conversations that ranged in subject matter from literature to Buddhism. Though they were political enemies in K'aifêng, among the rivers and hills they were friends. After seeing Su Shih off, Wang An-shih sighed: "How many hundreds of years must pass before there is another man like this!"

The greatest emperor-artist in Chinese history, Hui-tsung, enjoyed literary meetings like this one and neglected affairs of state. Upper right is his poem and calligraphy; he may have painted this picture.

Death mask of beaten silver came from northern border area under Liao rule, which was conquered by the Jurchen in 1125.

A National Shame

A gifted artist came to be a disastrous ruler when he devoted himself to aesthetic pursuits and neglected matters of state. He was the emperor Hui-tsung, whose calligraphy and painting displayed exquisite taste and consummate skill. When he ascended the throne in 1100, a most crafty minister, Ts'ai Ching, soon gained his complete trust. Under the guise of reform, Ts'ai set out to liquidate all opposition, conservatives as well as reformers. His entire family strengthened his position by joining the emperor in his pursuit of beauty and pleasure. One of the younger Ts'ai's even mingled with actors and courtesans to amuse the artistic monarch. Large ships transported fancy rocks, strange plants, rare antiques and art objects from the south to decorate the emperor's newly built palaces and gardens. Such extravagances were superimposed on an already shaky financial structure, and unrest was inevitable.

In the far northeast, the rising power of the Jurchen or Chin, a Tungusic people of Manchuria, threatened the now decadent Liao empire. Hoping to eliminate its traditional enemy, the Sung court proposed a concerted attack, with the understanding that Sung was to recover the border regions and the Jurchen would receive the annual tribute now collected by Liao. But the Sung forces met only defeat, while the Jurchen swiftly overran Liao territories all the way to Peking. Sung had to pay a large sum in addition to the tribute to buy back the city. A few years later, Jurchen forces swept south again. A payment of money induced them to leave but they came back the next year—1126—to capture K'ai-fêng and its inhabitants. The Jurchen took the now retired Hui-tsung and his son, Emperor Ch'in-tsung, as prisoners, together with his other sons, royal family members, attendants, court officials and the imperial treasures. This ended the Northern Sung dynasty.

A plump baby on its bed forms the base of this exquisite porcelain pillow. Children were a popular theme in Sung art.

To Sung painters, the story of the poetess Lady Wên-chi, captured by Tartars in the Han dynasty and taken to Mongolia, was current. The invaders are shown looting the house and bringing the lady to their commander. She was forced to marry

a Tartar chief, by whom she had two children. After twelve years she was ransomed. Her eighteen poems of lamentation inspired many paintings. Figures and setting are Sung period rather than Han; the Tartars here resemble the Khitan invaders.

177

An Uneasy Peace

The ninth of Hui-tsung's thirty-one sons was the only one to escape from the Jurchen's dragnet. He became known in history as Emperor Kao-tsung, the first ruler of the Southern Sung dynasty. Too disheartened to defend the north, he either dismissed or ignored his patriotic generals and headed south to seek safety, closely pursued by the invaders. The Jurchen commander-in-chief, Wu-chu, nearly captured Kao-tsung in a sea chase below the Yangtze delta and then decided to withdraw to avoid encirclement. At this juncture, Sung's military situation was by no means hopeless, for a few outstanding generals managed to exact heavy casualties from Wu-chu's returning army. Chances for a military victory ended when a Sung official, one Ch'in Kuei, who had seemingly escaped from the north but who favored the Jurchen regime, returned to the new Sung capital, Hangchow, with his family and servants. He persuaded Emperor Kao-tsung to adopt a policy of appeasement, rejecting the military gains as transient and unreliable. Thus in spite of decisive victories north of the Yangtze, an imperial edict went to all fronts to halt advances and withdraw. Yüeh Fei, whose soldiers had annihilated Wu-chu's best cavalry and armored troops, was framed with charges of treason and executed, along with other war advocates. The Sung court submitted to the Jurchen as a vassal state, agreeing to pay heavy annual tribute in exchange for a border settlement roughly midway between the Yellow and Yangtze rivers. Except for a brief rupture in 1161, this arrangement was generally observed until 1217.

The real victor in this uneasy peace was Chinese civilization. In spite of the Jurchen's determined efforts to preserve their identity and culture, they adopted Chinese governmental institutions, including the examination system and Confucian classics; and their people, contrary to repeated prohibition, assumed Chinese names. Meanwhile the Chinese south, though diminished in territory, expanded economically and culturally under pacifist emperors who continued to patronize the arts. Hangchow became a grander and more resplendent city than K'ai-fêng; the nation enjoyed a state income larger than that of Northern Sung; and Chinese merchants sustained the first great oceanic commerce of the world, trading with the rest of Asia and dominating routes eastward to Korea and Japan and southward to Indonesia.

In the arts, the Imperial Painting Academy, established by the ill-fated Hui-tsung, continued to attract talented artists. The practice of testing candidates for posts of court painters by having them illustrate given lines of poetry further cemented the bond between literary and pictorial traditions. Official taste for sensitive

Poet-painter-emperor Kao-tsung created this tranquil landscape painting and inscription, a poem on the life of a fisherman.

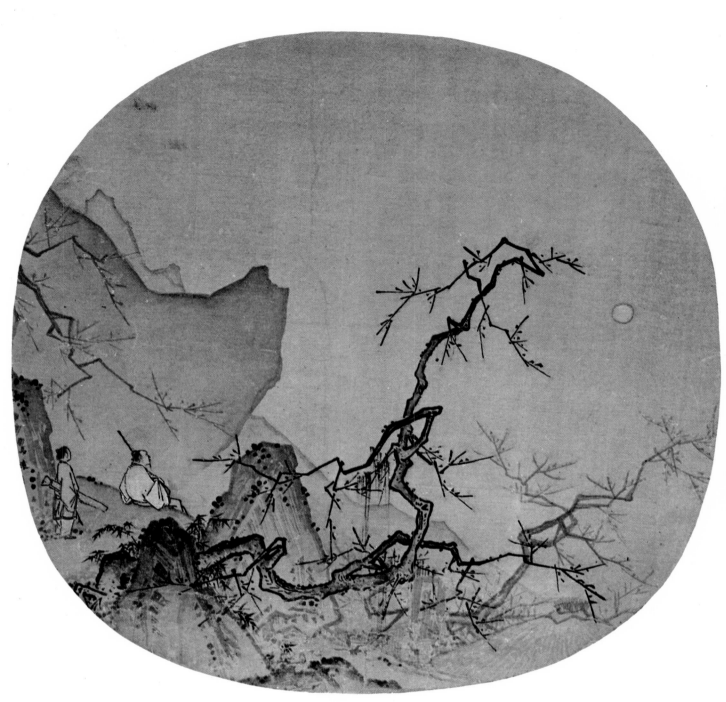

Scholar contemplates the moon beyond a plum tree. Attendant carries a musical instrument. By the master painter Ma Yüan.

A rice-paddy scene south of the Yangtze. A farmer and his wife use their legs and feet to work the square-pallet chain pump. At right a boy drives a large water buffalo to turn a larger water-pumping device. Boy in the background fishes.

Traveling peddler is laden with a variety of articles. Most are useful household notions, others are toys. Customer is a nursing mother with five small children whose ages seem to be not more than a year apart. It was painted by Li Sung.

and delicate works resulted in an Academic Style that contrasted with the free and powerful manner of Five Dynasty and Northern Sung landscapes. The most important transitional landscape artist, Li T'ang, retained much of the inspiration of the past while adding precision to his paintings. This technique was later simplified and transformed by Ma Yüan and Hsia Kuei, whose abbreviated brush strokes and atmospheric washes captured the lyricism of the southern countryside. In common with these twelfth- and thirteenth-century painters, the poets of this period conveyed in their short verses and *t'zu* strong power of suggestion. Nostalgia and despair for the lost central homeland were frequent themes. These were the words of Hsin Ch'i-chi (1140–1207):

In the clear water under the Yü-ku Cliff,
Tears of how many travelers?
Looking northwestward at Ch'ang-an,
A pity, such countless hills!
Blue mountains cannot hinder,
Eastward it finally flows.
Dusk on the river, sadness over me,
Deep in the mountains, hear the *chê-ku* bird sing!

But Lu Yu, though homesick, was hopeful to the end. His last words to his sons were:

Dying, one knows all is vain,
Yet I regret the nine regions as one not to see,
The day our army northward takes the central plain,
At ancestral offering forget not your father to inform.

A gathering of ballplayers and spectators shows the sport-loving side of the Sung people. The different and colorful costumes, which were strictly regulated by occupation, show a total disregard for social status in the sporting world.

Two actresses exchange greetings in one of "assorted plays," which were comic vignettes. Tiny feet were result of binding.

Humorous songs and dialogue in a popular play satirize a situation between an eye doctor and his tattooed patient.

183

From Faith to Philosophy

Buddhism, Taoism and Confucianism had achieved coexistence in T'ang, but continued to compete on religious and philosophical levels. By winning popular adherents and imperial patronage, Buddhism enjoyed an advantage over Taoism but could not shake the position held by Confucianism over officialdom. It was favored as the foundation of the political structure and the social order.

Neo-Confucianists scored a further victory on the philosophical level in the Sung dynasty. They freshened the time-worn teachings of the Sage by borrowing metaphysical concepts such as the universality of all beings from Buddhism and Taoism. The greatest Neo-Confucianist was Chu Hsi, historian, teacher, statesman and commentator on the classics. Chu Hsi analyzed and synthesized the thoughts of his predecessors to develop the *Li* School, which proposed that *li*, or principle, is the origin of all beings, while *ch'i*, or matter, is the substance. *Li* has the connotation of reason, rationality and essence; *ch'i*, of breath, spirit and force. Man's true nature, being fundamentally good, is one with the principle of the universe; thus man's mind is capable of probing into the essence of all beings, and the investigation of all things is his path to learning. Through *jên*, or humanity, man can overcome his limitations; by beginning with known principles and reaching for the utmost, he will find the universal principle and all things will become clear to him.

A great challenge was offered to Chu Hsi by Lu Chiu-yüan, who merged the Ch'an (Zen) Buddhist practice of meditation and insight with the philosophy of Mencius, who taught that to reach the mind's utmost is to recognize one's nature, and consequently the nature of the universe. Lu had the concept of a "great unity" through which all men have the same mind, and the mind has the same principle; therefore man's mind is identical with the universal principle. He mocked Chu Hsi's theory as one that promoted devotion to fragmentary and isolated trivia rather than concentration on intuitive simplicity and illumination. Two and a half centuries later, Lu would find his greatest advocates in the Ming dynasty.

Liang K'ai, famous for the simple free style of his later Ch'an (Zen) phase, probably painted "The Supreme Taoist Master Holding Court" during the years of the Painting Academy. Taoism had now adopted deities similar to those of Buddhism.

Inertia and Pressure

The most relevant criticism against Neo-Confucianism came from independent thinkers who considered their metaphysical speculations valueless in combating the major ills of the day—foreign military pressure and domestic economic troubles. Yet the rise of Neo-Confucianism may be directly attributed to the frustration of high-minded scholar-officials who vainly presented memorials on reform measures and protests against corruption and complacency without having any visible effects on the power structure of the expanding bureaucracy. The lofty Lu Chiu-yüan once wrote to a friend: "The people are too poor and hard pressed; the officials are haughtier by the day.... We must curb corrupt officials and let the people gain back some strength." But the remedy Lu offered for poverty and mistreatment—peace of mind, magnanimity of

Taking odes of the Chou dynasty as a theme, a thirteenth-century artist portrayed contemporary life: this section of a long scroll shows tenant farmers bringing the harvest to the landlord. In Sung dynasty rent was roughly half of annual yield.

Other sections of painting opposite describe different activities in various months. This scene shows hunting of raccoons, foxes, and wild hogs on foot and on horseback after the harvest. Peasants' catch was turned over to the landlord.

spirit and the serenity to look upon adversity as a blessing—was not likely to achieve either end.

Other more realistic reformers deplored the prevailing self-satisfied delusions of peace and suggested wisely that "what was taken from the people must be used to benefit the people." Yet they lacked the conviction to place heavier responsibilities upon rich merchants and big landowners, because they believed that the rich were the foundation of a nation's wealth; to diminish them in any way would result in destroying the national equilibrium. Even without external pressure, it might have been only a matter of time before the Sung administration collapsed under its own weight. But the end came sooner than that when a serious threat developed in the north: the rapidly rising Mongols conquered the Jurchen in 1234: In another forty-five years they succeeded in overcoming the resistance of Chinese armies and forcing the last Sung emperor into the South China Sea.

187

Sung painting captures a critical moment as a Han beauty crosses a northern river in a camel-drawn carriage. She was

a gift from the emperor to a Hsiung-nu ruler. Khitan, Jurchen and Mongol invasions made such themes relevant in Sung.

Lung-ch'üan or Dragon Spring ware from Chekiang. This kiln flourished in the eleventh and twelfth centuries.

Small brush basin in the shape of a lotus leaf was made in Hsiang-hu kiln in central Yangtze valley.

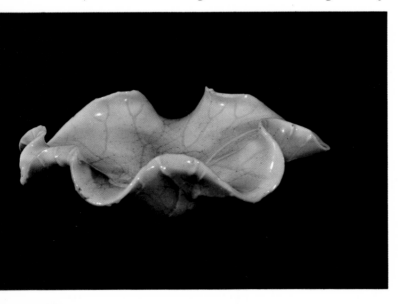

Changing the Whole Face of the World

Scientific and technological progress continued under the Five Dynasties and Sung. During these 370 years, the three discoveries that Francis Bacon (1561–1626) considered as having "changed the whole face and state of things throughout the world" either took place or advanced tremendously. The first was printing, to which Sung added the invention of the movable type in the 1040's. Inventor Pi Shêng fashioned type out of sticky clay hardened by fire and composed on an iron plate, using an even spread of paste made from pine resin, wax and paper ashes. The paste would melt under heat to accept the types but solidify after cooling to hold them for printing. This innovation took place four centuries before Gutenberg.

The second invention on Bacon's list was gunpowder. Taoist alchemists acquired an early knowledge of gunpowder and pyrotechnics through experimentation with sulfur and saltpeter. The firecracker, designed as a substitute for crackling heated bamboo sticks used to ward off evil spirits, was known in the sixth century and a Chinese military handbook compiled about 1042 recorded the formula for preparing explosive powder in making "fire balls." In the twelfth century, Sung armies utilized projectile explosive weaponry both on land and water against the Jurchen. By the thirteenth century, the Jurchen were employing this ingenious agent of destruction against the militarily superior Mongols, who lost no time in improving it for attacks on Chinese strongholds.

The third item mentioned by Bacon was the magnetic compass. The same 1042 military handbook described the making of a floating south-pointing fish from thin iron leaf, first heated, then rapidly cooled while oriented in the earth's magnetic field. Around 1088 Shên Kua, who had ample opportunity to travel during his varied career that ranged from ambassadorship to military command, recorded in his encyclopedic *Mêng-ch'i pi-t'an* or "Dream

Stream Essays" that a needle tip became south-pointing after having been rubbed by lodestone, and that it always inclined slightly to the east. This observation predated by four centuries the discovery of declination traditionally attributed to Columbus in 1492. Shên also described the floating needle, the balanced needle, and the suspended needle that hung by a single fiber of new cocoon silk. Around 1111, Chu Yü, whose father was a high official stationed at the port of Canton, wrote of seagoing ships that carried several hundred persons and the dependence of their pilots on south-pointing needles in dark weather. A century or so later a book on foreign peoples told of ships sailing in the boundless ocean solely by means of the south-pointing needle, closely watched day and night, since life and death depended upon the slightest fraction of error.

Bacon did not know the origins of what he correctly perceived to be epoch-making discoveries, for he had limited access to Chinese literature. He would have been astonished to read Shên Kua's book; it contains information on mathematics, astronomy, meteorology, geology and mineralogy (with references to fossils), geography and cartography (including the making of relief maps), biological observations and a host of other subjects. Sung was a great period for the publication of high-quality botanical and zoological monographs and books on pharmaceutical plants. Scholarly physicians codified traditional systems to pharmaceutics and acupuncture. To intensify cultivation and expand the area of arable land available to support a greatly increased population that probably exceeded one hundred million, irrigation and hydraulic engineers made great strides in lockgates and new surveying instruments. Since minerals were a major source of government income, metallurgical processes in gold, silver, copper, iron, lead, tin and mercury were highly developed.

The making of porcelain, which began in T'ang, became fully refined in Sung. Innovations in paste, glaze and firing made possible almost all forms, textures and colors. Porcelain has remained to this day the most universally admired of Chinese inventions. Sung porcelain, in particular, transcends mere utility and expresses the true spirit of a most civilized era in Chinese history.

Shaped like an ancient bronze and colored lilac, this Chün ware came from kiln in Honan, Central China.

Teapot in shape of wrapped bundle is fine Chi-chou ware. It competed with white northern Ting ware.

Considered the greatest prime minister in Southern Sung, Chao Ting's nationalistic policies against the Jurchen clashed with the pacifism of Ch'in Kuei. Chao committed suicide in exile.

Under the Mongols A.D. 1279–1368

For the first time all of China is ruled by a foreign conqueror . . . She becomes the cornerstone of the Mongol Empire, which includes Persia and Russia . . . Imperial highways link the land mass from Korea to Poland, encouraging the flow of trade and cultural exchange . . . Arabs, Russians, Venetians and other non-Chinese serve the Yüan court, while Chinese are distrusted . . . Native revolt succeeds in ending Mongol domination in less than a century.

HISTORICAL CHRONOLOGY

A.D.

1281   Mongol invasion fleet meets heavy resistance and typhoon in Japan; they are defeated.
Kubilai Khan repeats order of 1258 to seize and burn all Taoist books except Tao-tê ching.

1283   Burma is conquered.

1285–88   Repeated expeditions to Annam and Champa suffer defeats, partly due to diseases and guerrilla attacks.

1287   Kubilai eliminates kinsman Nayan, a claimant to the throne, in South Manchuria.

1290   Yüan helps vassal Korea to crush residual Nayan forces.

1291   Buddhist establishments, mainly Lamaist, counted at more than 42,000, with over 213,000 monks and nuns.

1293   Expedition in Java succeeds initially, but ends in disaster after surprise attack by natives.

1294   Kubilai Khan dies. Preparations for further campaigns to Annam and Champa ended.

1308   White Lotus Society, a Chinese Buddhist cult, is banned.

1308–33   Succession of seven rulers.

1315   Competitive examinations resumed, separating Mongols and non-Chinese from the Chinese.

1351   Liu Fu-t'ung leads Red Turbans in revolt.

1352   Chu Yüan-chang joins a rebel group.

1358   Liu Fu-t'ung's forces take the old Northern Sung capital K'ai-fêng, cross the Great Wall and reach South Manchuria and Korea.

1362   Liu Fu-t'ung is crushed by Yüan army and dies next year.

1364   Chu Yüan-chang declares himself king of Wu.

1368   Chu declares himself emperor of Ming dynasty, after having defeated all major contenders. The last Yüan emperor escapes to Shang-tu (Xanadu).

ART CHRONOLOGY

A.D.

c.1280   Poetic plays in northern style reach peak in Peking. Best writers are Kuan Han-ch'ing, Wang Shih-fu, Po P'u and Ma Chih-yüan. Wang Ying-lin (1223–96) writes San-tzu ching, a children's primer on history and philosophy.
Ch'ien Hsüan (c.1235–after 1300), archaic-style painter.
Chêng Ssu-hsiao (1241–1318), famous for ink orchids without soil, symbolizing loss of country.
Chao Mêng-fu (1254–1322), most versatile man of period, excels in painting, calligraphy, poetry and essay.

c.1300   Greatest Yüan poet and essayist is Yü Chi (1272–1348).

1306   Confucian Temple in Peking completed.

1308   Lamaist Temple in Mount Wu-t'ai built.

c.1310–50   Poetic play writing shifts center to Hangchow. Chêng Kuang-tsu and Ch'iao Chi-fu are outstanding playwrights.

1311–20   Chu Ssu-pên (1273–1337) compiles great atlas of China.

1324   Wall painting in a Shansi temple depicts actors.

c.1325   Wang Chên-p'êng, leading figure painter. Huang Kung-wang (1269–1354) and Wu Chèn (1280–1354), both Taoist landscape masters.

1342–45   Buddhist figures in marble relief on gate passage of Chü-yung Kuan, north of Peking.

1343–45   Sung, Liao and Chin histories are compiled.

c.1350   Ni Tsan (1301–74) and Wang Mêng (c.1309–85), literati landscape painters. K'o Chiu-ssu (1312–65), ink bamboo painter and calligrapher.

1351   Temple vases, white porcelain with underglaze blue decoration, indicate maturity of this important innovation in ceramic art.

Fine horses were highly prized in Mongol China. Two handsome stallions, with grooms, are seen in two sections of a

Two bearers of tribute from an Asian country painted by Jên Po-wên are from a scroll on previous page.

The Conquerors

The Mongol Empire began at the northern fringe of Chinese civilization. On the upper reaches of the Amur, Temujin built his power from a handful of followers to become Jenghis Khan (the "Emperor of the Seas"). Temujin was destined to lead. He gave unequivocal commands to his subordinates, which were never rescinded. To his enemies, surrender meant life and resistance meant death. To the talented, he offered high posts and generous compensation without regard to race or origin. He united the diverse Mongol tribes for a single purpose: to defeat their enemies and share their treasure.

Jenghis' personal guard, an elite corps made up of his leaders' sons, served as hostages for their fathers as well as officer-trainees for the army. Eventually grown to ten thousand in number, they endured harsh discipline but enjoyed special privileges and the opportunity to rise to high posts. The striking force of the army came from its hard-riding horsemen, capable of covering long distances at great speed. Superior mobility and coordination enabled

short scroll by artist Jên Jên-fa, famous for his sensitive yet realistic painting of horses. He was grandfather of Jên Po-wên.

Older Sung painting style was used by Ch'ien Hsüan, who remained loyal to the former Chinese dynasty.

them to maneuver the enemy into encirclement and entrapment.

Jenghis Khan governed the Mongol nation with a code of law called the Great Yasa. Its measures were stern. Stealing a horse was as serious as killing a man: both were punishable by death unless specified fines were paid. A deserter, as well as any officer who sheltered him, would be executed. Capital punishment was also meted out to the thrice-bankrupt.

In a final campaign before his death in 1227, Jenghis Khan destroyed the Hsi Hsia and took over much of the Jurchen land in North China. He overwhelmed the Kara-Khitan Empire in Central Asia, and captured the Turkish empire of Khorezem east of the Caspian. But he gained far more than territory: he acquired the services of Chinese generals and administrators, Moslem merchants and financiers, Turkish warriors and Uighur scholars, who adapted their script for a Mongolian written language. Thus, with some 130,000 warriors and a population of only a million, Jenghis Khan laid the foundation for the Mongol Century.

During the second phase of conquest, through the reign of three successive Khans lasting thirty-three years, Mongol armies

triumphed over Persia, Mesopotamia, Armenia, Georgia and the Abbassid Caliphate at Baghdad. Westward they crossed the Volga, took Moscow and Kiev, penetrated Poland, Bohemia, Hungary and the Danube valley, and reached the Adriatic Sea. In the east, the whole of North China and Korea came under their control. One of the most important figures in this period was the Sinicized Khitan nobleman Yeh-lü Ch'u-ts'ai, the empire's chief civil administrator from 1231 until his death. Ogodai Khan, successor to Jenghis Khan, almost invariably followed Yeh-lü's thoughtful advice. When many Mongols urged putting the population of North China to the sword and reducing the land to a vast grazing ground, Yeh-lü pointed out that the living could work, produce and pay taxes, but not the dead. This one admonition saved the lives of millions.

The final conquest was accomplished by Jenghis Khan's grandson Kubilai Khan, who adopted the Chinese dynastic name of Yüan and reconstructed Peking as his winter capital. After the conquest of Southern Sung, Kubilai Khan became the first foreign ruler of all China. He retained Yeh-lü Ch'u-ts'ai's government structure, including a Central Chancellery which directly controlled provincial governments by natural geographical divisions. To keep the local Chinese officials under surveillance, several grades of supervisors descending to the town level were usually filled by Mongols or non-Chinese. As the famous Venetian traveler Marco Polo later observed, the Khan had no confidence in the natives; he put all authority in the hands of Tartars, Saracens or Christians. The Mongols divided the people into four classes, with themselves at the top, the non-Chinese collaborators next, the North Chinese third, and the "Southerners," the Chinese who resisted them the longest and hardest, on the lowest level.

But some countries in East and Southeast Asia remained unconquerable. The Japanese, well prepared and aided by a hurricane, annihilated a Yüan armada in 1281, Champa and Annam routed several Mongol expeditions and Java repulsed an invasion. With the death of Kubilai in 1294, the tide of the Mongols began to recede.

◁ *A band of Mongol horsemen, with their leader Kubilai Khan, cross a desert region. Note camel caravan in the sand dunes.*
▽ *Detail: Magnificent in ermine, Kubilai Khan is accompanied by a woman. Dog in right corner is of the greyhound family.*

The harshness of the North China winter and the interdependency of horse and man are strikingly revealed in this masterpiece painted by Chao Mêng-fu. His mastery of both painting and calligraphy influenced Chinese artists for centuries.

The Conquered

After Sung fell to Kubilai Khan, the south continued to be inhabited with men the Mongols considered bandits, some of whom resisted the imperial armies for years. In 1288, a Mongol official reported to Kubilai Khan that uprisings took place in more than four hundred areas. But the Mongol policy of rewarding turncoats did not always work. The last Sung minister, General Wên T'ien-hsiang, was held captive in a windowless mud hut for three years before his execution. He refused every offer from Ku-

bilai Khan, who secretly held him in great esteem because of his indomitable spirit. Many Confucianists refused to serve the conqueror and devoted themselves to teaching and writing; others took upon themselves the duty of civilizing the "barbarians." The chief Neo-Confucianist influence on Kubilai Khan was Chao Fu, who presided over a college in the north and taught many of Kubilai's advisers. On the whole, the Chinese scholar-gentry class suffered psychological humiliation and economic deprivation under the Mongols. Their access to success closed when the competitive examination system was suspended in the north and later in the south. It was revived in 1315, but openings for southerners were restricted.

Common farmers fared no better than they

had under Sung. Heavy taxation forced them to borrow from the government's loan agencies, which charged an interest rate of one hundred per cent, compounded annually. Various tax-collection privileges were auctioned off to the highest bidder, who could collect many times his investment. Later such piecemeal auctions were abolished, only to be replaced by a centralized auction.

With Arab and Turk interference eliminated, communications between the East and West improved, facilitating trade and commerce. They were also aided by the paper currency, issued initially with reserve backing. But as government expenditures exceeded income, the temptation to print paper money without reserve became irresistible. The resulting in-

flation, together with measures against the use and sale of gold, silver and copper, impoverished the people and ruined the economy. During the last years of Mongol rule, the never-ceasing resistance movement seriously challenged the central authority, which had little success in coping with famine, flood, locusts and epidemics. The Chinese soldiers who made up most of the armies surrendered to native rebels as soon as their foreign commanders proved incompetent in battle and the local Chinese administrators were no more loyal to their non-Chinese supervisors or the court. In addition, the strongest generals engaged in power struggles among themselves in Peking and the northwest. The end of Yüan came less than a century after the conquest of Sung.

Mixed Culture and Counterculture

The account of the Venetian Marco Polo, who stayed in China from 1275 to 1292 in the service of Kubilai Khan, aroused wide curiosity about Cathay among generations of Europeans, but even more lasting were the impact of Chinese civilization on Mongol-controlled areas and the influence of foreign cultures that came to the Central Kingdom with the Mongols. Sung innovations such as printing, the magnetic compass, gunpowder, porcelain, textile and medical discoveries were brought to the West, as sorghum, the distillation process, sugar refining and musical instruments found their way to China. In religion, Islam took root in western and southwestern China; Tibetan Lamaism, a form of Buddhism, won support from the Mongol court; Nestorian Christianity and Roman Catholicism gained a few adherents. A Persian astronomer reached China in 1267 with models of six instruments and a terrestrial globe, but the Chinese engineer-astronomer Kuo Shou-ching found the Greco-Muslim ecliptic coordinates unsuited to the Chinese polar-equatorial system—a system which three hundred years later was hailed in

Europe as one of the main advances of Renaissance astronomy. Kuo's invention of equatorial mounting is used in our modern telescopes, although the telescope itself did not exist in his time. He also developed an elementary form of

These cone-shaped mountains rising out of a lake were painted by Taoist recluse artist Wu Chên. His favorite subject was

Man as part of the landscape is shown in "Dwelling in the Fu-ch'un Mountains" by Taoist priest-painter Huang Kung-wang.

spherical trigonometry, and directed the restoration of the Grand Canal.

The great majority of Chinese intellectuals, however, had to find outlets other than government service, in which they were often relegated to clerical jobs. Taoism, a native religion tolerated by the Mongols, provided a haven for a counterculture of recluse writers and artists. Its influence, together with Ch'an (Zen) Buddhism and Confucianism, nourished the defiant

fishermen in spacious landscapes. He and Huang (above), Ni and Wang (next pages), are the Four Great Yüan Masters.

No movement disturbs the tranquillity of this quiet landscape by the wealthy and eccentric master painter Ni Tsan.

spirit to create an expressive and individualistic type of literati paintings. The subject matter was landscapes, bamboos, orchids, trees and rocks and the style paid scant regard to rationality, realism or formalism, which were identified with the taste of kings.

No longer fettered by the examination system, literary men sought an audience among the masses. They combined two or three short songs to give fuller expression to feelings and moods, linked these combinations into a set for telling a story and then joined four sets into a play. In performance, each set was sung by a single character, while other actors provided the dialogue and action. The popularity of this dramatic form is shown by the fact that one early Ming book recorded 535 Yüan plays. The four finest playwrights were Wang Shih-fu, celebrated for his *Western Chamber*; Ma Chih-yüan, author of *Autumn in the Han Palace*; Po P'u, for *Rain on the Wu-t'ung Tree*; and Kuan Han-shêng, for *Injustice Suffered by Widow Tou*. The first three plays are love stories; the last, a social tragedy. Kuan Han-shêng, who lived among actors and occasionally took a part himself, used the vernacular extensively to achieve realism and heighten drama.

Some material used in these early plays came from storytellers' prompt-books, which eventually formed the basis for novels. During the turn of the dynasty from Yüan to Ming, countless anonymous authors rewrote these stories and gave birth to a truly popular form of fiction.

The music seems to fill the air as a scholar (far left) plays the ch'in *for his monk friend in a painting by Wang Mêng.*

"Street Scenes in Peace Time" is a twenty-four-foot scroll by artist Chu Yü. In this section a small gathering of men, women and children watch a portable puppet show. The manipulators of the puppets are hidden within the curtains; a drum-

mer accompanies the action. The audience appears to be southerners still wearing clothing of the Sung period. In left foreground an old man is followed by a boy in red carrying a wrapped ch'in, *a seven-stringed, hand-plucked musical instrument.*

205

△ An acrobat demonstrates his skill with a lance in another section of the "Street Scenes" scroll. Some spectators hold shoulder poles used for transporting merchandise. At top is a cripple, two beggars and a boy who calls to them.

▷ In this monkey show the trainer puts the animal through an acrobatic routine. Holding hat, belt and decorative sword are probably delivery men who have been distracted by the entertainment. Donkey driver with badly balanced load moves on.

▽ As scroll unrolls a street fight has started between two men who may be drunk. Their friends try to keep them apart. A concerned woman in the foreground calls to her stray child; her friend holds the baby on her shoulder.

Painted decorations in underglaze cobalt blue was the most important innovation in the ceramics of the Yüan period. It was most likely introduced from Mesopotamia and Persia, where the color had been used for several centuries. The Chinese called it "Mohammedan blue". From the fourteenth century on, a great variety of Chinese blue and white porcelain and other ceramic ware was made and exported, inspiring an ever widening circle of imitators in the Near East and Europe.

A Chinese Revival
A.D. 1368–1644

The founder of Ming dynasty restores Chinese rule and establishes political institutions to last for the next five centuries . . . Building activities abound: city walls, canals, highways and the great architectural gem of Peking . . . Early fifteenth-century reaches height in Chinese maritime explorations, adding tribute states south to Java and west to the Persian Gulf . . . As decline sets in, Annam becomes independent, Japanese pirates prey on coastal cities . . . In closing decades, Jesuits bring Western science to the court . . . The Manchus are invited to help quell rebels who break into Peking, and they stay on.

HISTORICAL CHRONOLOGY

A.D.

1368	*The first emperor of Ming takes reign title Hung-wu in Nanking.*
1368–88	*Ming army enters Xanadu; Yüan emperor escapes.*
1371–82	*Hung-wu conquers Szechwan, Yünnan and Kwei-chow.*
1380	*After liquidating prime minister for treason, Hung-wu takes over executive duties.*
1390–95	*Liquidation of top aides, with execution of whole clans.*
1398	*Hung-wu's death makes grandson emperor.*
1402	*Hung-wu's fourth son wins civil war, begins reign Yung-lo next year.*
1405–33	*Eunuch admiral Chêng Ho heads seven maritime expeditions to South Seas and Indian Ocean.*
1407	*Annam becomes a Ming province.*
1410–24	*Yung-lo leads five campaigns against Mongols, who prove to be elusive; he dies on return from last expedition; Mongol raiders continue to harass border areas.*
1421	*Yung-lo moves capital to Peking.*
1427	*Ming abandons Annam.*
1449	*Mongol tribal leader Esen captures Ming emperor after crushing imperial expeditionary force.*
1514	*Portuguese reach Chinese shores for the first time.*
1552	*Japanese pirates plunder Yangtze delta, Hangchow Bay and other coastal areas until checked by Ming forces ten years later.*
1573–82	*Chang Chü-chêng, grand secretary, pushes reforms.*
1592–98	*Ming forces help Koreans expel Japanese invaders.*
1616	*Nurhachi (c.1559–1626) founds Manchu state.*
1624–27	*Eunuch Wei Chung-hsien conducts reign of terror against scholar-officials.*
1628	*Misrule and famines produce roving rebels; leader Li Tzu-ch'êng rises to power.*
1636	*Nurhachi's successor proclaims Ch'ing dynasty in Mukden.*
1644	*Li Tzu-ch'êng takes Peking; the last Ming emperor hangs himself.*

ART CHRONOLOGY

A.D.

1369	*New imperial factory started in Ching-tê Chên, soon to become ceramic center of China.*
c.1398	*Hung-wu's tomb is built near Nanking.*
1407–21	*Rebuilt Peking is greatest Ming architectural gem.*
1408	Encyclopedia of the Yung-lo Period *is completed.*
c.1424	*Yung-lo's tomb is built near Peking.*
1426–35	*Technique of blue-and-white porcelain developed.*
1465–87	*"Painting in contrasted colors" (tou ts'ai) on porcelain, an innovation of Ch'êng-hua period.*
c.1430	*Hsia Ch'ang (1388–1470), leading ink-bamboo painter. Tai Chin (active to 1450's) founds the Chê School of painting.*
c.1450	*Shên Chou (1427–1509) founds the Wu School of painting based on Yüan masters.*
1450–56	*Cloisonné work excels in Ching-t'ai reign.*
c.1500	*Wang Shou-jên (1472–1528), thinker with great influence on philosophy, literature and art. Li Mêng-yang (1472–1529) revives ancient literary styles. Kuei Yu-kuang (1506–71) creates simple essays. Wên Chêng-ming (1470–1559) and T'ang Yin (1470–1523) excel in painting and calligraphy.*
c.1520	*Ch'iu Ying rises from artisan to master painter.*
1522–66	*Printing displays technical excellence. Wu Ch'êng-ên (c.1500-80) writes picaresque novel* A Journey to the West. *An anonymous scholar writes Chin-p'ing-mei, the first realistic Chinese novel. The* Three Kingdoms *and* Water Margin, *attributed to Lo Kuan-chung (died c.1400), are rewritten.*
c.1550	*Li Chih (1527–1602) and Yüan Hung-tao (1568–1610) champion self-expression and creativity in writing. Hsiang Yüan-pien (1525–90) collects art and rare books.*
c.1600	*T'ang Hsien-tsu (1550–1617) writes play* Peony Pavilion. *Tung Ch'i-ch'ang (1555–1636) becomes pivotal painter-calligrapher and art historian.*
1606	*Earliest woodcut book in color, Ch'êng-shih mo-yüan.*
c.1625	*Fêng Mêng-lung (active 1620–44) compiles short-story collections.*

China for the Chinese

Chu Yüan-chang was confronted by a major crisis at the age of sixteen when drought, locusts and epidemics struck his home in the Huai River valley. His parents and oldest brother died within a few days of each other. Unable to help his second brother feed the remainder of the family, he entered monkhood. But the local temple soon ran out of food and he left with an alms bowl, wandering and begging for the next few years. In this vagabond period, he joined a secret cult that prophesied the rebirth of the Maitreya, or Future Buddha, as "Ming Wang," the Brilliant Ruler. Called the White Lotus Society, this sect was apparently a fusion of Manichaeism, which worshipped light against darkness, and the Maitreya Society. It had been repeatedly banned by the Mongol regime, and had gone underground to become a center of resistance. In 1351, one member, Liu Fu-t'ung, led a rebellion which gathered a sizable force and occupied several cities. Supporting groups soon appeared, all wearing red turbans as a badge and offering incense to the Maitreya.

Chu Yüan-chang joined one of these groups and soon proved himself an able fighter and organizer. Within seven years, his victorious troops won control over a large area in the lower Yangtze valley including Nanking and Yangchow. He sought out the great strategist Liu Chi and plotted the unification of China. Meanwhile, Liu Fu-t'ung campaigned in North China, marching through the Great Wall, taking Xanadu and reaching South Manchuria and Korea. His success ended when he was betrayed and killed by another rebel. Although Chu Yüan-chang did not arrive in time to rescue Liu, his efforts in the south were more successful. He soon eliminated his major rivals. When he announced his intention to take the north, Chu described himself as a sage sent by Heaven to save the suffering multitude (a Confucian version of the Maitreya). He told the people they had nothing to fear from his well-disciplined troops. Early in 1368, Chu proclaimed the founding of Ming dynasty and his title Hung-wu, by which he is better known. By the fall of that year, his main forces under Marshall Hsü Ta had taken Peking and the last Yüan emperor escaped to the Mongol home territory beyond the Great Wall. After two and a half centuries, North China was once again Chinese.

In the next fourteen years Ming armies succeeded in bringing all of China proper under control. Hung-wu's main military force, however, concentrated on the destruction of the Yüan ruling house in the Mongol homeland. Three of his best generals, each with fifty thousand cavalry, penetrated deep into the Mongolian heartland beyond the Gobi Desert with costly but indecisive results. Repeated campaigns took thousands of enemy captives but never the ruler or his heir. The Mongols were so weakened by 1388 by internal conflicts that Hung-wu ceased his operations against them.

The phenomenal rise of Hung-wu from pauper to founder of a dynasty had no parallel in Chinese history; even the first emperor of Han had begun as a minor official. He owed his success to native intelligence, an intimate understanding of the needs of the common people, shrewd application of the power of superstition and psychology, and a respect for organization and learning.

In 1380, a corrupt prime minister attempted to assassinate Hung-wu; he was accused of seeking help from the Japanese and Mongols as well as most of Hung-wu's former comrades. The aborted coup resulted in tens of thousands of executions over thirteen years. With the death of Empress Ma in 1382, Hung-wu lost his only confidante and he became increasingly paranoid as the cooperative spirit which existed during empire-building days deteriorated into suspicion. Hung-wu's decision to act as his own prime minister after 1380 concentrated more power and more duties in his own hands than were held by any other monarch in Chinese history. Before his death in 1398 he confessed that, "During thirty-one years I have shouldered the Mandate of Heaven, worries and fears have accumulated in my heart, and I have labored daily without relaxation." Such power and consequent burden could have been disastrous to any man. It was remarkable that in this case, the dynasty he founded would endure for another two and a half centuries.

Legend describes Ming's founder as having an ugly porcine face. This official portrait contradicts it.

大明太祖高皇帝

The Three Yangs were celebrated for their exemplary service to the empire. Left to right, Yang P'u, Yang Jung, both in official robes indicating rank, and Yang Shih-ch'i, in informal attire. All three were grand secretaries.

The Foundation for Stability

Hung-wu's ambition was to complete the reconquest of China. Mongol occupation and native resistance had laid waste large areas, especially in the Huai River and lower Yellow River valleys. He understood the need for returning uprooted refugees and peasants to the abandoned fields and offered incentives such as land ownership, a three-year tax exemption, seeds, farm implements and draft animals. He also required that a percentage of the land be used for planting cotton, hemp and mulberry trees, an indication of the importance of fibers in the national economy. To distribute the tax burden and increase treasury receipts, population census and land surveys were initiated. Trained officials led local laborers in repairing irrigation works all over the country and every male between sixteen and sixty was subject to labor draft. Craftsmen in Nanking and Peking either served the government for ten days out of each month or paid a tax; those outside the capitals served three months every three years, but had the right to sell products they made in their free time.

The traditional three components of government—civil administration, supervisory apparatus, and military hierarchy—were retained. The ministries of civil appointments, revenues, rites, war, justice and public works bore the main burden of executive functions. Local gar-

A gathering of scholar-officials was held in Yang Jung's Apricot Garden on April 6, 1437, and painted by Hsieh T'ing-hsün.

This view of the life of these elderly scholar-artists shows something of the respect for learning and creativity in the fifteenth century. Ch'en Hsün (right) ranked first in the palace examination; later he reached the eminence of the Yangs.

risons of 5,600 men each were placed under the direct control of five commands within the Ministry of War. Hung-wu took special pride in creating a system that separated the army from the civilians and boasted that one million fighting men did not cost the treasury a single coin. Military families were required to supply men for the army while civilians were free from the draft. Seventy per cent of the border garrisons and eighty per cent of the interior garrisons were diverted to cultivate land belonging to the army—a little over one-tenth of the nation's total arable acreage.

To share decision-making and paper work, grand secretaries were established to review memorials, make recommendations and draft edicts, but they were given no authority to take executive action. These consultants were mainly scholars from the Hanlin Academy, recruited through examinations. They also served in the personal bureau of the crown prince, providing a valuable link between rulers. The most celebrated consultants were the Three Yangs: Yang Shih-ch'i, Yang Jung and Yang P'u, who entered the Hanlin Academy about the same time and served five rulers in roles of increasing importance. Their scholarship, brilliance and justice contributed greatly to the stability and moderation of the Ming empire up to 1440, when old age and death began to eliminate them from the court. A few others, notably the Minister of Civil Appointments Chien I and Minister of Revenue Hsia Hsün-chi, were also sturdy pillars of the administration. Both served several rulers with tireless devotion until their deaths.

Two of Three Yangs were in power longer; the third, Yang P'u, not in this section, suffered unjust punishment for ten years.

The Desert and the Ocean

The beloved eldest son of Hung-wu died prematurely. This tragedy led to a disaster when the Emperor passed over his fourth and ablest son and placed his grandson on the throne. Within a year, the new Emperor, Chien-wên, imprisoned four princes and caused the suicide of a fifth. Prince Yen revolted, starting a civil war. When his forces entered the capital, Nanking, young Chien-wên disappeared. The former Prince Yen became Emperor as Yung-lo and hunted his deposed nephew for years, suspecting that Chien-wên had escaped. Where he was and whether he escaped has remained a most intriguing mystery.

Yung-lo's cruelty in punishing his opposition matched that of his father. He liquidated whole clans of Chien-wên's supporters, including those who had already surrendered to him. He was also aggressive and followed an expansionist policy. During a twenty-two-year reign, he led five expeditions into the heart of Mongol territory, first defeating the eastern tribe, the Tartar, and then the western tribe, the Oirat. But Yung-lo's failure to capture the Tartar chief made his conquests temporary.

He continued preparations for moving the capital from Nanking to Peking. Thousands of wealthy families were transferred from the lower Yangtze valley to fill the northern city and criminals were employed to till the land around it. After fourteen years, the great plan was completed and Peking became the Ming capital. To supply the north with southern grain and lessen the dependence on coastal shipping, which was perilous and vulnerable to piracy, the Grand Canal was also repaired and improved.

But Yung-lo did not confine his interests to the north. He waged another major series of campaigns in the extreme south, directed at Annam, the present-day North Vietnam. He succeeded in annexing Annam as a province, but the area remained a trouble spot for many years. The local rebellions—which became es-

A powerful portrait of a powerful emperor. Yung-lo raised the Ming dynasty to the top of its splendor.

The eunuch Chêng Ho led Ming's naval expeditions. Early seventeenth-century woodblock gives idea of his ships.

pecially serious toward the end of his reign—made it necessary for him to carry on continuous costly campaigns in the area. In its relations with other nations, the Ming court pursued the tribute system successfully and received missions from Korea, the Ryukyu Islands, Annam, Champa, Cambodia, Siam, Borneo, Java, Sumatra, Malacca and some states on the southeast coast of India. Japan, which the Mongols failed to subdue, complied on and off with requests to keep their pirates from raiding China's coastal ports, but not until Yung-lo's reign did the third Ashikaga Shogun acknowledge China as their superior and pay lavish tribute.

Yung-lo's most successful exploits were great maritime expeditions to Southeast Asia led by Chêng Ho, a Moslem eunuch. His first good will voyage to India involved sixty-two vessels with twenty-eight thousand mon. Some of the other six voyages, the last after Yung-lo's death, went as far as Aden on the Red Sea and Hormur on the Persian Gulf. Chinese vessels touched the east coast of Africa and some representatives reached Mecca. These armadas are believed to have sailed farther, with more vessels and men, than any other up to that time.

Lifelike jade figurine of a man grooming a horse. The common people were not allowed to buy Mongol horses before 1438.

The Resurgence of Eunuchs

The extensive appointment of eunuchs by Yung-lo as ambassadors and army superintendents directly contradicted his father's admonition: "Eunuchs should not be allowed to interfere with affairs of state; death to the offender." The former emperor also prohibited teaching the eunuchs to read and forbade them to correspond with outside officials. When Yung-lo died during the return from his fifth northern campaign of 1424, his eldest son succeeded him for one year, then a grandson took over with the title Hsüan-tê. In the interval, some eunuchs had become army commanders in charge of cities or regions. A palace school

for eunuchs had been established, with members of the Hanlin Academy as teachers. Fortunately, the court was still dominated by wise advisers from previous regimes including the Minister of Civil Appointments Chien I, Minister of Revenue Hsia Yüan-chi, and the Three Yangs, who were imperial counselors. It was not until after Hsüan-tê died that the full effect of relying on eunuchs became evident.

Hsüan-tê inherited a legacy of inflation from his activist grandfather. Yung-lo's astronomical expenditures for military expansion, naval operations and building far exceeded income from taxes and savings made during Hung-wu's reign. The price of rice increased fifty times from the beginning of Hung-wu to the end of Yung-lo, a period of fifty-odd years. Hsüan-tê took various measures to fight this inflation. He

◁ *Statue of a civil official. Such images, which include military figures and animals, line the avenue to Yung-lo's tomb.*

Proficient in riding and archery, Hsüan-tê emperor was the only really talented artist-emperor after Hui-tsung of Sung. He made frequent journeys on horseback to personally inspect northern border defenses. Name of the painter is unknown.

reduced the circulation of paper money by accepting it in place of goods for taxes, salt and fines, put a stop to the costly Vietnam wars and dropped large-scale maritime expeditions.

Having accompanied his grandfather on northern campaigns, Hsüan-tê learned the art of war and having been tutored by Hanlin scholars, he knew the ways of peace. But Hsüan-tê neglected to give such education to his heir. Chêng-t'ung grew up in the Inner Court, where the chief eunuch, Wang Chên, became his closest adviser. The first seven years of Chêng-t'ung's reign were guided by his level-headed grandmother and the Three Yangs, but when they died, Wang Chên took control. By this time the Oirat tribe had grown strong under their leader Esen, who resented Wang's hard bargaining over tribute horses. He launched an invasion in 1449. Wang Chên responded by staging a display of half a million men, a host of ministers and generals, and the

emperor himself to discourage the enemy, and incidentally, impress his hometown just beyond the Great Wall. The result was a catastrophe. The empire's best troops were annihilated, Wang Chên met death in the confusion of battle and the emperor was captured. This might have been another 1127, when Northern Sung ended with the seizure of its emperor by invaders, but fortunately Esen did not press his gains. Ming's resolute war minister, Yü Ch'ien, persuaded the new emperor, Ching-t'ai, to make a stand in Peking. When Esen finally came south, he found the defense forces ready with cannon to engage him outside the city wall. After a few defeats, Esen withdrew to Mongolia. Several months later he released the ex-emperor in exchange for ransom and trading privileges. When Ching-t'ai contracted a fatal illness, the ex-emperor regained his throne, and once again surrounded himself with schemers and eunuchs.

Birds and rabbits in snow were painted by Hsüan-tê for one of his generals. The work reflects the style of the Sung Painting Academy, a source of his inspiration. Court painters of the Ming period tended to comply with imperial taste.

These two hounds, also from the brush of Hsüan-tê, were painted in an easy manner, displaying the emperor's ability to put his sensitive observations into ink impressions with colors playing a minor role. The literati preferred this style.

Avenues to Officialdom

Two years after its founding, Ming restored and improved the examination system, which then remained essentially unaltered for the next five hundred years. This process of elimination through progressively more difficult tests became the main avenue to high officialdom for a commoner of low origin. The first hurdle consisted of district examinations for the degree of *hsiu-ts'ai* or "flowering talent." If the candidate qualified, he went on to the provincial examinations to seek the credentials of *chü-jên*, the "elevated man," which entitled him to take the metropolitan examinations in Peking. When he passed those, he became a *chin-shih* or "presented scholar," and was summoned to the palace examinations. The man who ranked highest in the summit test, together with the second and third ranked, were appointed to the Hanlin Academy as editor-compiler and compilers; the rest had to undergo further tests for entering Hanlin and receiving appointments. Starting from tens of thousands of *hsiu-ts'ai*, about three hundred *chin-shih* degrees were conferred for every triennial metropolitan examination during the Ming period.

Strictly supervised and on the whole impartial, this system provided an opportunity for the talented to rise without discrimination. But the restriction of subject matter to the nine Confucian classics with Sung commentaries, and a fixed literary format using parallel structure of sentences, suppressed all other kinds of learning. It also discouraged the development of science and technology, which gradually became identified with Western civilization. Two other avenues to officialdom were special recommendations by high officials and a degree of *chien-shêng* from the Imperial Academy, whose student body consisted of children of high officials or "tribute students" chosen from *hsiu-ts'ai* degree-holders by local officials. Thus the competitive examinations were the only avenue upward that could be called "open."

◁ *Young scholar-official with book and attendant epitomizes in porcelain the dream of students in Ming China.*

▽ *The hero-explorer of the Han dynasty Chang Ch'ien is immortalized in Ming jade. He is shown floating in a hollow log.*

Shên Chou went into the mountains during a spring rain to enjoy the mist and the greenery. In a poem accompanying his painting, he mused that in such an enchanting realm, beautiful lines were lying about waiting to be picked up.

On this self-portrait at eighty, Shên Chou wrote that others criticized the likeness, but claimed he could not know himself, hence could not see the deficiency. He expressed the thought that virtue was more important than appearance.

The Perfect Gentlemen

The examination system became in a sense the Chinese social system. By Late Chou, Chinese society ranked the people into four major groups: scholars, farmers, artisans and merchants, in that order. Mencius had asserted sweepingly, "One who labors with his mind rules; one who labors with his body is ruled." Through the energetic empires of Han and T'ang, and the sophisticated rule of Sung, the examination system underwent constant refinement, reaching final development during the Ming dynasty. The whole of society seemed to

Recognized with Shên Chou as one of the Four Great Ming Masters, T'ang Yin painted these secluded fishermen on a river in autumn with strong and sure strokes. His technique is reminiscent of a Sung master, unlike Shên Chou who owed much

live by its rules. A holder of the lowest educational degree was exempt from labor service and assumed a status of gentility. The winner of higher degrees was entitled to fly a red silk banner over his residence, with his honors emblazoned in gold characters. His family and clan, even the townspeople, shared in his pride and the glory. Official appointment awaited him; his future was limited only by the "Son of Heaven." Money and gifts flowed to him from favor-seekers even if he was incorruptible. For most people, there was no better means for achieving such eminence except birth or marriage, both of which depended largely on fate rather than ability.

There were a few exceptional men who shunned the examination system but still enjoyed the respect of all society, even ministers

to the Yüan landscape artists. T'ang's scholarly career began brilliantly in examinations, but ended when he was implicated in a bribery case. He drowned his sorrows in the taverns and brothels of Soochow and channeled his great gifts into art.

and royalty. These were the untitled gentlemen of high artistic and literary achievements, whose influence lasted beyond the dynasties. A prime example was Shên Chou. He came from three generations of scholar-painters who inherited some wealth and an aversion for the despotism of the court. Although his learning and talent won him special recommendation from the local officials, Shên declined an offer to serve the government. Instead he chose a private life in Soochow, then the cultural center of the Yangtze delta. His home resembled an artists' colony: poetry, calligraphy and painting occupied all members of the family; outings in neighboring scenic areas and drinking parties with literati friends were their recreation. For them, education meant life, not livelihood.

The other two of Four Great Ming Masters are Wên Chêng-ming and Ch'iu Ying. Wên's austere character contrasted sharply with his friend T'ang Yin's romanticism. Simplicity and purity shine through Wên's snow scene with a lonely fisherman.

Shên Chou delighted in helping needy friends and relatives, with the result that he never accumulated savings. Once a friend identified a set of rare books in Shên's studio as being stolen from him by reciting specific passages from it. After listening, Shên Chou gave him the books without revealing the name of the seller. As Shên Chou's fame grew, purchasers for his paintings would line up at the gate; he could not escape for long even by hiding in remote temples. Unable to refuse the most humble of admirers, such as peddlers and herd-boys, he was swamped by requests and his students often had to take over his obligations. He would good-naturedly put his signature on passable fake paintings, especially to help someone in financial need, such as a poor scholar with an ill mother. But in his authentic works, it is easy to see the qualities that established Shên as the first of the Four Great Ming Masters and the founder of the Wu (Soochow) School. He was active until his death at the age of eighty-two.

The second of the Four Masters was his star pupil, Wên Chêng-ming, who proved that a comfortable income was not necessary for a scholar-gentleman. Wên was fifteen when his father died in office, leaving no savings; yet he refused a sizable funeral gift from the local gentry. He found contentment in simple food and worn-out clothing, tactfully declining financial help from a sympathetic family friend. On another occasion, Wên returned money sent to him by Prince Ning, sending word he was ill, and did not even reply to the letter offering him a position. After the age of fifty, he had a short and unhappy career at the Hanlin Academy, but the prospect of promotion and deeper involvement in politics only increased his desire to retire. When his resignation was finally granted, Wên left Peking to continue his artistic life in Soochow. He died at eighty-nine, as he was laying down his brush after having written an essay.

Individuals like Shên and Wên represented the Chinese ideal of scholar-gentleman, the counterpoint of the scholar-officials who climbed the ladder of worldly success.

Beginning as a humble artisan,
Ch'iu Ying was greatly admired by the scholar-gentry, who
helped him to become a professional painter. He illustrated
popular literature; the scene is from a Yüan period play.

A noted calligrapher
Wang Ch'ung, befriended by Wên and T'ang, copied this
selection from Western Chamber. *This play was the mas-*
terpiece of playwright Wang Shi-fu of the Yüan dynasty.

Artist makes use of the pun, such as a horse with bee and monkeys (or ma-shang fêng-hou). *The meaning is "Immediately became a marquis" (or instant nobility). An immortal monkey in a novel was also a groom in the Heavenly Kingdom.*

The Rise of Popular Literature

The traditional literary output of Ming was undistinguished in comparison with that of preceding major dynasties, but its popular literature reached new heights. Around the 1360's two novels, *San-kuo-chih yen-i* ("The Three Kingdoms") and *Shui-hu chuan* ("Water Margin," translated into English also as "All Men Are Brothers"), were put into coherent forms from the prompt-books of storytellers, marking the division between oral and written traditions in full-length tales. "The Three Kingdoms" was written in an appealing mixture of literary and vernacular languages, while "Water Margin" even contained colloquial expressions from a local dialect. The name Lo Kuan-chung was connected with both; he was probably the author of the first and the editor of the second.

"The Three Kingdoms" was based on the conflict among the divided states after the collapse of Han. All its characters and episodes came from standard history, partially fictionalized to sustain a fascinating narrative. "Water Margin," although also historical, was much less faithful to the record of a group of thirty-six outlaws of the early twelfth century. As in the tales of Robin Hood in England, they came from all walks of life; they were forced by injustice into acts of crime and fled to a rural hideout where they organized to help the oppressed. Lo's original editions of these novels were lost and it was not until the middle sixteenth century that extensively rewritten versions appeared. By then, many scholars were repelled by the corruption of the Ming court and began to find creative and financial satisfaction in writing and polishing popular literature to meet the demand of a prosperous urban population. In contrast to mainstream writers, who tried to revive dying ancient styles, these slighted novelists explored new horizons in theme and rhetoric.

The first novel built on fairy tales was the *Hsi-yu chi* or "A Journey to the West," written by Wu Ch'êng-ên. Using Hsüan-tsang's seventh-century pilgrimage to India as a starting point, Wu created an escort for the Buddhist monk—a fearless and resourceful monkey—and wove a picaresque tale involving eighty-one dangers and demons that had to be overcome before the monk reached the Western Paradise and obtained the sacred sutras. Humorous and engrossing, the novel also satirizes through supernatural characters the degenerate court and corrupt bureaucracy.

The first realistic novel to describe contemporary society was *Chin-p'ing mei* or "Prunus in a Golden Vase." The talented author chose to remain anonymous, due no doubt to the many erotic passages in the story. Borrowing a single episode from "Water Margin," he placed the action in the Sung Dynasty, but his vivid description of the sex life of a bourgeois businessman accurately reflects life during Late Ming and was a strong indictment against the merchants and officials of that time.

Known as the "Four Marvelous Books" of Ming, these novels are still read by most literate Chinese. Ming also produced a great dramatist in the tradition of Yüan. T'ang Hsien-tsu considered official duties a bore, choosing a life of art and poverty instead. His play entitled "Four Dreams" earned him a permanent place in Chinese literature. The most famous of his works is *Mu-tan t'ing* or the "Peony Pavilion," a complex tale of the union of two lovers through a dream in which the impossible is mixed with the realistic. The magic of this work lies in its moving poetry celebrating the eternal nature of love.

Woodcut illustration of a Yüan play called The Lute Story *shows farewell scene. Late Ming published many fine plays.*

Cultural Isolation

If time had stopped all over the world just after Chêng Ho's last voyage in 1433, Chinese civilization would have represented the height of human endeavor. Never before had a single nation with so large a population (some sixty million) achieved such cultural unity and continuity over so large an area (more than half the size of Europe). Unfortunately, China isolated itself culturally just at the beginning of the great European transformation which included the Renaissance, Reformation, growth of nationalism, discovery of the New World, Commercial Revolution, advent of scientific methods, Industrial Revolution and imperialism. What Chêng Ho learned from his trips to Southeast Asia, India and Africa only confirmed the ideas of superiority held by the ruling houses of Ming. Age-old tendencies to downgrade artisans and merchants blocked advances toward industrialization and commercialism and hampered expansion through capital accumulation or organized foreign trade. Most of the brains of the empire were channeled into the civil service examinations and imperial projects such as the *Yung-lo ta-tien*, the great encyclopedia compiled between 1403 and 1408. More than 2,180 scholars selected and transcribed Chinese works in all phases of human knowledge existing up to 1400, producing an encyclopedia made up of 22,937 chapters in 11,095 volumes. It was too vast to be printed, and only small portions of two hand-copied sets survive today.

This reverence for the past contrasted sharply with the low estate of contemporary work. A few individuals made original contributions in some fields, including two useful handbooks. The medical handbook *Pên-ts'ao kang-mu* was completed in 1578 by Li Shih-chên, who took twenty-six years to record some two thousand animal, vegetable and mineral

Ming ceramic art moved away from Sung austerity and returned to T'ang's energy and color.

Top, monk's hat jug, named for shape of its lid, Hsüan-tê reign (1426–35); middle, jar with rope-shaped handles, Hung-chih (1488–1505); bottom, stemcup with decorations of children at play, Chia-ching (1522–66).

230

drugs, and over eight thousand prescriptions. The illustrated industrial handbook *T'ien-kung k'ai-wu* by Sung Ying-hsing was published in 1637. Sung investigated the technology of producing rice, silk, salt, ceramics, metals, coal, paper, weapons and other items in which, even at that late hour, China held world leadership.

Top, dish with dragon painted in overglaze green and black enamel, Hung-chih; middle, broad bowl decorated on the outside with fish painted in underglaze copper red, Ch'êng-hua (1465–87); bottom, tripod with sculptured decoration after ancient bronze, from the kiln of Chou Tan-ch'üan, without time marking.

A 21.5-inch-high Wan-li vase with interesting enamel-painted decorations of birds, flowers and insects.

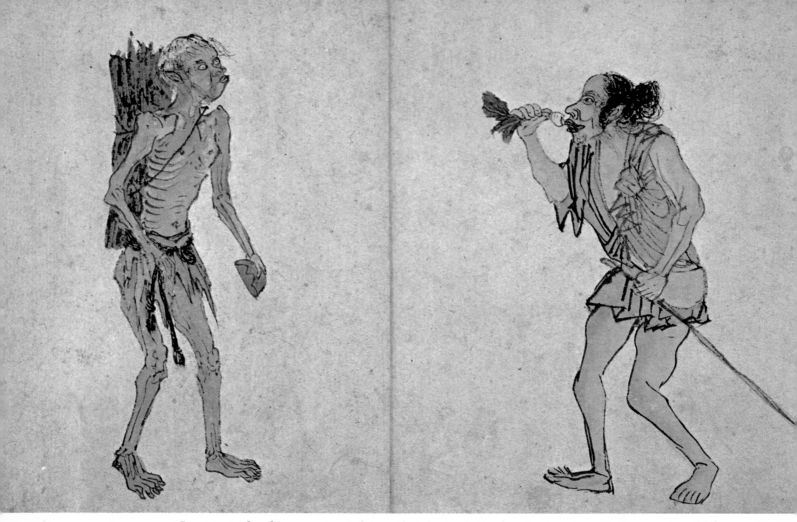

Poverty-stricken beggars uprooted from their homes by famine, flood, unbearable taxes or forced labor were painted by Chou Ch'ên, teacher of both T'ang Yin and Ch'iu Ying. Such poor people roamed aimlessly about, only one meal

Power Without Responsibility

The two centuries of Ming rule from the middle of the fifteenth century to the middle of the seventeenth, mostly under irresponsible emperors and their intimates, demonstrated the durability of Chinese institutions. During this period, only fifty years were led by sound governments, and out of nine sovereigns, only two could be considered good rulers. Serious deterioration began with Chêng-tê, an emperor who preferred to be a general and bestowed military titles on himself with a lavish hand. He loved to display his physical prowess in riding, archery and wrestling, sought pleasure in disguise outside the palace and rounded up beautiful women for sexual orgies with his drinking companions, which included foreign monks. At his death, a courageous Grand Secretary managed to dismiss 148,000 superfluous palace guards and other parasitical personnel in one stroke, and to execute many officials who had led Chêng-tê astray.

His successor, Chia-ching, was a completely different kind of man but no better as a ruler. Concerned more with his own lifespan than the people's livelihood, he left the affairs of state in the hands of Yen Sung, one of the more unpleasant top officials in the entire dynasty. Chia-ching devoted himself to seclusion and self-cultivation under the direction of Taoist monks. His forty-five-year reign ended, ironically, with a fatal dose of "longevity pills."

The next emperor, Lung-ch'ing, placed his trust in worthy men and managed to maintain a strong, stable government for the five years of his reign. His untimely death left the direction of the state in the capable hands of the statesman Chang Chü-chêng, who took over on behalf of the ten-year-old monarch, Wan-li. Chang rose from a family of poor scholars to the pinnacle of power. For ten years until his death in 1582, he was, in effect, the emperor. A man steeped in Confucian principles and dedicated to the revitalization of Ming, he directed the affairs of state without concern for vested interests, declaring that he would do what was best for the nation, without regard for his own life. Chang believed in pragmatism and the existing system. With infinite patience, he checked his subordinates' deeds against their words to ensure truthfulness.

He was also a legalist in the sense that he did not rely on moral restraints but rather on re-

away from hunger and death. Some learned skills such as snake-catching to entertain the curious or supply exotic menus. These dispossessed and desperate people were the natural followers of strong rebel leaders who sought to destroy the dynasty.

wards and punishments to control the people. Firmness and simplicity, to him, were the essence of good government; wealth and strength the foundation of a healthy and just society. One of his reform measures concerned taxation: land surveys and censuses were carried out strictly to form a solid base for applying the "single whip" tax collection method, a system gradually developed by combining many different levies on land and labor into one or more items payable in silver. This arrangement eliminated many opportunities for extortion, fraud and interference with the people's productivity. The strength of Chang's character gave his decade a flash of light before the sunset of Ming, but his selfless autocracy produced numerous enemies. As soon as he died, his titles were stripped, his properties confiscated, his family imprisoned and his eldest son forced to commit suicide.

In the absence of this stern and fatherly man, the new emperor, Wan-li, indulged himself: drinking, opium-smoking, philandering, squandering the state funds and ordering harsh punishment to all opposition. During his unfortunately long reign, Wan li decimated his bureaucracy by avoiding the business of state, including the appointment of public officials. By the end of his reign, only five out of more than one hundred censors remained; of six ministers, only one. In the supervisory staff for the provincial governments and provincial and local magistrates, half of the vacancies were left unfulfilled. In addition, peasants were driven off their land to create great domains for members of the imperial family and other court favorites. One example was the prince of Fu, Wan-li's third son, who received land in Hukuang, Honan and Shantung totaling over 250,000 acres. Naturally the peasants, removed to make way for these domains, were unhappy with their lot and formed bands who roamed the countryside robbing and looting. A debacle followed.

In 1620 a fifteen-year-old boy, whose sole interest was carpentry, ascended the throne, and the ruthless eunuch Wei Chung-hsien took over the government for his own profit. With his private eunuch army and a network of spies, he systematically persecuted opposing scholars and made Confucian martyrs out of many loyal men. Official robbery and extortion against the people were committed in the name of tax collection. The end-of-the-dynasty syndrome was complete when rebellions erupted throughout the country.

Long scroll depicts the Ming campaign of 1598 to help Koreans resist Japanese invaders. In detail above, Chinese commander with two generals in camp; below, Japanese entrenched in their fortress with firearms made after Portuguese models.

A Ming ship is under full sail in a detail from scroll. The banner is marked "Commander of Three Armies." While land forces were storming the Japanese stronghold, the Ming and Korean navy engaged the enemy reinforcements arriving by sea.

The Japanese Pirates

The Ming dynasty's relationship with Japan was an unhappy one from the beginning. Japanese pirates had disturbed Chinese coasts even before the founding of the dynasty and early Ming attempts to curb them through diplomatic negotiations proved futile, for the man the Chinese considered the king of Japan had little power over these buccaneers. The situation was worsened by the Japanese practice of sending tribute missions composed of profiteers who trafficked in illegal trade and used force to gain their goals. Matters deteriorated further when the islanders started coming en masse. In 1419, twenty ships carrying several thousand men attacked the Liao-tung peninsula, and twenty years later, forty shiploads of raiders plundered the Chekiang coast. From the mid-sixteenth century on, these sporadic raids escalated into full-fledged invasions in which Chinese local bandits and offshore pirates joined forces with the Japanese. Major cities and ports in the Yangtze delta and Hangchow Bay were pillaged, while in the south, other prosperous trading ports along the Chekiang and Fukien coasts suffered severely. One of the strangest cases involved an elusive band of sixty to seventy swordsmen who terrorized the countryside from Hangchow to Nanking, killing thousands before they were finally destroyed.

Although it was not until the 1560's that specially trained Chinese defenders and massive armies stamped out the invaders, the Japanese campaigns in Korea became even more punishing. In 1592, Japan's unifier Hideyoshi moved his army into Korea as a first step in a march to Peking. The invasion army swiftly took over the whole peninsula, but it was beaten back to a foothold near Pusan by a combination of Ming rescue forces, guerrilla outbreaks, and Korean naval defenders. Inconclusive peace negotiations ended when Hideyoshi brought in a second wave of fresh troops, which proved no more successful. The death of Hideyoshi in 1598 hastened the invaders' complete withdrawal, but this empty "victory" drained Ming's military and financial resources and made it easier for the growing Manchu power to conquer the Chinese empire fifty years later.

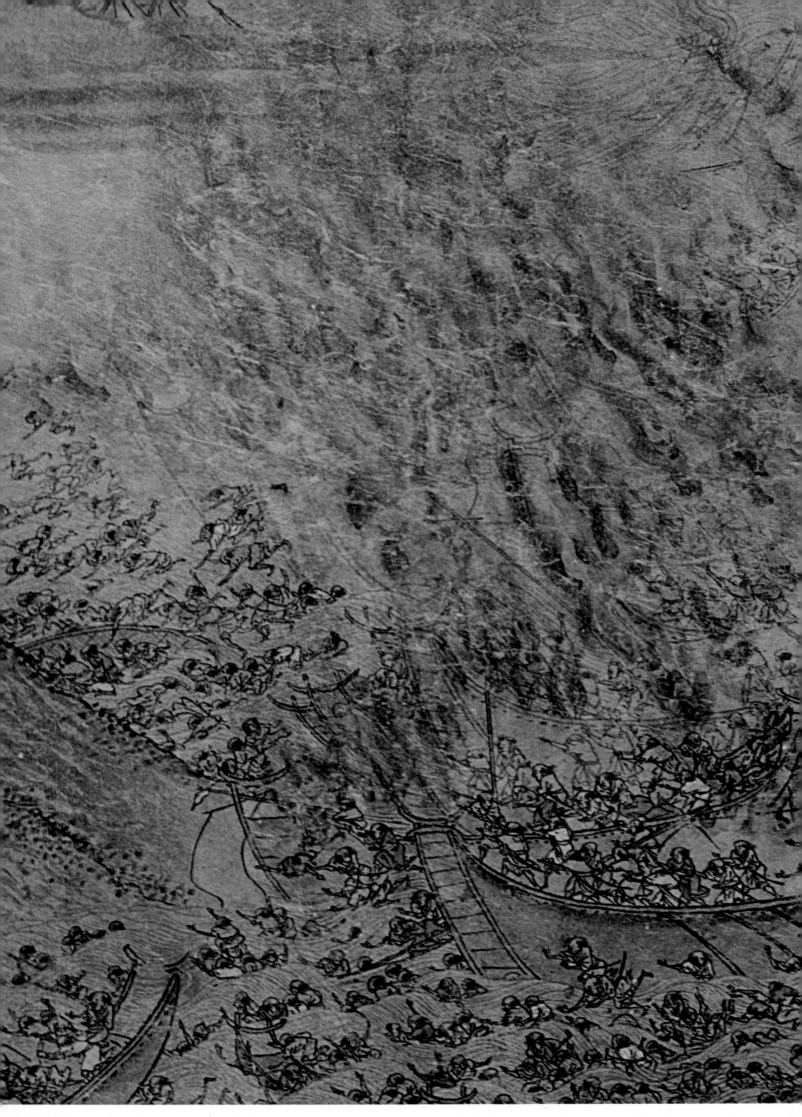

In a dramatic view of the holocaust, Japanese who are leaping off the burning vessels are pursued by Ming vessels intent

upon spearing the survivors. This final battle lasted only five weeks and ended with complete withdrawal of the Japanese.

The Ming Legacy

The greatest philosopher of Ming was Wang Shou-jên, better known as Wang Yang-ming, who developed the "idealism" of Sung thinker Lu Chiu-yüan into a powerful influence in East Asia that has lasted into the modern times. Starting from Lu's premise that the universal principle is in man's mind, Wang urged the removal of all selfish desires and prejudices to discover this innate knowledge. He taught that knowledge is the beginning of action, and action the completion of knowledge. This unity of knowledge and action results in the unity of spiritual and moral convictions with conduct and in the expression of inner strength through outer achievement. This to-know-is-to-do concept, together with reliance on one's mind for ultimate authority, stimulated the independent spirit of many late Ming scholar-activists.

Wang's philosophy spurred profoundly significant movements in late Ming literature. The individualist movement theorized that true creativity comes from the individual's mind and heart and should not be tainted by external influence or learning. In denouncing all forms of imitation and hypocrisy, it went to the extreme of confusing strangeness with inventiveness. By placing folk songs, novels and plays on the same level as Confucian classics, literati poetry and prose, it contributed enormously to the continuing growth of popular literature. The mainstream movement, on the other hand, emphasized Wang's concept that knowledge and action are inseparable. And since knowledge was synonymous with Confucian teaching, it concluded that only a man of superior character and great learning could produce meritorious work. The resulting demand that philosophy and scholarship be synthesized with literature placed a great burden on the creative talent.

In the field of art, Tung Ch'i-ch'ang became the thinkers' artist and the artists' thinker by considering theory as knowledge and practice as action. Ignoring the other famous painter-calligraphers of his time, Tung chose to compete with the thirteenth-century master Chao

Two decorative jade pieces display themes of good omen. Left, an ancient fisherman with a basket and children holding carp and, below, a buffalo with a cub of ch'i-lin, a creature symbolizing both benevolence and wisdom.

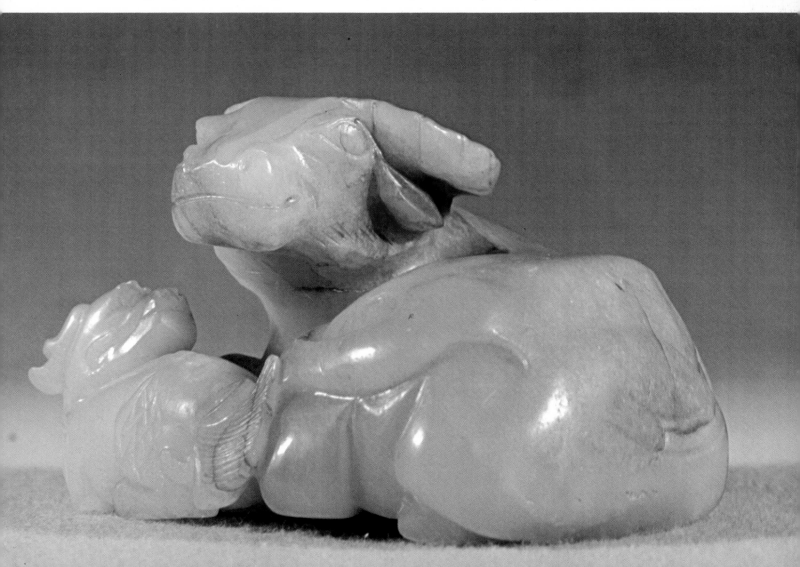

An episode from a Ming period historical novel, probably The Three Kingdoms, *based on a happening some thirteen hundred years earlier. Such literature inspired Ming craftsmen. In the colorful scene above a messenger reports to officials.*

Mêng-fu and openly claimed to be the most important man in three hundred years of Chinese art. He was the first to put forward the thesis that there had been a Northern and a Southern School in Chinese painting, the former. excelling in technical proficiency and the latter in intellectual inspiration. As an art historian, he was more inventive than scholarly, but as the leader of a movement which extended and unified the techniques of painting and calligraphy to express ideas, he left an indelible mark on later painters. From this point onward, literary and calligraphic elements gained at the expense of the pictorial. Claiming authority from the ancients he admired, Tung's Southern School was the form of the literati, but not the professional.

Another intellectual development in Ming was the inductive method in research. The pioneer was Ch'ên Ti, who succeeded in determining the ancient pronunciation of several hundred words by classifying and comparing rhymes in ancient poetry. Chinese scholars, however, applied such scientific thinking largely to their favorite fields of historical and textual criticism, phonetics and etymology rather than science and technology.

By this time a trickle of the new European learning also began to penetrate China's cultural citadel. A Jesuit priest, Matteo Ricci, traveled to Peking from Rome via Macao and became famous for his ability to learn the Chinese language and make friends among influential intellectuals and officials. One of them, Hsü Kuang-ch'i, became a Christian and co-translated with Ricci and other Jesuits useful books on mathematics and hydraulics. The Jesuit Mission in Peking by 1620 boasted a library of some seven thousand volumes of Western books. But the Ming court in its last hours was more appreciative of Western armaments. A deeper knowledge of the civilization that produced big cannons and gunboats was not to come until some two centuries later, under much more painful circumstances.

The Ming dynasty ended dramatically when the rebel leader Li Tzu-ch'êng rose to power on the tide of hungry masses; he took control of Peking and the last emperor hanged himself. But the social, political and military events that followed affirmed the durability of the Ming legacy in institutions and culture.

The Manchu Dynasty
A.D. 1644–1912

The Ch'ing dynasty rules China through Chinese institutions and Manchu military power ... Early emperors expand territory and maintain domestic peace, resulting in prosperity and population explosion ... Military spending and corruption deplete the national strength, making China susceptible to the Western thrust in the nineteenth century ... Pride and ignorance compound the calamities ... Seven decades of rebellion and invasion bring the empire to collapse, and the ancient civilization faces its first test of survival.

HISTORICAL CHRONOLOGY

A.D.

1644   *Ch'ing dynasty regent Dorgon enters Peking.*

1683   *Ch'ing naval forces occupy Taiwan.*

1685–89   *K'ang-hsi's campaigns against Russia result in favorable treaty.*

1696   *K'ang-hsi wins control over Outer Mongolia and Hami.*

1699   *East India Company establishes trading post.*

1720   *Ch'ing armies enter Lhasa, making Tibet part of the empire.*

1755–59   *Dzungars and Mohammedans defeated by Ch'ien-lung in Turkestan and Ili, conquered area becomes "New Dominion."*

1766–70   *War with Burma.*

1788–89   *Ch'ing makes Annam (Vietnam) a tributary.*

1795–1804   *White Lotus Society rebels ravage countryside.*

1839–42   *Opium War: British impose peace terms at Nanking.*

1844   *Similar treaties with the United States and France.*

1847   *The first Chinese student enters Yale.*

1850–73   *T'ai-p'ing Rebellion.*

1856–58   *British and French show of force results in Treaty of Tientsin. United States and Russia join.*

1860   *British-French enter Peking; take punitive action. Russia gains territory in Siberia from China.*

1862   *Ch'ing government begins to adopt Western technology.*

1879   *Loss of Ryukyu Islands, including Okinawa, to Japan.*

1884–85   *Sino-French War: France occupies Vietnam.*

1894–95   *Sino-Japanese War: ceding of Taiwan and the Pescadores to Japan and loss of suzerainty over Korea.*

1897   *Germany occupies Tsingtao.*

1898   *Kuang-hsü emperor begins Hundred Days of Reform. Empress dowager imprisons him.*

1900   *Anti-foreign Boxers sponsored by Manchu court. Foreign allies attack Peking.*

1901   *Ch'ing, with eleven powers, signs Boxer Protocol.*

1905   *Russo-Japanese War on Chinese territory.*

1911   *Republican Revolution ends the Ch'ing dynasty.*

ART CHRONOLOGY

A.D.

1644–1720   *Mainstream Landscapes represented by the Six Masters. Individualistic landscapes painted by Nanking Group and by monk-painters.*

c.1650   *Historical and philosophical studies written by Ming loyalists Huang Tsung-hsi (1610–95), Ku Yen-wu (1613–82), and Wang Fu-chih (1619–92).*

1679   *Strange Stories of Liao-chai, mostly supernatural tales, completed by P'u Sung-ling (1640–1715).*

1680–1722   *Great dictionaries, a compendium on painting and calligraphy, and other literary projects completed.*

17th–18th c.   *K'un-ch'ü and other local varieties of singing drama flourish, precursors of the Peking Opera. Porcelains attain perfection in monochrome, blue-and-white and enameled wares. Eighteenth-century export porcelains influence European craftsmen.*

1728   *Synthesis of Books and Illustrations of Ancient and Modern Times printed.*

c.1750   *The Dream of the Red Chamber, novel begun by Ts'ao Hsüeh-ch'in (c. 1715–63).*

c.1760   *Scientific method in studying history advocated by Chang Hsüeh-ch'êng (1738–1801).*

1773–82   *Imperial Manuscript Library compiled.*

1826   *Collected Essays on Statecraft edited by Wei Yüan (1794–1857). His Gazetteer of Maritime Nations completed in 1844.*

c.1830   *Scholarship in art, poetry, classics, antiquity and mathematics advanced by Juan Yüan (1764–1849).*

c.1880   *Western fiction translated by Lin Shu (1852–1924). Western liberalism introduced by Yen Fu (1853–1921).*

c.1890   *New poetry created by Huang Tsun-hsien (1848–1905).*

1891   *Study of forged classics by K'ang Yu-wei (1858–1927).*

1898   *Exhortation to Study, written by Chang Chih-tung (1837–1909).*

1906   *Adventures of Lao-ts'an, exposé novel, written by Liu Ê (1857–1909).*

241

Banners Over China

Manchu troops entered North China in 1644 at the request of Ming general Wu San-kuei, who asked for their help in defeating Chinese rebels led by Li Tzu-ch'êng. The Manchus smashed the rebel forces, forced them out of Peking and then refused to leave. General Wu surrendered and the Manchus gradually gained control over the rest of the Central Kingdom.

The Manchu takeover in 1644 marked the final step in a conquest which started about sixty years earlier when a Manchu tribal chief, Nurhachi, avenged the murder of his grandfather and father by killing off his closest rival. He then began to unify other Manchu tribes into a state, organizing the soldiers under a "banner system" consisting of four and later eight commands, each with a different-colored banner. In 1616, he proclaimed the Later Chin dynasty in memory of the glorious Jurchen empire, Chin (1122–34), with which the Manchus shared a common racial background. He openly rebelled against Ming and captured a portion of Liaotung. After Nurhachi's death, his son, known as Ch'ing T'ai-tsung, gained control over Inner Mongolia, the Amur River region and Korea. He raided North China five times, and by treating the Chinese well, attracted many Ming generals and officials to his side. As an administrator, he followed the Ming example by setting up six ministries or boards. In cultural matters, he ordered the translation of Chinese classics and histories, Ming laws and military books and even the previously mentioned novel "The Three Kingdoms" into the newly perfected Manchu writing based upon the Mongolian alphabet. He adopted the Ming system of examinations, which were given in Manchu, Mongol and Chinese languages.

In 1636 T'ai-tsung changed the name of his dynasty to Ch'ing, no doubt thinking ahead to the conquest of all China, but he died one year before his troops entered Peking. His brother Dorgon took over as regent for his six-year-old son. During the next twenty years, Dorgon and the young Shun-chih emperor concentrated on overcoming resistance from the various Ming

princes and the other scattered remnants of Ming forces. The most stubborn opposition came from a pirate's son named Chêng Ch'êng-kung, who controlled much of the Fukien coast. Chêng staged an unsuccessful attempt to recover Nanking, and then fell back to Amoy and Taiwan, where he expelled the Dutch and established his own island fortress in 1662. The same year the great K'ang-hsi ascended the

A walled city near mouth of the Yangtze had not changed for centuries before the Manchus came. Wang Hui painted timeless scenes along this longest river in East Asia from the sea to its source in a long scroll. This is one section.

Manchu throne.

He faced opposition from the Ming traitor, Wu San-kuei, who had entrenched himself in the southwest, and from two other defectors who held the far south and southeast. Sensing that the court would not tolerate their semi-independence, they decided to strike first. This "Revolt of the Three Feudatories" was put down in 1681 and two years later Ch'ing naval forces took Taiwan, making K'ang-hsi emperor of China in fact as well as in name. In the far north, K'ang-hsi fought off Russian encroachment on the Amur River and earned a favorable settlement, the first treaty between China and a Western power. Prosperous trade and cordial diplomatic relations followed. In Mongolia, K'ang-hsi personally led some eighty thousand troops across the Gobi Desert to rout

Domesticated water buffalo pulls harrow in one of the paintings on farm life commissioned by emperor.

The growing shoots now must be separated. Men and children help transplant the fast-growing stalks.

Galdan, khan of the Dzungar, a western Mongol tribe also known as Eleuth. With this victory he won control of Outer Mongolia and the northwestern border. In 1720, Manchu armies entered Lhasa, installed a new leader and placed Tibet under Ch'ing control. For the first time in the history of China, peace reigned on the northern frontiers. The enormous savings in military expenditure enabled the Man-

chu treasury to overflow even after reducing the taxes.

The success of Manchu rule over China owed much to K'ang-hsi's tolerant and conciliatory policy toward the natives. To win over recalcitrant Chinese scholars, he initiated a series of monumental projects to absorb their energy: the compilation of the Ming history; a dictionary containing more than fifty thousand

In flooded paddies, bounded by dikes, men carefully seed the rice. Note artist's attention to detail.

It is harvest time, and most of the large family is out in the fields reaping the bountiful rice crop.

Silkworm culture is traditionally handled by women but men (as shown here) help pick mulberry leaves.

The silkworms are fed on mulberry leaves. They are cultivated, graded and harvested as pictured here.

characters; a phrase dictionary; a compendium on painting and calligraphy; the complete works of the Sung Neo-Confucian Chu Hsi and other literary works. The imperial studio for painters, mechanics and architects employed not only the Chinese but also European missionaries with artistic and mechanical skills. K'ang-hsi's intellectual curiosity led to his involvement in a controversy over the Chinese

A child fans the fire as cocoons boil in caldron. The cocoon must be cooked before thread can be drawn.

and Western calendars. He decided in favor of the West and had Jesuits tutor young Chinese and Manchus in Western sciences. The missionaries were also responsible for the production of a general map of the empire in 1718. It was owing to Rome's insistence upon controlling its Chinese converts that the emperor decided to restrict Christian evangelism in China.

Silk weaving on a wooden loom. China has been the leading exporter of silk for more than two thousand years.

Immense wealth which he amassed from the regional salt monopoly made An Ch'i, shown above, a leading collector and art patron of the early Ch'ing period. His portrait is by the artist Chiao Ping-chên, with a background painted by Wang Hui.

Salt merchants were consistently wealthy, as shown in this well-documented painting of the Ma brothers (the fifth and ninth figures from left). It was painted by Yeh Fang-Lin and Fang Shih-Shu some fifty years after the painting of An Ch'i shown above.

The Uninterrupted Flow

With the Manchu emperors enthusiastically absorbing Chinese learning, the cultural life in Early Ch'ing differed little from that of Late Ming. The mainstream painters pushed toward new horizons from bases established by old masters, while individualists followed their own visions in various new directions. The combination made the seventeenth to mid-eighteenth century the last great period of Chinese painting in the traditional style. The literati movement championed by Tung Ch'ich'ang continued through his friends Wang Shih-min, whose generosity and achievements inspired many younger men, and Wang Chien, a brilliant interpreter of Sung and Yüan styles. Their protégé Wang Hui synthesized the essence of both Northern and Southern schools. Wang Yüan-ch'i, a grandson of Wang Shih-min, held high offices, but apparently devoted all his leisure time to painting. He developed into an artist whose brushstrokes were as intricate as his forms. These giants of the orthodox school are known as the Four Wangs; together with Wu Li and Yün Shou-p'ing, they comprise the Six Masters of Ch'ing.

Among personalities, two descendants of the Ming royal house were as defiant toward entrenched traditions in art as they were toward the alien rule. Chu Ta had a natural sense of composition enabling him to place his powerful and simple strokes in ingenious spatial relationships. Tao-chi responded to the limitless lessons of nature with brush and ink, creating his own free style. Both artists entered monkhood to avoid involvement with the new order, following the tradition of Chinese intellectual recluses under the Mongols. Even the officially praised Wang Hui and Wang Yüanch'i did not cater to the imperial taste, which remained superficial and leaned toward the decorative. Private art patrons, such as the salt merchants of Yangchow, helped to encourage eccentric artists centered in the city. As the strength of the empire declined toward 1800, art declined as well.

"Drunk in Autumn Woods," painted by Tao-chi, recalls happy days with friends. He wrote the poems at top.

During the sixty-year reign of Emperor Ch'ien-lung, China became the world's richest and most populous nation. Ch'ien-lung abdicated in 1796 but dominated the government until his death at eighty-eight in the year 1799.

The Dynastic Apogee

K'ang-hsi's exemplary reign was marred by his tolerance toward unscrupulous subordinates and his indecisiveness in naming another heir when his first choice became mentally ill. The fourth son, who became Yung-chêng emperor, was suspected of having changed his father's will or even shortening his life in order to gain the throne. His obsession with his right of succession revealed an inner insecurity which he expressed through cruelty toward his brothers as well as by extensive tampering with the archives to assure his "rightful" place in history. He confiscated the manuscripts of the *Synthesis of Books and Illustrations of Ancient and Modern Times* to deny credit to a brother who opposed his succession to the throne. This five-thousand-volume project was printed with brass movable types in 1728 without any mention of the original editor. Yung-chêng also jealously guarded imperial power by taking control of banner forces from the princes and by educating the younger princes in a special palace school. He kept his selection of an heir in a sealed box, to be opened only after his death.

As emperor, Yung-chêng proved highly competent and hard-working. He corrected his father's permissiveness toward corrupt aides by close surveillance over officials, enforcing the laws of the empire strictly and reforming national finances. The civil servants received an adequate income to "cultivate incorruptibility." And to avoid delays and leaking of secrets in times of war, he created the Grand Council, a small group of able, trusted men who streamlined the process of decision-making at the highest level. This innovation was so responsive to imperial wishes that it was retained during times of peace. Yung-chêng also wanted to remake prevailing religions. He transformed the palace where he lived as a prince into a Lama temple, assembled a group to study Ch'an (Zen) Buddhism, and may have believed in the longevity theories of the Taoists. His death at fifty-seven gave rise to a host of rumors concerning its cause, including murder for revenge or lethal Taoist pills. Yet his firm rule had rejuvenated the government and prepared the way for the reign of his son Ch'ien-lung.

Ch'ien-lung was an outstanding emperor, who had the good fortune to rule a nation at peace during the height of its dynastic power. The empire left to him was in excellent shape: a centralized power structure without contenders, well-disciplined officials and a treasury with a sizable surplus. Admiring his grandfather K'ang-hsi for his benevolent rule of sixty years, Ch'ien-lung aspired to at least equal his record. He followed a strict regimen in per-

For recording court events, the Italian Jesuit Castiglione became Ch'ien-lung emperor's favorite artist. Detail shows the monarch attending an archery contest. Note the Manchu queue was imposed on all Chinese.

The attacking Manchu troops with superior cavalry and war camels have overwhelmed the Dzungars who are in full re-

sonal life: rising at six in the morning; breakfast at eight; reading of reports and acting upon them in consultation with ministers; giving instructions to new officials. A second meal was at two in the afternoon; the afternoons he spent reading, painting, or writing verse, with light refreshments served in the evening.

Ch'ien-lung exercised power with reason, a keen sense of responsibility, and seemingly, a constant awareness of history. He promoted the military spirit among his people and never hesitated to assert the dignity of the empire with force. The unquiet western border area dominated by the Dzungars seemed ready for pacification when their general, Amursara, surrendered to the Manchu expeditionary force.

treat. This dramatic battle scene was engraved after an original by Catholic priests in the service of the emperor.

But this first success was short-lived, for Amursara rebelled as soon as the conquering armies were withdrawn. When Manchu troops were sent to reoccupy the Ili area, Amursara fled; then slipped back to direct renewed resistance and almost annihilated the emperor's army. Manchu general Chao-hui managed to escape and returned with a strong force in 1757. He completely routed the rebels, slaughtering them ruthlessly. The next year Chao-hui succeeded in suppressing a Mohammedan rebellion south of Ili and transformed the whole Chinese Turkestan region into Sinkiang or the "New Dominion." When Chao-hui led the victorious army home with captives, the emperor greeted the returning hero outside Peking.

Hollow Victories

As he grew older, Ch'ien-lung looked back on his reign with self-satisfaction, taking particular pride in his "Ten Victories." Three of them, the 1755 and 1756–57 campaigns against the Dzungars and the 1758–59 pacification of the Mohammedans, were historically significant. The other seven victories, however, were much less noteworthy. The war to suppress the rebels of Taiwan could be considered a successful police action, but the expeditions to subjugate the Chin-ch'uan aborigines in the Upper Yangtze, the Burmese, the Vietnamese and the Gurkhas in Nepal were neither wholly justified nor completely effective. The Dzungar and Mohamme-

dan campaigns cost twenty-three million taels (Chinese units of silver) and the Chin-ch'uan wars three times as much. Furthermore, military operations far away from the court gave Manchu generals ample opportunity to enrich themselves from the huge sums of money passing through their hands.

Ch'ien-lung could afford such extravagance only because of unparalleled prosperity. The unofficial population estimate in 1741 was 142,000,000, which might have been somewhat low. The amount of arable land was increased considerably and new crops introduced from the Americas in Late Ming dynasty—corn, sweet potatoes and peanuts capable of growing on marginal or sandy soil, as well as fast-ripening types of rice from Champa—were planted on a large scale. Both improvements broadened the economic base for a population explosion which was beneficial to national revenue. No wonder Ch'ien-lung indulged in luxuries. He grew more and more fond of using the old summer palace called Yüan-ming Yüan as his residence, and made it into a unique pleasure resort. Buildings and gardens were constructed in

Many Mohammedan captives kneel at the entrance to the Purple Light Hall awaiting the arrival of the emperor who attended a victory feast there on April 18, 1760. The versatile artist-priest Castiglione signed his Chinese name, Lang Shih-ning.

The emperor's impressive arrival on his sedan chair is shown in another section of the same scroll. Castiglione was born in Milan in 1688, went to Peking in 1715, served two emperors and enjoyed imperial patronage until his death in 1766.

the Italian style with several Jesuit missionaries, including Castiglione, as architects and designers. He encouraged decorative arts such as porcelain and cloisonné, and employed European mechanics to maintain clocks and other machines sent from Europe as gifts. Since South China had been the citadel of native resistance, Ch'ien-lung's six tours in the Yangtze valley from 1751 to 1784 could be considered the mixing of business and pleasure but the estimated travel expense of two hundred million taels indicates the scale of his extravagance.

Ch'ien-lung took great pride in his Chinese education. One year after enthronement, he published notes on his studies, followed next year by a collection of prose and verse. His lifelong literary output, although indifferent in quality, was astonishing in quantity; verse alone amounted to more than 42,000 poems, certainly not composed without help. His poems, calligraphy and seals graced (or marred) hundreds of masterpieces in his extensive collection of paintings and calligraphy. Among the many projects he sponsored, none surpassed the compiling of the Imperial Manuscript Library, which resulted in some 3,450 complete works in more than 36,000 volumes.

As many as 15,000 scribes spent nearly twenty years hand-copying seven sets. The printed catalogue went beyond books selected for copying, commenting on a total of 10,230 titles, more than any other Chinese bibliography.

This project, however, was basically political rather than scholarly, since its purpose was to expunge all unfavorable references to the Manchus and other alien rulers. Thousands of works were destroyed or abridged. Known titles of such censored books amount to more than 2,300. Ever since the Manchus had entered the Great Wall, they had tried to control the thoughts of Chinese subjects, especially any outright or implied sympathy for the previous dynasty. They forbade discourses on border defenses or differences between the Chinese and the "barbarians." During Ch'ien-lung's reign, cases of literary inquisition increased several times over those of all previous reigns combined. Family members, proofreaders, editors and printers paid with their lives for as little as one or two lines of poetry which could be interpreted as treasonous. The nephew of a high Manchu official was ordered to commit suicide because he referred to the Mongols as "Hu," or foreign nomads, in writing a Chinese poem.

The Manchus waged successful warfare on both land and sea. Here a Manchu fleet of the Emperor Ch'ien-lung lands

Such terrorism frightened many scholars away from political and economic subjects, costing the services of many of China's most gifted men.

Ch'ien-lung's last period was marked by the meteoric rise of his protégé, Ho-shên. When this handsome and clever Manchu guard caught the eye of the sixty-five-year-old emperor, he was promoted to high office within a year, becoming a Grand Councilor and Minister of the Imperial Household. As the emperor's confidence in him continued to mount, he acquired additional privileges and control over revenue, personnel and capital security. Holding the power to advance or ruin officials at will, he set up a network of intimates and collaborators all over the empire to exact gifts

富良江之
戰

門戶黎城日

富良彼雛

回疆氛名

皇靈舟獨入

真稱壯既

男知方深

首藏復國一

their cavalry in an attack on the Vietnamese. At the top of the picture is a poem by the emperor commemorating the victory.

from hapless victims. The last two decades of Ch'ien-lung, including three years as the "Super Emperor" after he abdicated the throne to his son in 1796, may be called the "Era of Ho-shên," who held as many as twenty important offices at one time. His sordid campaign against a rebellion of impoverished people in Central and Western China led by the White Lotus So-ciety, a secret religious sect, began in 1795 and lasted beyond the death of Ch'ien-lung in 1799. Vast sums of money intended for military expenditure found their way into Ho-shên's personal fund and thousands of innocent people were slaughtered to confirm his reports. This was one "victory" that not even Ch'ien-lung could afford.

A fisherman with his net, his wife at the oar and his cat on the roof, is carried along in delicately crafted jade boat.

Ladies are shown weighing a piece of jade in this seventeenth-century soapstone carving. Costumes are Ming.

The Point of No Return

The empire that Ch'ien-lung left when he died was far different from the one he had inherited. Devastation caused by rebellions and suppression, depletion of the treasury, corrupt officialdom and a burdensome population of three hundred million marked the year 1799 as the turning point for traditional China. The new emperor Chia-ch'ing's first acts were laudatory: Five days after his father's death, he put Ho-shên in jail and ordered him to take his own life. The confiscation of Ho-shên's property yielded a fantastic hoard of gold, silver, jade, pearls, bronze, silk and furs, in addition to five houses with 2,790 rooms, two large gardens and many pawnshops—the total value estimated at 900 million taels, too vast a sum to imagine. Though a dramatic act, the elimination of Ho-shên cut out only the most obvious tumor from a very sick body. The White Lotus Rebellion was halted in 1804, but another secret religious cult called *T'ien-li chiao,* or "Heavenly Reason Society," suspected of being linked to the White Lotus, plotted to capture Peking and key provinces in North China. Two hundred rebels stormed the Forbidden City in a suicidal attempt that was quickly quashed, but hard-fighting massive armed bands in the provinces took the government troops another year to suppress. In the south, pirates harassed Chekiang coasts and attacked Taiwan with more than a hundred ships and ten thousand men. As if there were not

Servants attend their mistress, who drinks from a decorated cup. The architecture is of the Ming style.

enough man-made misery, the Yellow River overflowed at least seventeen times during Chia-ch'ing's twenty-four-year reign. A substantial part of the relief cost, as in any other governmental expenditure, fell into the hands of the officials in charge.

Chia-ch'ing was a conscientious, diligent monarch, but unequal to the task of arresting the steady decline of the empire. He tried hard to balance income and outgo by stringent personal economies, such as cutting court expenses, eliminating his fiftieth birthday celebration, and reducing allotments to relatives and members of the imperial household. After his death, his son Tao-kuang continued this policy of frugality. It was reported that he wore old and patched garments, and gave up the luxury of summering at Jehol.

As soon as a fresh uprising of Muslims in Turkestan was put down, he turned his attention to internal affairs: the seemingly insoluble problems of the Yellow River; the inadequacy of the Grand Canal for transporting northbound grains; and the inefficiency of the ad-

ministration of the salt industry, from which Peking derived one-eighth to one-quarter of its total revenue. His attack on the first two of these problems was ineffectual. Instructions to river conservation officials to increase effectiveness and eliminate waste met with only superficial compliance and a plan to reopen sea routes was discontinued when it threatened hundreds of thousands of Grand Canal workers with unemployment. In the case of the salt monopoly, he succeeded in reforming its administration and increasing revenue.

In normal times, Tao-kuang would have been an adequate emperor, but in the second decade of his reign China was heading heedlessly toward a collision with the West. Even before the confrontation—one which threatened the whole Chinese civilization, not just a single reign or dynasty, as in the past—the entire empire was collapsing from her own cultural senility, economic breakdown and military impotency. The heavy costs of dealing with internal rebellions thoroughly exposed the deterioration of the Manchu war machine,

The dragon-boat contest which is held on the Fifth Month Festival was originally created to honor the patriot poet, Ch'ü Yüan, who, in 277 B.C., drowned himself in a river. This once-solemn occasion became a happy and spectacular sporting event.

Cloissonné, a technique introduced into China during the Ming dynasty, continued to be favored in the decorative arts. This plaque is designed in the T'ang style, using blue and green with the added richness of brilliant enamels and metal wires.

whose bannermen were preoccupied with balancing their accounts under rising prices, insufficient stipends and expanding families, and whose officers were becoming adept in siphoning off military funds and falsifying reports. The Ming and other local forces that surrendered during the first years of Ch'ing were organized into an "Army of the Green Standard" for internal security, but in time they, too, became ineffective.

The economy of China in the early nineteenth century was severely strained by the need to produce enough for 350 to 400 million people, resulting in a lowering of per capita productivity and the standard of living. Perhaps the most fundamental problem was a delusion of cultural superiority, which might have been justified during the two thousand years before the fifteenth century, when China dominated East Asia, but which became increasingly self-defeating. The totality of Confucian institutions, enthusiastically promoted by autocratic emperors, produced a closed-circuit civilization, which constantly searched the past for the future. Its response to challenges was to harden time-honored attitudes rather than adapt to new ideas and situations. Such Western concepts as the search for profit in foreign trade, risk-taking with accumulated capital, credit utilization and legal protection for inventions were beyond the comprehension of Confucian scholar-officials who considered the profit motive evil, commerce undignified and industry a minor complement to agriculture. The application of such sixth-century B.C. concepts to a crumbling nineteenth-century empire would have resulted in economic disaster even without Western intervention. The single-ruler system proved overtaxing even in the best of times, to such outstanding emperors as Hung-wu and Yung-lo of Ming, K'ang-hsi, Yung-chêng, and Ch'ien-lung of Ch'ing, yet the great scholars were blind to any other alternative for the political structure. When the West burst upon the scene in the mid-nineteenth century, it was not merely a new alien invader, and the result was not just another change of dynasty. A new civilization had come to crush the old, and nothing in the Chinese experience was equal to it.

A Taoist sage and his young pupil gathering sacred mushrooms, the food of immortality, in the center of this carved mountain of lapis. It was inspired by an earlier Ming painting. The reverse side bears an inscription by Ch'ien-lung emperor.

The Future in the Past

Long before the mid-nineteenth century upheaval, leading intellectuals were probing the past for a better future. They included independent thinkers such as Huang Tsung-hsi (1610–95), whose systematic studies of Sung, Yüan and Ming philosophers and political critiques were part of his passionate quest for the causes of Ming failure and remedies for imperial despotism. The travels and research of Ku Yen-wu produced a wide-ranging interest in farming, trade, banking, industry and mining, and convinced him of the futility of Neo-Confucian metaphysical speculations. Ku believed that every statement must be reinforced by evidence and pioneered the school of "Han Learning," which advocated the return to Han texts. This emphasis on evidence led to Yen Jo-chü's discovery that the Book of History in the so-called "ancient text" was actually a forgery.

Two other important scholars were Tai Chên and Chang Hsüeh-ch'êng. Tai proposed that the natural principle does not exist subjectively in the mind but objectively in various physical manifestations to be found through careful observation and analysis, verified by the findings of others. He applied his theory to the studies of philology, phonology, historical geography and mathematical history. Chang, dissatisfied with Han Learning's preoccupation with textual evidence, searched for historical meanings relevant to current events. Significantly, these great scientific spirits concentrated on the humanities, and Ku Yen-wu's example of studying agriculture, commerce and industry for practical use was not followed until after the shocking impact of Western military power.

Popular literature offered other insights into the mental and cultural state of the times. The greatest traditional Chinese novel ever written is probably *Hung-lou-mêng* ("The Dream of the Red Chamber"). Created by Ts'ao Hsüeh-ch'in, who died before finishing it, the last third was completed by Kao Ê around 1791. It is the saga of a powerful and wealthy family whose sudden downfall is interwoven with the story of unfulfilled love between two cousins. Though romantic in theme, the "Dream" is a realistic novel set in a symbolic frame. The hero, Pao-yü, was the reincarnation of a primeval rock left unused by the sky-mending goddess Nü-wo. Carried into the Heavenly Palace by a Buddhist monk and a Taoist priest, it became an attendant there before descending into the world through birth into a great family. A plant that the attendant had watered in the Heavenly Palace also achieved human incarnation as his cousin, Tai-yü. The two fell madly in love, but it was her fate to return his kindness with tears. Near the end of the tale, when Tai-yü lay dying, Pao-yü was tricked into marrying another cousin. He became mentally ill after discovering the ruse. The family suddenly incurred imperial wrath through corruption and suffered the confiscation of its properties, followed by a rapid decline of fortune and the scattering of its members. Pao-yü recovered from his illness, but disappeared after taking the examinations, which he passed with high honors. Later, on a voyage, his father caught a brief glimpse of him in monk's garb before he was taken away by a Buddhist monk and a Taoist priest, never to return.

Noted for its true-to-life characterizations and descriptions of daily activities, the novel's Buddhist-Taoist view of the world reaches deep into the Chinese mind. It owes part of its realism to the fact that the author's grandfather met a reversal in fortune similar to that of the family in the novel. In retrospect, the "Dream" is symbolic and prophetic: The glorious family could have been the Manchu dynasty or even Chinese civilization, with its members immersed in the pleasures of literature and art and its social structure built on Confucian principles. When the storm came, the intellectual consciousness did not readily awaken from the dream of finding the ideal future in the past.

Two favorite Bodhisattvas identified by their attributes, elephant and lion, meet on a jade mountain, which is carved in high relief. Buddhism and Taoism dominated the Chinese imagination, while Confucianism governed Chinese conduct.

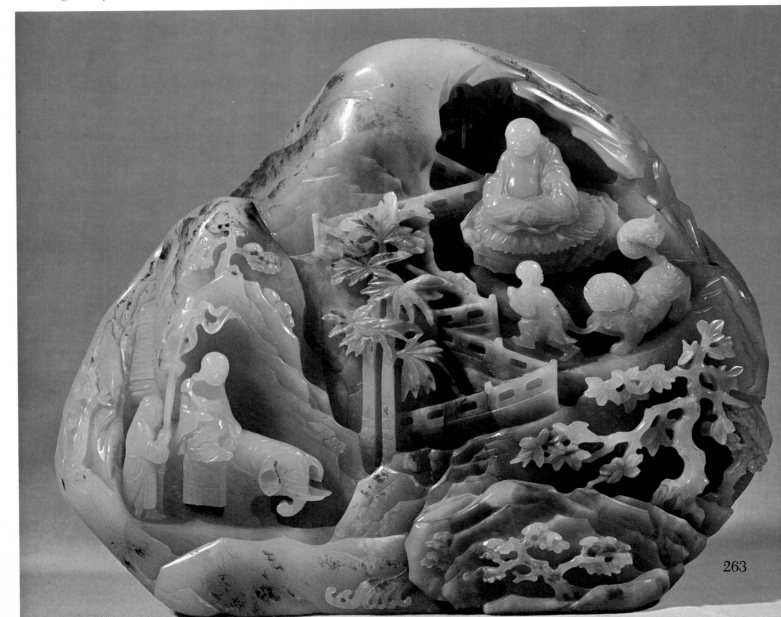

Chinese children play alongside a traditional house with lake in background in this porcelain plate made for export. The native artist has painted the scene in what he considered Western technique, resulting in a curious stylistic mixture.

The Coming of the West

In 1494, the Ming emperor in Peking could never have dreamed that the entire globe was being divided between Portugal and Spain for sea trade and colonization, with Portugal claiming Brazil and all non-Christian areas to the east, up to the edge of the Spanish sphere at the Philippines. Four years later Vasco da

Gama succeeded in sailing around Africa to India and opening direct commerce with South and East Asia. The Portuguese dominated, if not monopolized, the spice trade between Asia and Europe as well as trade within the Asian seas in the sixteenth century. The end of their era saw fierce trade competition between the Dutch and the British. The Dutch won monopoly of the Indonesian archipelago and its spice trade, but their outposts established on Taiwan were taken by a Ming loyalist general in 1661. As this was happening, the British consolidated India into their main base, with the crown granting the monopoly of trade throughout the Indian and Pacific oceans to the East India Company, which by the end of the seventeenth century entrenched itself firmly in Madras,

A Chinese interpretation of the baptism of Jesus (an unusual subject) is revealed in this export porcelain. The native artist's lack of knowledge of the subject matter and the anatomy of the figures gives the work a primitive appearance.

Bombay and Calcutta. After 1763, the East India Company began direct rule over Bengal, whose opium, together with Bombay's raw cotton, found an increasing demand in China. Another important connection came when, in the mid-eighteenth century, the British Empire adopted tea as a national beverage. Tea soon produced most of the Company's profits and an important tax revenue for the Crown. Thus commerce, which the Confucian scholars considered the lowest of occupations, moved England, India and China toward a rendezvous with destiny at Canton.

Canton derived its importance from being the center of Chinese overseas trade, carried southeast to Manila, the Moluccas and Java, and southwest to Siam and beyond by numerous seagoing junks. The officially appointed merchant firms called "hongs" had long experiences in handling such commerce. With the advent of European trade, a group of hongs banded together into a cohong and was given a monopoly over it. They retained tight control through large sums paid to local officials and powerful men near the emperor. All Western trade, dominated by the British toward the end of the eighteenth century, was restricted to this port. Pressure gradually built to break this monopoly. The British private traders grew in number and importance as the Industrial Revolution increased production at home and invigorated commerce abroad. This prompted the unsuccessful Macartney mission to the court of Ch'ien-lung in 1793 to request permission for trade in other places, island depots for storage and refitting ships and a fixed and printed tariff. Behind the failure of this mission were several irreconcilable issues: the Chinese treatment of foreign nations as tributaries versus the British expectation of equal diplomatic relations; Chinese reluctance to grant privileges to troublesome foreigners within their own borders versus the British drive to expand international trade for its national livelihood and the British refusal to submit their citizens to the local legal system, which countenanced arbitrary arrest and punishment.

When the East India Company's monopoly of China trade was abolished in 1834, the British government sent Lord Napier as official superintendent of trade to negotiate. Chinese officials refused to recognize the British as equals and Lord Napier countered with force. His frigates did not overcome the Chinese blockade, and a compromise pressured by hong merchants and British free traders prevented the incident from escalating further. But by now the Canton control system no longer worked, for neither side had effective representation in dealing with trade problems, and it became a paradise for smugglers. A high percentage of the smuggled goods was opium.

▷ *The rich and famous Woo Pingkien who was also known as Howqua, was a well-known Cohong merchant of eighteenth–nineteenth-century China. This is a Chinese copy of a Western painting by George Chinnery.*
▽ *The Dutch ship* Vryburg *is shown arriving in China in 1756. A meticulous copy of a Western drawing of the vessel decorates this excellent example of the type of china then popular in Europe.*

A *full-rigged Yankee clipper in the China trade,
painted by a Chinese artist in Western medium and style.*

Foreign factories were set afire by Chinese
during 1856 war. In retaliation, the British burned houses.

The Opium War and T'ai-P'ing Rebellion

The amount of opium imported into China
soared from an annual average of five thousand
chests of 133 pounds each during 1800–20 to
twenty-two thousand chests in 1834 and forty
thousand in 1838. This was a bonanza for the
British traders, since it not only paid for tea
and silk but also earned increasing amounts of
silver. In the 1830's China began to suffer a silver shortage and inflation. This economic pressure and the moral stigma compelled Tao-
kuang emperor to strictly prohibit the use and
import of opium. In 1838 he sent Lin Tsê-hsü,
a courageous scholar-official, to enforce his
edict in Canton. Lin burned the stock of
twenty thousand chests brought in by British
traders and drove them out of the city to Hong
Kong after they refused to deliver an English
sailor accused of killing a Chinese villager.
Hostilities began in November 1839. The superior British fleet with up-to-date weaponry
found the Manchu empire a paper dragon; the
invaders easily blockaded the Chinese coast
and sailed to the port near Peking. Lin was
cashiered by the emperor, whose indecision
and ignorance produced only ineffectual resistance to the reinforced British striking force. In
August 1842, the Manchu court, worried over
its hold on the Chinese populace after this ex-
posure of weakness, signed the first of a series of
unequal treaties with foreign powers.

The Treaty of Nanking included the ceding
of Hong Kong, the opening of five ports to

268

A British side-wheeler arrived in Canton in 1840. It is seen in the riverbank area against the foreign enclaves, flying their own flags. Before the Opium War, the Western merchants were confined to this area outside the city walls.

British residences and trade, the abolishing of the cohong monopoly in Canton, the promise of a fair and regular tariff and a huge indemnity. Such humiliation inspired the people to express their resentment forcefully. In 1850,

Hung Hsiu-ch'üan, the founder of a strange cult mixing Christianity with Confucianism, began a rebellion which lasted until 1864. He eventually occupied Nanking, making it his capital, penetrated sixteen of the eighteen

provinces, captured some six hundred cities and pressed northward to threaten Peking. Hung's *T'ai-p'ing T'ien-kuo*, or the "Celestial Kingdom of Peace," almost overturned the Manchu dynasty.

In a painting that resembles a garden scene with toy soldiers the rebels of T'ai-p'ing are under siege and being rapidly annihilated by the concentrated firepower of the Manchus. This detailed painting was commissioned by the Ch'ing court.

271

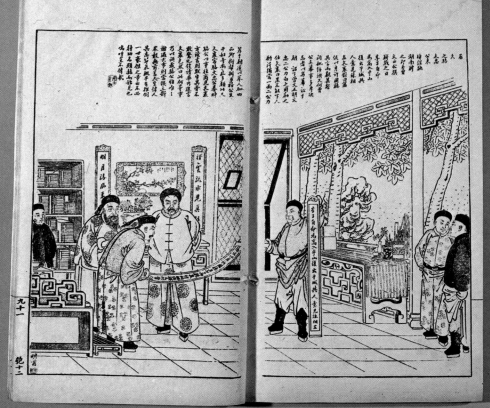

The campaign against the Moslem rebels from 1876 to 1878 recovered Chinese Turkestan and maintained it as a province. The army was led by Tso Tsung-t'ang, general and administrator, portrayed here.

The beared figure at left, Tsêng Kuo-fan, rescued the Manchu court from the T'ai-p'ing Rebellion. Shanghai artist portrayed him relaxing with Li Hung-chang (leaning forward to read) and Tso (next to Li).

Opium addicts in a commercial smoking house. The reclining figure is puffing away on a long pipe, the others rest between smokes. Toward the late nineteenth century, there were from two to ten million addicts.

First railway in China, the Shanghai-Wusung Line, opened in 1876. It was short and short-lived. Not until 1888 did railroad building become an accepted idea; by 1900 major lines were under construction.

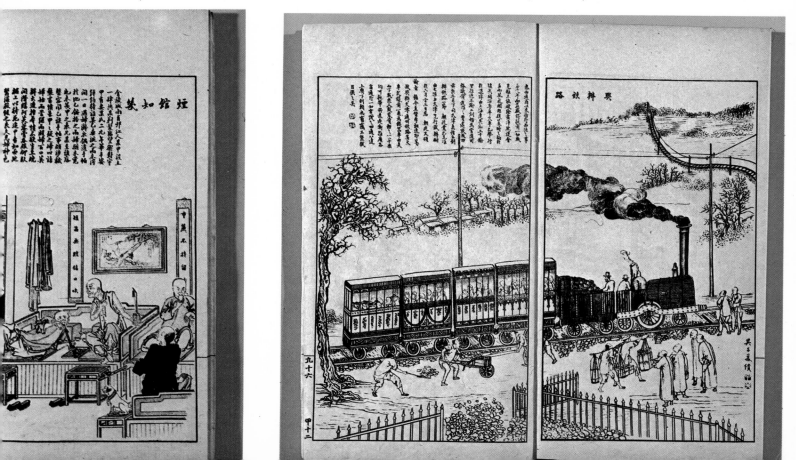

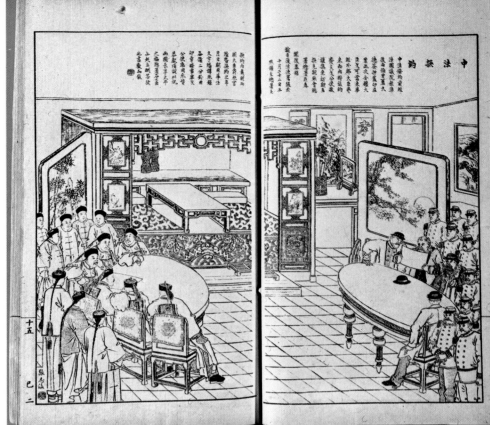

The most important figure in Chinese foreign relations for the last three decades of the nineteenth century was Li Hung-chang. His policy was peace at all cost and progress—with Western industry and arms.

Li and French envoys signed a treaty in 1885, recognizing Vietnam as a French colony, no longer a tributary to China. Shanghai pictorial journal sketched the scene of exchange of treaties in Peking.

To Strengthen Oneself

Hung's *T'ai-p'ing T'ien-kuo*, or the "Celestial Kingdom of Peace," failed to overturn the Manchu dynasty because of Hung's ignorance about administration, his purge of top lieutenants, the deterioration of his movement from austerity to corruption and his unique religion, which was unacceptable to the tradition-bound society. The Hsien-fêng emperor, who reigned from 1850, realized that the Manchu bannermen and the Chinese Green Standard troops were no longer effective and decided to entrust the task of suppressing Hung to Tsêng Kuo-fan, a Hanlin scholar who had organized a strong militia army to defend his home province of Hunan. Tsêng had moral fortitude and the ability to inspire loyalty and courage in his men. When he was given supreme authority over the middle and lower Yangtze valley; his aides included unusually able governors such as Hu Lin-i, Tso Tsung-t'ang and Li Hung-chang. Tsêng instructed Li to build up the Anhwei Army and model it after his Hunan militia. Financed by revenues from the rich Yangtze delta and the Shanghai trade, Li purchased foreign arms and trained his soldiers into the most modern force in China.

Concurrently, there was considerable military and diplomatic activity between the Manchu court and the West. The British and French used force to win new privileges in the Treaties of Tientsin. But when their ministers came to the northern port of Taku in 1859 to exchange the ratified treaties, the Chinese opened fire and the foreign gunboats had to withdraw. The next year the French and British sent a retaliatory force which chased the emperor out of Peking and destroyed his summer palace Yüan-ming Yüan. The resulting settlement opened the whole empire to Western trade and evangelism. In the meantime, the Russians gained large Siberian territories through the Sino-Russian Treaty of Peking.

By now the Western powers had a vested interest in the submissive Manchu regime. Thus when the T'ai-p'ing forces under Hung Hsiuch'üan threatened Shanghai in 1862, they were met by both foreign and imperial defenders. Two small mercenary forces, one led in turn by an American and a British and the other led by a French, scored impressive victories along the coast. To powerful Chinese officials like Tsêng and Li, whose slogan was "strengthen yourself," China's strength could only be restored with the aid of Western technology and especially with guns and steamships.

形上同海盗 英商怡和行之高陞轮船為李得相在威海二十餘里處名咜當中日未经闢戰之光緒朝萬國公法平無不雅之理方慎人坪迨今船上懼将官下政碩有慎有船兵間艦數視如兵坪内共出兵殺之氣瀰漫如不浮已降倭已降倭已浮后降倭我船泥大沽口逃可见後事詳倭詳中国間伏多致斗前退顾折拆回大洁口逃諸砲一齐闢立時四面放沉入海巴華人坪六主水面浮洗候本備挂英国折旗舉之二尔圆水下战書備刮収紫生集死不如此倭条惨被人一坪不测之禍不知此倭条高不主残恶罙之英律师謂於海之無珠吾浅可逃

A British steamer carrying Chinese troops to Korea was sunk by the Japanese.
More than one thousand soldiers were drowned. This incident led directly to the outbreak of the first Sino-Japanese war.

The Ultimate Humiliation

Beginning in 1862, the last half century of Manchu rule was dominated by the Empress Dowager Tz'u-hsi, who directly and indirectly controlled both her son, T'ung-chih emperor, and her nephew, Kuang-hsü emperor. Internal unrest continued with the Nien rebels, adherents of a secret society, in North China and the Moslems in the southwest and the northwest. After more than fifteen years of persistent effort, domestic order was restored, but millions were killed and vast areas laid waste. Foreign encroachments increased in tempo and severity, for imperialistic powers found the prostrate regime fair game, and their rivalry hastened the race for choice concessions.

In the crucial last thirty years of the nine-teenth century, Li Hung-chang emerged as the architect and executor of China's foreign policy and a leading force for industrialization. His enterprises, based upon government-supervised merchant operations, ranged from a steamship line to textile mills—all unfortunately used for profiteering rather than transforming the agrarian economy. His intrigue of setting one power against another only succeeded in postponing calamities.

Political and economic oppression was accompanied by Western cultural penetration. The Christian Church, which competed with the local gentry in influencing the public and enjoying the protection of extraterritoriality, aroused mounting resentment and sporadic violence. On the positive side, the missionary work in education and medicine had profound influence on Chinese intellectuals striving for modernization. The same, unfortunately, could not be said for Chinese officials. Although they realized the superiority of Western arms and industry, they did not understand the civilization which produced such technology and were unwilling to make the necessary fundamental changes in institutions. The initial attempts to know the West, such as the opening of an official bureau for the study of foreign languages in 1862, the sending of 120 students to America in 1872, and the establishment of diplomatic missions abroad in 1879, were reluctant and half-hearted.

In dramatic contrast was the speed and thoroughness of Japan's modernization after Commodore Perry's visit in 1853. In 1868 the island nation made the pursuit of knowledge of the world a national policy. Its wholesale adaptation of Western technology and institutions had made such headway by the 1870's that it entered the competition with Western powers to dismember China. Japan took the Ryukyu Islands, which included Okinawa, and in 1874 sent a punitive expedition against aborigines on Taiwan. In 1876 it signed a treaty with Korea to deny China's suzerainty over that peninsula. In the decade after 1880, rivalry intensified between China and Japan for the domination of Korea, and the two neighboring states moved inexorably toward a confrontation in 1894, the final test of whether China had learned from the West as well as Japan. The complete destruction of the North Sea fleet and the defeat of Chinese land forces in Manchuria sealed the fate of Confucian institutions as a viable base for modernization.

The loss of Taiwan and the Pescadores, the recognition of Korea's independence and the then astronomical sum of 230,000,000 taels indemnity, three times Peking's annual revenue, made the peace treaty with Japan a yoke on the empire's neck. In the midst of general grief and rage, K'ang Yu-wei presented a memorial with the support of some twelve hundred scholars gathered in Peking for the metropolitan examinations. This signaled the Reform

Chinese journal depicted a jubilant "victory" over Japanese army, which actually routed the Chinese troops.

This naval battle was indecisive, but China lost more ships. Chinese journal again claimed "victory."

Russia, Germany and France "advised" Japan to modify treaty; their ships are shown observing Japanese.

This expensive silk jacket, heavy with gold thread, was once worn by the empress dowager Tz'u-hsi. It gives an impression of her extravagance at the expense of the tottering nation. She diverted navy funds to build a new summer palace.

Movement, which finally resulted in the Hundred Days of 1898, during which the Kuanghsü emperor issued some forty edicts on westernization drafted by K'ang and his followers. The empress dowager, alarmed by the attack on her personal power, seized the emperor and imprisoned him, putting the Manchu diehards back at the helm. Their hatred of foreigners found expression in a secret society called *I-ho ch'üan,* better known as the "Boxers," many of whom believed in supernatural powers which could make them impervious to bullets. The Boxers' slogan of "Support the Ch'ing and destroy the foreigner" convinced the empress dowager that for once she could utilize the people's rebellious force.

On June 21, 1900, she declared war against the foreign powers and unleashed the fury of the fanatics. The Boxers massacred Chinese Christians, besieged the foreign settlements of Tientsin and attacked the legation quarter of Peking. Fortunately, the regional officials saw this desperate move as suicidal. Assuring the foreign powers of their peaceful intentions, they maintained order in Shantung, as well as Central and South China. When the large international force entered Peking in August, the empress dowager had fled, instructing Li Hung-chang to again assume his familiar role as peacemaker. The Boxer Protocol of 1901 rendered the capital defenseless against foreign forces and shackled China with a staggering indemnity of 450,000,000 taels. From this point on, the Chinese patriots gave up hope of saving the nation through the existing power structure, which finally fell in 1911.

Twentieth-Century China
A.D. 1912–1949

Sun Yat-sen leads the Republican Revolution to end imperial rule in China . . . Remnant feudalistic forces breed warlordism . . . Japanese expansionists tighten their hold on China . . . Chiang Kai-shek establishes the National Government and suppresses the Communists . . . Japanese invasion forces Nationalists and Communists to combine their resistance . . . Civil war after Japanese defeat ends in Communist victory under Mao Tse-tung.

HISTORICAL CHRONOLOGY

A.D.

1912   *Sun Yat-sen is elected first provisional president of the Republic of China, then resigns in favor of Yüan Shih-k'ai. Sun transforms his revolutionary society (T'ung-mêng-hui) into the Nationalist Party (Kuomintang).*

1915   *Yüan's Peking government capitulates to Japan's Twenty-One Demands.*

1916   *Yüan's death ushers in a decade of warlordism.*

1919   *Students demonstrate on May 4 against the acquiescence of Western powers to Japanese gains in China. Mao Tse-tung leads study group on Marxism in Hunan.*

1921   *Founding of the Chinese Communist Party.*

1924   *Nationalist Party admits individual Communists.*

1925   *Sun dies in March. In July, Chiang Kai-shek establishes National Government and the National Revolutionary Army.*

1926   *Chiang launches Northern Expedition.*

1927   *Chiang captures Shanghai, establishes Nanking as capital and purges Communists.*

1930–35   *Chiang stages five campaigns against Communists in Kiangsi and Hunan, finally drives them to northwest.*

1931   *Japanese militarists seize Manchuria and set up puppet regime Manchukuo the next year.*

1932   *Mao Tse-tung, chairman of the first Chinese Soviet Republic, declares war on Japan.*

1936   *Chang Hsüeh-liang detains Chiang Kai-shek at Sian to join Nationalist and Communist efforts against Japan.*

1937   *Anti-Japanese United Front created, Japan begins war on July 7, takes major cities. National Government retreats to the west.*

1938   *Chungking becomes wartime capital of China.*

1945–46   *General George C. Marshall mediates between the Nationalists and the Communists.*

1946–49   *Civil war.*

1949   *Communists achieve victory. October 1, the People's Republic of China is founded with Peking as capital. The Nationalists withdraw to Taiwan and continue the Republic of China.*

ART CHRONOLOGY

A.D.

1910's   *Painter-calligrapher-poet Ch'i Pai-shih, creates style of simplicity and vigor.*

1917   *Center of cultural renaissance is National University of Peking (Peita) under Ts'ai Yüan-p'ei. Hu Shih (1891–1962) suggests reform of literature in the magazine* New Youth. *Editor Ch'ên Tu-hsiu (1879–1942) calls for Literary Revolution.*

1918   *Lu Hsün (1881–1936) begins writing career with* The Diary of a Madman, *indicting hypocrisy.*

1919   *May Fourth Movement spurs intellectual revolution in learning and arts.*

1920   *Literary Association takes over* The Short Story Monthly. *Editor Mao Tun (born 1896), major novelist, endorses realism.*

       New Poetry in vernacular and Western styles.

1921   *Founding of the Creation Society by Kuo Mo-jo. Member Yü Ta-fu (1896–1945) writes novels of sex and patriotism.*

1923   *Crescent Society formed by Hsü-Chih-mo, influenced by European Romantic writers.*

1924   *Marxist principle of "literature for propaganda" adopted by Kuo's group.*

1925   *Hsü Pei-hung (1895–1953) returns from studying in Paris and Berlin, incorporates Western training into Chinese painting. In 1946 he heads National Art Academy in Peking.*

1926   The Philosophy of Lao Chang *is the first of Lao Shê's satirical novels.*

1930–37   *Short stories, autobiography and novelette* The Border Town *written by Shên Ts'ung-wên. Farcical stories and the novel* The Strange Knight of Shanghai *written by Chang T'ien-i.*

1930's   *Most versatile traditional painter is Chang Ta-ch'ien.*

1933–40   *Autobiographical trilogy* Family, Spring, *and* Autumn *by Pa Chin.*

1942   *Mao Tse-tung lectures on "Problems of Art and Literature," directing the Communist cultural movement.*

1949   *Art treasures from former imperial collections moved to Taiwan.*

277

Wearing western clothing, Dr. Sun Yat-sen was photographed in 1911 while on a world tour to enlist the support of overseas Chinese. This painting was made from one of the photographs. Below, Sun's calligraphy reads "Universal Love." He has signed the work and affixed his seal.

The Birth of the Republics

Twentieth-century China moved toward nationhood powered by two basic drives: nationalism and modernization. During the last seventy years of the Manchu rule, the greatest empire in the East had disintegrated into a semicolony. On the eve of the revolution which historically began on October 10, 1911, China was divided into five "spheres of influence." The British controlled the Yangtze valley, the Canton region and Tibet; the French dominated the southwestern provinces adjacent to Vietnam; the Germans dominated the Shantung peninsula; the Russians dominated Outer Mongolia and Sinkiang; and the Japanese controlled Manchuria and Fukien. Shanghai and Tientsin became international cities with foreign concessions.

A promise of a constitutional monarchy was forced from the empress dowager by an increasingly angry people. She also agreed to follow her governor-general Chang Chih-tung's halfway measures of modernization, as suggested in his slogan, "Chinese learning as essence and Western learning for application," a concept that proved to be as unworkable as it sounded. Unrealistically, in the first decade of the twentieth century, the dying imperial house still dreamed that the emperor could be the symbol of national unity and that Western technology alone would be sufficient to shore up the ancient civilization. But the future, in fact, belonged to the vision of Dr. Sun Yat-sen, the revolutionary leader. Born in a village north of Macao in 1866, Sun was a patriot from childhood. At thirteen he began his international education in Honolulu in an American school. He returned to Hong Kong and attended medical college graduating in 1892.

Near the summit of this wooded hillside in Nanking stands the mausoleum of Sun Yat-sen. It was built by the Nationalist Government in 1929. The scene was painted by Fu Pao-shih, who headed the Kiangsu Academy.

But Dr. Sun was more interested in curing his sick country than sick men. In 1894 he formed a revolutionary society, Hsing-chung-hui, in Honolulu. The next year he staged the first of many unsuccessful attempts to foment an uprising in China. To rally the support of overseas Chinese students and to raise funds, he traveled extensively around the world, and in 1905 he formed T'ung-mêng-hui, the Revolutionary Comrades' Association, in Tokyo. Their cry was "Drive out the Tartars, recover China, establish the republic and equalize landownership." Not until six years later, when Sun's revolutionaries infiltrated the Manchu army in the Central Yangtze industrial city of Wuchang, did the Ch'ing dynasty fall. It was the beginning of the work of reform and revolution that was to surge over the nation.

The only remaining strong man of traditional China was Yüan Shih-k'ai, who commanded the imperial army of Ch'ing. When Dr. Sun was elected the first provisional president of the Republic on January 1, 1912, at Nanking, Yüan maneuvered to bring about the last emperor's abdication and Sun's resignation, which assured his own election to the presidency in Peking. Yüan crushed all opposition, engineering the assassination of Sung Chiao-jên, the chief organizer in the Kuomintang (KMT), or Nationalist Party.

Japan took full advantage of the Western powers' involvement in World War I to drive the Germans from Shantung. Yüan's Peking government was forced to accept Japan's Twenty-One Demands, turning China into a vassal state. Aroused Chinese students, merchants and workers organized nationwide anti-Japanese and anti-Yüan movements, including boycotts of Japanese goods. After his failure to install himself as emperor, Yüan died. Resulting regional revolts ushered in an era of chaos for the common people as warlords with shifting alliances ravaged the countryside. When the Western powers acquiesced to Japan's gains in

On the eve of the Sino-Japanese war, Chiang Kai-shek addressed the nation. He warned that the moment of sacrifice had arrived; that every citizen must fight for his country.

China, students from Peita, the National University of Peking and other institutions participated in strong demonstrations against the Versailles Treaty on May 4, 1919. This expression of nationalism, known as the May Fourth Movement, exploded into an intellectual revolution, championing democracy and science while condemning imperialism and Confucianism.

To spread literacy and modern ideas, Dr. Hu Shih, a philosopher who bridged the Chinese classics and Western liberalism, advocated writing in the living tongue of the vernacular instead of in the "dead" language of the ancients. In this critical year of 1919, the effects of the Russian Revolution began to influence China's fate. An entire issue of the magazine *New Youth*, edited by a Peita professor, was devoted to Marxism. His assistant in the university library, Mao Tse-tung, returned to his

On the "Long March" of 1934–35, Mao Tse-tung and his army traveled through deep snow as in this painting called "Red

native province, Hunan, where he led a study group on social theories. In July 1921, Mao and his comrades, along with an agent of the Comintern who was called Maring, attended the First Congress of the Chinese Communist Party (CCP) in Shanghai. Aiming at the reorganization of the Kuomintang two years later, Dr. Sun sent his compatriot, General Chiang Kai-shek, to Moscow to investigate the party, governmental and military establishments of the Soviet Union. Upon his return, Chiang became head of the new Whampoa Military Academy at Canton, with a Soviet general as chief of staff, and the French-educated Communist Chou En-lai as his deputy political commissar. The Comintern's man in China, Michael Borodin, advised Dr. Sun on propaganda and organization. The expanded Kuomintang admitted these Communists as individuals. Nationalism, democracy and people's

Mao as he looked around 1949 is shown in this recent portrait called "Chairman Mao Walks All Over the Country."

Army Over Snowy Mountain." Only twenty thousand of Mao's army of ninety thousand reached their new base in Shensi.

兩家的父親

倉皇

向故鄉

轟炸 一

征夫語征婦 死生不可知
欲慰泉下魂 但視輿中兒

命中

戰苦軍猶樂

黔道 二

醜劇

livelihood, comprising the Three People's Principles, were the subject of Dr. Sun's lectures to the reorganized Nationalist Party. Three stages of nation-building were projected: military, tutelage and constitutional.

But Sun Yat-sen did not live to see the launching of the northern expedition of the Nationalist Revolutionary Army in 1926. In the next year, Chiang Kai-shek led revolutionary troops victoriously from Canton to the Yangtze River. He established his capital at Nanking, and purged all Communists from the Kuomintang. The great power struggle between the two parties led by Chiang and Mao began. Chiang was on his way to unifying China under the Nationalist Government, but in the spring of 1927, a small number of Communists escaped to the rural mountain area of Kiangsi province. A triangular struggle raged above and underground in China in the ten years from 1927, when the Nationalists established their capital at Nanking, to 1937, when the Japanese sacked that city. The two main antagonists were Generalissimo Chiang Kai-shek's National Government, whose aim was a unified independent China, and the Japanese militarists, whose aim was to dominate and control China. The third force, a minor one at the time, was Chairman Mao Tse-tung's Communist Party. The Communists, whose aims were similar to Chiang's but whose ideology was different, barely survived Chiang's persecution, but won the sympathies of many intellectuals for their intense nationalistic and anti-Japanese stand. Chiang's policy was first to create order within the country, then resist the outside invader, even at the temporary expense of nationalism. He vigorously purged the Communists, yet negotiated cautiously with the Japanese. While he was conducting his successful campaign to drive the Communists out of their base area in the south and gain control over the remaining warlords, the Japanese

"Flood of Wrath" by Li Hwa depicts the rage of the Chinese peasants against the invaders.

were racing against him to extend their conquests from Manchuria to Inner Mongolia and North China. Undeclared war broke out in the fall of 1937. Within a few months, the Japanese wiped out Chiang's ten-year work of unification and construction. Under the pressure of attack, survival depended on the cooperation of both Chinese parties against the common enemy. Thus began an uneasy alliance between the Nationalists and the Communists. Chiang continued his policy of "trading space for time," preserving his military strength by retreating into China's vast interior. He was waiting for the ultimate collision of Japan with the Western powers as well as the inevitable showdown with the Communists after Japan's collapse. Mao, however, read history from the Marxist-Leninist point of view. He believed

A beggar under the occupation, painted by Chen Chi, who advocates the blending of styles of East and West.

*People rioting and scrambling for rice. The
shortage of food was caused by hoarding and profiteering.*

imperialism had prepared the material as well as the moral conditions for a Communist victory in China. The deeper the invaders penetrated into Chinese towns and villages, the greater became the awakening of the Chinese masses and the release of revolutionary power.

As the protracted war with its accompanying vices of inflation, corruption and profiteering demoralized the urban bourgeoisie, the army and the bureaucracy under both the Nationalists and the Japanese conquerors, the Communists indoctrinated and or-

As the population exceeded seven hundred million, China rebuilt by mobilizing manpower. In "Moving Mountains and Filling Valleys," Li Shih-ch'ing painted a railroad construction scene in 1958 against a landscape reminiscent of Sung master Li T'ang.

▽ An industrial town since the turn of the century, Wu-hsi now has many smokestacks dwarfing a lonely pagoda. The lyrical villa in midriver seems out of place among the freight boats. A detail from a modern painting by Ch'ien Sung-yen.

ganized the peasantry, slowly establishing a disciplined government in the areas they controlled. As the Communists predicted, the imperalist war, made in Japan and exported to China, could lead only to the success of a social revolution.

The American victory over Japan entangled the United States in China's internal affairs. The Russians, who had marched into Manchuria on the eve of Japan's surrender, quickly became involved. Yet neither Washington nor Moscow could have influencd the outcome of China's civil war; that rested with the decisions of Chiang Kai-shek and Mao Tse-tung.

The end of the Civil War came on October 1, 1949. Mao's People's Republic of China established its capital at Peking and Chiang's National Government withdrew to Taiwan. During the two decades which followed, China withdrew into itself. Vast internal convulsions and struggles, only dimly visible to the outside world, kept the country in turmoil. The passing years witnessed the crumbling of Sino-Soviet friendship, the easing of the United States containment policy, and as the nineteen seventies began, the renewal of China's contacts with the other powers of the world. Yet China's national goal, sought by all but with different methods, is still that of the revolutionary Three People's Principles of Dr. Sun Yat-sen, as quoted from the selected works of Mao Tse-tung: "a China independent and free, democratic and united, prosperous and powerful."

For the most enduring of all civilizations and the most populous of all nations, there is a much older vision shared by the Chinese people from the earliest dynasties to today:

> When the Great Way held its sway, the world was for all. The worthy and the able were selected; people lived in faith and affection. Thus one did not treat only his own parents as parents, nor only his sons as sons. The aged found their retirement, the full-bodied their employment, the young their upbringing, the widow and the widower, the orphaned and the sick, their care. Men had their duties and women their homes. Goods would not be hoarded for oneself and lie in waste; energies would not be spared for oneself and kept idle. Evil schemes would not be initiated; thievery and rebellion would not arise; outer gates did not need to be closed. This was Grand Unity. [*An Early Han text attributed to Confucius.*]

Ch'i Pai-shih painted this plant called "Forever Green" and inscribed it: "Long Live Our Ancestral Country."

Works of Art

Legend into History

The Forming of a Civilization

The First Empires

silk; by G. Castiglione (Lang Shih-ning, 1688-1766); private collection.

255 Same as above (section showing Emperor Ch'ien-lung).

256-257 *Vietnam Campaign;* engraving; by anonymous artists, 1789; The Library of Congress, Washington, D.C.

258a *Fishing boat with fisherman, his wife and cat;* jade; Ch'ing; Seattle Art Museum.

258b *Virtuous ladies* (one of four panels); soapstone on satin; 17th-18th century; Metropolitan Museum of Art, New York.

259 Same as above (another panel).

260 *Dragon Boats* (detail); cloisonné; 18th century; The Avery Brundage Collection.

261 *Dragon boats, design on box cover;* cloisonné; 18th century; The Avery Brundage Collection.

262 *Picking sacred mushrooms on mountain;* jade; Ch'ing, Ch'ien-lung period (1736-1795); The Avery Brundage Collection.

263 *Bodhisattvas on mountain;* jade; 17th-18th century; The Avery Brundage Collection.

264 *Plate decorated with children at play;* porcelain; Ch'ing; Metropolitan Museum of Art, New York.

265 *Plate decorated with Jesus Baptized;* porcelain; Ch'ing; Metropolitan Museum of Art, New York.

266 *Plate decorated with 1756 ship Vryburg;* porcelain; Ch'ing; Metropolitan Museum of Art, New York.

267 *Portrait of How-qua;* oil color; by anonymous Chinese painter after George Chinnery; Metropolitan Museum of Art, New York.

268 *U.S. Clipper Ship;* oil color; by anonymous Chinese painter, 19th century; Metropolitan Museum of Art, New York.

268-269a *Canton Harbor;* oil color; by anonymous Chinese painter, 19th century; Metropolitan Museum of Art, New York.

268-269b *Burning of Canton Harbor;* oil color; by anonymous Chinese painter, 19th century; Metropolitan Museum of Art, New York.

270-271 *Attacking T'ai-p'ing Rebels;* color on paper; by anonymous painter, 1860's; Chaoying Fang, Englewood, New Jersey.

272a *Portrait of Tso Tsung-t'ang;* color on silk; by anonymous painter, 19th century; Wan-go H. C. Weng, New York.

272b *Tso Tsung-t'ang, Tsêng Kuo-fan, and Li Hung-chang, looking at calligraphy;* from *Tien-shih-chai huo-pao,* a Shanghai picture magazine, 1885 or later; Columbia University, New York.

272c *Opium eaters;* same source as 272b.

272d *First railroad in China;* same source as 272b.

273a *Portrait of Li Hung-chang;* same source as 272b.

273b *Chinese signing treaty with French envoys;* same source as 272b.

274 *Japanese sinking Chinese troopship;* same source as 272b; 1895.

275a *Fighting at Ya Shan in Korea;* same source as 272b; 1895.

275b *Naval battle at Yalu;* same source as 272b; 1895.

275c *Foreign powers interfering in the Sino-Japanese Treaty;* same source as 272b; 1895.

276 *Silk jacket of the Empress Dowager Tz'u-hsi;* embroidery and k'o-ssu; c. 1900; Metropolitan Museum of Art, New York.

Twentieth-Century China

277 *Two horses;* ink and color on paper; by Hsü Pei-hung (1895-1953), 1950's.

278a *Portrait of Sun Yat-sen;* oil color; by Liao Wei-lin, 1965.

278b *Universal Love;* calligraphy, ink on paper; by Sun Yat-sen (1866-1925), c. 1918.

279 *Sun Yat-sen's Mausoleum;* ink and color on paper; by Fu Pao-shih (1904-1965), 1950's.

280 *Portrait of Chiang Kai-shek;* watercolor; by Chang Chien-p'ing, 1966.

280-281 *Red Army Over the Snowy Mountain;* oil color; by Ai Chung-hsin, 1950's.

281 *Portrait of Mao Tse-tung;* ink and color on paper; by Li Ch'i, 1960.

282, 283 *Cartoons,* ink on paper; by Fêng Tzu-k'ai, dated from 1931 to 1940.

284a *Flood of Wrath;* woodcut; by Li Hwa, c. 1947.

284b *Old Woman Beggar;* ink and color on paper; by Chen Chi, 1943.

285 *Scramble for Rice;* woodcut; by Chao Yen-nien, 1947.

286 *On the Lake Fu-jung (Wu-hsi);* ink and color on paper; by Ch'ien Sung-yen, 1958.

287 *Moving Mountain to Fill Valley;* ink and color on paper; by Li Shih-ch'ing, 1958.

288 *Long Live Our Ancestral Country;* ink and color on paper; by Ch'i Pai-shih, 1955.

Bibliography

1. General History and Biography

Chang, Kwang-chih. *The Archaeology of Ancient China.* Rev. ed. New Haven and London, 1968.

Chow, Tse-tsung. *The May Fourth Movement.* Stanford, 1960.

Clubb, Edmund. *Twentieth Century China.* 2d. ed. New York and London, 1972.

Eberhard, Wolfram. *A History of China.* Berkeley and Los Angeles, 1960.

Erh-shih-wu shih [Twenty-five histories of China]. Wu-ying-tien ed. 26 vols. Reprint. Taipei, 1962.

Fairbank, John K. *The United States and China.* New York, 1962.

Fairbank, John K.; Reischauer, Edwin O.; and Craig, Albert M. *East Asia: The Modern Transformation.* Boston, 1965.

Fan, Wên-lan. *Chung-kuo t'ung-shih chien-pien* [A brief general history of China]. Rev. ed. 4 vols. Peking, 1965.

Fitzgerald, C. P. *China, A Short Cultural History.* New York, 1961.

Goodrich, L. Carrington. *A Short History of the Chinese People.* London, 1969.

Grousset, René. *The Rise and Splendour of the Chinese Empire.* Berkeley, 1965.

Ho, Ping-ti. *The Ladder of Success in Imperial China.* New York, 1964.

Hsu, Cho-yun. *Ancient China in Transition.* Stanford, 1965.

Hummel, Arthur. W., ed. *Eminent Chinese of the Ch'ing Period.* 2 vols. Washington, D.C., 1943.

Latourette, Kenneth Scott. *China.* Englewood Cliffs, 1964.

Reischauer, Edwin O., and Fairbank, John K. *East Asia: The Great Tradition.* Boston, 1960.

Schurmann, Franz, and Schell, Orville, ed. *The China Reader:* vol. 1, *Imperial China;* vol. 2, *Republican China;* vol. 3, *Communist China.* New York, 1967.

Snow, Edgar. *Red Star Over China.* Rev. ed. New York, 1968.

Snow, Edgar. *Red China Today: The Other Side of the River.* Rev. ed. New York, 1971.

Têng, Chih-ch'êng. *Chung-hua erh-ch'ien-nien shih* [Two thousand years of Chinese history]. 5 vols. Hong Kong, 1964.

Wang, Gungwu. *The Structure of Power in North China During the Five Dynasties.* Stanford, 1963.

Watson, Burton, trans. *Records of the Historian, Chapters from the Shih chi of Ssu-ma Ch'ien.* New York and London, 1969.

Watson, Burton. *Ssu-ma Ch'ien, Grand Historian of China.* New York, 1958.

Watson, William. *Early Civilization in China.* New York, 1966.

2. Philosophy and Religion

de Bary, William Theodore, ed. *The Buddhist Tradition.* New York, 1969.

de Bary, William Theodore, ed. *Sources of Chinese Tradition.* 2 vols. New York and London, 1960.

Bodde, Derk. *China's Cultural Tradition.* New York, 1957.

Chan, Wing-tsit. *A Source Book of Chinese Philosophy.* Princeton, 1963.

Chan, Wing-tsit, trans. *The Way of Lao Tzu.* Indianapolis, 1963.

Ch'en, Kenneth. *Buddhism in China.* Princeton, 1964.

Creel, H. G. *Chinese Thought, from Confucius to Mao Tse-tung.* New York, 1953.

Fairbank, John K., ed. *Chinese Thought and Institutions.* Chicago and London, 1957.

Fung, Yu-lan. *A Short History of Chinese Philosophy.* New York, 1966.

Hu, Shih. *Chung-kuo chê-hsüeh shih ta-kang* [A general outline of the history of Chinese philosophy]. Hong Kong, no date.

Hughes, E. R. *The Great Learning and the Mean-in-Action.* London and New York, 1943.

Legge, James, trans. and annot. *The Chinese Classics.* 5 vols. Hong Kong, 1960.

Lin, Yutang. *The Wisdom of Confucius.* New York, 1938.

Liu, Wu-chi. *Confucius, His Life and Time.* New York, 1955.

Liu, Wu-chi. *A Short History of Confucian Philosophy.* Harmondsworth, 1955.

Wright, Arthur F., ed. *Studies in Chinese Thought.* Chicago, 1953.

3. Literature

Birch, Cyril, comp. and ed., and Acker, William, et al., trans. *Anthology of Chinese Literature.* New York, 1965.

Buck, Pearl S., trans. *All Men Are Brothers,* translated from *Shui-hu chuan* [Water margin] of undetermined authorship. New York, 1937.

Bynner, Witter, trans. *The Jade Mountain, A Chinese Anthology.* New York, 1964.

Chêng, Chên-to. *Chung-kuo su-wên-hsüeh shih* [A history of Chinese popular literature]. Peking, 1959.

Christie, Anthony. *Chinese Mythology.* Middlesex, 1968.

Fêng, Ming-chih. *Chung-kuo wên-hsüeh-shih t'i-kang* [An outline of the history of Chinese literature]. Hong Kong, 1964.

Kuo, Shao-yü. *Chung-kuo wên-hsüeh p'i-p'ing shih* [A history of Chinese literary criticism]. Shanghai, 1964.

Giles, Herbert A., ed. *Gems of Chinese Literature.* 2 vols bd. as one. New York, 1965.

Giles, Herbert A. *A History of Chinese Literature.* 2d ed. New York, 1958.

Hawkes, David, trans. and comment. *Ch'u Tz'u, the Songs of the South.* Boston, 1959.

Hsia, C. T. *A History of Modern Chinese Fiction, 1917-1957.* New Haven and London, 1961.

Hsu, Kai-yu, trans. and ed. *Twentieth Century Chinese Poetry: An Anthology.* New York, 1963.

Hung, William. *Tu Fu, China's Greatest Poet* and *Notes.* 2 vols. Cambridge, Mass., 1952.

Lai, Ming. *A History of Chinese Literature.* New York, 1964.

Liu, James J. Y. *The Art of Chinese Poetry.* Chicago, 1962.

Lu, Hsün (Chou Shu-jên). *A Brief History of Chinese Fiction,* translated by Yang Hsien-yi and Gladys Yang. Peking, 1959.

Payne, Robert. *The White Pony, An Anthology of Chinese Poetry.* New York, 1960.

Waley, Arthur, trans. *Chinese Poems, selected from One Hundred Seventy Chinese Poems, More Translations from the Chinese, The Temple,* and *The Book of Songs.* Rev. ed. London, 1962.

Waley, Arthur, trans. *Monkey,* translated from *Hsi-yu chi* [A journey to the West] by Wu Ch'êng-ên. New York, 1943.

Waley, Arthur. *The Life and Times of Po Chü-i.* London, 1949.

Waley, Arthur. *The Poetry and Career of Li Po.* New York, 1950.

Wang, Chi-chen, trans. *Dream of the Red Chamber,* translated from *Hung-lou-mêng* by Ts'ao Hsüeh-ch'in. Abridged ed. New York, 1958.

Wang, Chi-chen, trans. *Traditional Chinese Tales.* New York, 1944.

Watson, Burton. *Early Chinese Literature.* New York, 1962.

Yang, Hsien-yi and Yang, Gladys. *Li Sao and Other Poems of Chu Yuan.* Peking, 1953.

4. Art and Architecture

Akiyama, Terukazu, et al. *Arts of China: Neolithic Cultures to the T'ang Dynasty, Recent Discoveries.* Tokyo and Palo Alto, 1968.

Akiyama, Terukazu, and Matsubara, Saburo. *Arts of China: Buddhist Cave Temples.* Tokyo and Palo Alto, 1969.

d'Argencé, René-Yvon Lefebvre. *Chinese Treasures from the Avery Brundage Collection.* New York, 1968.

Arthaud, Claude; Hébert-Stevens, F.; and Swann, Peter C. *Chinese Monumental Art.* New York, 1963.

Boyd, Andrew. *Chinese Architecture.* Chicago, 1962.

Cahill, James. *Chinese Painting.* Geneva, 1960.

Cahill, James. *Fantastics and Eccentrics in Chinese Painting.* New York, 1967.

Ch'en, Chih-mai. *Chinese Calligraphers and Their Art.* London and New York, 1966.

Chiang, Yee. *Chinese Calligraphy.* London, 1938.

Ecke, Tseng Yu-ho. *Chinese Calligraphy.* Philadelphia, 1971.

Fontein, Jan, and Hickman, Money L. *Zen Painting and Calligraphy.* Boston, 1970.

Honey, William Bowyer. *The Ceramic Art of China and Other Countries of the Far East.* London, 1944.

Lee, Sherman E. *A History of Far Eastern Art.* Englewood Cliffs and New York, no date.

Lee, Sherman E., and Ho, Wai-kam. *Chinese Art Under the Mongols: The Yüan Dynasty.* Cleveland, 1968.

Sickman, Laurence, ed. *Chinese Calligraphy and Painting in the Collection of John M. Crawford, Jr.* New York, 1962.

Sickman, Laurence, and Soper, Alexander. *The Art and Architecture of China.* Baltimore, 1971.

Siren, Osvald. *Chinese Painting: Leading Masters and Principles.* 7 vols. New York, 1956-58.

Siren, Osvald, trans. and comment. *The Chinese on the Art of Painting.* New York and Hong Kong, 1963.

Sullivan, Michael. *A Short History of Chinese Art.* Berkeley and Los Angeles, 1967.

Swann, Peter. *Art of China, Korea and Japan.* New York, 1963.

Trubner, Henry. *The Far Eastern Collection.* Toronto, 1968.

Whitfield, Roderick. *In Pursuit of Antiquity.* Princeton, 1969.

Willetts, William. *Foundations of Chinese Art.* London, 1965.

Wu, Nelson I. *Chinese and Indian Architecture.* New York, 1963.

Yonezawa, Yoshiho, and Kawakita, Michiaki. *Arts of China: Paintings in Chinese Museums, New Collections.* Tokyo and Palo Alto, 1970.

5. Science and Technology

Bernard, Henri. *Matteo Ricci's Scientific Contribution to China.* Peiping, 1935.

Carter, Thomas Francis. *The Invention of Printing in China and Its Spread Westward.* 2d ed. rev. by Carrington L. Goodrich. New York, 1955.

Li, Ch'iao-p'ing. *The Chemical Arts of Old China.* Easton, 1948.

Needham, Joseph. *Science and Civilization in China.* 4 vols to date. Cambridge, England, 1961-1971.

6. Chronology and Map

Ao, Shih-ying. *Chung-kuo wên-hsüeh nien-piao* [Literature chronology of China]. First section, 3 vols. Peiping, 1935.

Cheng, Peter. *A Chronology of the People's Republic of China.* New Jersey, 1972.

Chien, Po-tsan, ed.-in-chief. *Chung-wai li-shih nien-piao* [Historical chronology of China and foreign countries]. Peking, 1958.

Fu, Pao-shih. *Chung-kuo mei-shu nien-piao* [Art chronology of China]. Shanghai, 1937.

Herrmann, Albert. *An Historical Atlas of China.* Edited by Norton Ginsburg. Chicago, 1966.

CHINA: A HISTORY IN ART

Index